And God Answered:

A Memoir

And God Answered:
A Memoir

by Jean Bell Mosley

Southeast Missouri State University Press • 2007

And God Answered: A Memoir

Written by Jean Bell Mosley

First published in 2006 in the United States of America by:

Southeast Missouri State University Press
MS 2650, One University Plaza
Cape Girardeau, MO 63701

http://www6.semo.edu/universitypress

paper ISBN: 978-0-9760413-7-5
cloth ISBN: 978-0-9760413-8-2

Cover photo of Jean Bell Mosley taken by:
Pat Patterson Photography, Cape Girardeau, MO.

The royalties from the sale of this book will be used to assist in the preservation of the 57-year writing career of Jean Bell Mosley. For more information, visit the website: www.jeanbellmosley.com.

For Viney;

Without my wonderful wife's love of Mom and her writing, this book would have never come into being.

— Steve Mosley

Acknowledgements

Special thanks to Dr. Susan Swartwout and the Southeast Missouri State University Press. Dr. Swartwout's commitment to this publication is appreciated by the family, friends, and relatives of Jean Bell Mosley.

Table of Contents

1980–1990

1990

Column Selections 237

Jean Bell Mosley's Vitae 257

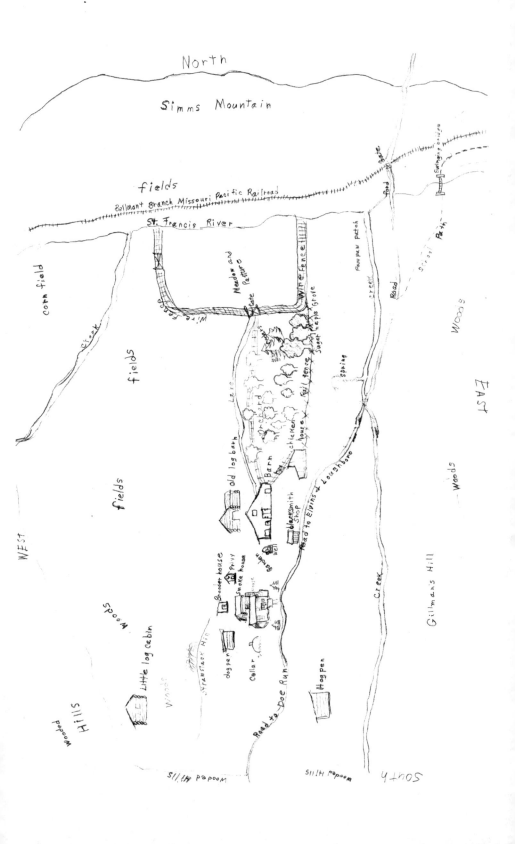

Prelude

Things were shaping up for my arrival. The ice-cream cone and the hot dog had been invented at the 1904 World's Fair in St. Louis, Missouri! Grandpa and Grandma Bell were there to witness the event. An old photo shows them in one of Henry Ford's newest contraptions: Grandpa at the steering wheel, which was on the right; Grandma on the left with a stern expression, as if she wasn't sure of this peculiar vehicle that needed no horses to pull it. A placard on the dashboard declared in bold letters that they were SEEING ST. LOUIS.

Grandma Bell, nee Josephine Lyons, from Carroll County, Virginia, and Grandpa Stephen Bell from Wythe County, Virginia, had married in Virginia and had five children before coming from the mining country around Austinville, Virginia, to the Lead Belt mining country of Missouri. Two other children were born to them after arrival in Bonne Terre, Missouri, one of them being my father, Wilson Leroy Bell, born in 1888.

Grandpa Stephen Bell (1857–1944) and Grandma Josephine Lyons Bell (1855–1932).

My maternal grandpa, Moses Casey, and Grandma Casey, nee Mary Alice Razor, had met and married in Madison County, Missouri. They had eight children; the youngest daughter, Myrtle, born in 1886, was destined to be my mother.

Of course, other things of importance were going on in that first decade of the twentieth century, which I learned about later. Three United States presidents served during this period: William McKinley for the last year of his term; Theodore Roosevelt,

13

often called Teddy, for eight years; and William H. Taft for the first year of his term.

The Spanish-American War, wherein we were involved with Cuba, had been over for two years before the first decade of the twentieth century. In the lst decade, we were still involved with Cuba.

Teddy Roosevelt fought corruption in politics during this first decade. We were still fighting that in the last decade. He organized conservation. In the 1990s, we were still arguing about a lot of conservation projects.

Grandpa Moses Carlyle Casey (1840–1912)
Civil War Veteran

I'm sure all these things were being talked about between 1900 and 1910, but until I had to study about them later in school, the only big things to come out of national affairs during this time, for me, were the ice-cream cone, the hot dog, and the fact that my brown, fuzzy teddy bear had been named for someone who had once been called President.

A part-log, part-frame farmhouse, barn, and outbuildings had been built in St. Francois County, Missouri, near the St. Francis River, sometime way back before the beginning of

Grandma Mary Alice (Razor) Casey
(1850–1936)

the twentieth century. This farmhouse was, later, to be my home during my formative years. The frame part of the house was put together with square nails, and wooden pegs held together the inner structure of the great barn.

More important to me than all these things, though, was that Mama and Daddy had met and married during this first decade of the twentieth century and had two young daughters, Lillian and Lucille. I had a ready-made family to welcome me, the third daughter, in the next decade.

1910–1920

Arrival

"Bells were ringing all over town when you were born," Mama was fond of telling me. I liked this and wasn't above repeating it to my little friends until I learned that September 21, 1913, was a Sunday morning, and church bells were calling the citizens to worship in the little town of Elvins, Missouri.

Thus I began my journey through the century, or, as I like to describe it, my first stitch was added to the great, ever-unrolling tapestry of time that began on that bright day of creation.

Elvins was known as a tough little town because of the hard life of the miners in the early days of mining in that area of Missouri known as the Lead Belt. Spending their working hours in the damp underground, picking out chunks of limestone that contained the precious lead ore, they were prone to "celebrate" after hours, gathering at the local saloons or livery stables where tempers sometimes flared and fights ensued.

I knew nothing of this rough-and-tumble life, have no memories of my life in Elvins at all, since my parents, two older sisters, and paternal grandparents moved about ten miles southeastward to a farm near the headwaters of the St. Francis River before my memory faculties began to develop.

My memories of Elvins resulted from later visits there, most often with Mama, in a horse-drawn buggy. She would take pounds of molded butter and dozens of crated eggs to Langdon's Store and trade them for what groceries we had to buy, such as coffee, sugar, flour, cornmeal — things we couldn't raise or manufacture on the farm. Sometimes, after these trade transactions, she would take me by the hand to cross the "dangerous" street, alive with other horse- or mule-drawn wagons and buggies and men on horseback, to Woods' Drugstore.

First photograph of Jean Bell Mosley (1913–2003)

The drugstore odor was a distillation of rose or violet talcum powder, soaps, cough syrups, and numerous other items to be found in such early emporiums. Past all these things we would go, I in my plain gingham dress and Buster Brown shoes, she in her Indianhead linen and leather slippers, all the way to the back where the ice-cream tables and chairs were, the kind with curly metal legs and backs.

We did not have to wait long until a waiter came. Then Mama, with a demeanor that it was an everyday occurrence, would say, "Two orange ice-cream sodas, please."

I tried to sit still and appear as calm as Mama, but inside I would be quivering with excitement. Two ice-cream sodas!

Other points of interest in the Elvins that I knew were Fatty Klein's Shoe Shop, Tlapke's Meat Market, Sizemore's Barber Shop, and the train depot. The little, approximately six-by-eight feet, concrete jail with tiny high-up windows was behind the depot and was not even to be looked at, should we have to pass by. Bad people were in there, they said. I did not know who or what bad people were.

Grandpa and Grandma Bell's Home in Leadwod, MO
From left to right: Wilson Bell, Stephen Bell, Luzena Bell (Jean's aunt), Jose-
phine Lyons Bell, Hugh Bell (Jean's uncle).

I had been christened at an early age in the Elvins Methodist Episcopal Church South, but, naturally, have no memory of that either, since such sacrament and ceremony is a vow of the parents to raise the infant child in a Christian manner.

Before moving to the farm, Grandpa and Grandma Bell and those of their children still at home had lived in Leadwood and Bonne Terre, Missouri, two other mining towns of the Lead Belt. Because of the Bell family's leading role in the mining operations, by not only Grandpa but also Uncle Frank Bell, streets in both of these towns were named Bell Street in their honor.

Other towns in this Lead Belt area, all bunched together, were Flat River, Deslodge, Rivermines, St. Francois, Esther, Cantwell, and Leadington. Doe Run, once the headquarters for the St. Joe Lead Company, was a bit geographically detached, about ten miles southeast, as was Farmington, the county seat of St. Francois County. Farmington was never considered a mining town. There were no shafts there leading to the underground mines as there were in the other "bunched up" towns. Now, in the twentieth century, four of these towns, Flat River, Elvins, Esther, and River-mines, have consolidated and are known by one name: Park Hills.

17

Quoting from Robert Sidney Douglass' *History of Southeast Missouri*, published in 1912,

> *[Stephen Bell] has been a resident of Missouri for fully thirty years, and his entire active career has been one of close identification with the mining industry. For a number of years past he has been captain of the mines of the Federal Lead Company at Elvins, St. Francois County, and he is well known in connection with this line of industry in Missouri, where his long experience in practical and executive capacities has made him an authority in his chosen vocation, the while he has so ordered his course as to retain the unqualified confidence and regard of his fellow men. He and his wife maintain their home at Elvins, and of their seven children, four sons and one daughter are living. Stephen Bell is a staunch supporter of the principles for which the Republican party stands sponsor, is affiliated with the Ancient Order of United Workmen, and his wife holds membership in the Methodist Episcopal Church, South. The Bell family was founded in Virginia in an early day and is of staunch Scotch lineage.*

There may have been several reasons why the move was made to the farm in 1915. Grandpa was fifty-eight years old and maybe wanted more of a touch of rural life for his remaining years. There was growing discontent among the miners, which finally led to riots in 1917.

Dad and George Maxton operated a livery stable and blacksmith shop at Elvins. A livery stable was a "hotel" for horses which, for one reason or another, needed stabling overnight or even longer. Also, surreys, buggies, and other wheeled conveyances, plus horses, could be rented as one would rent a car these days.

The blacksmith part of the business was for making horseshoes and fitting them to the hooves of horses or mules that needed to be shod. Wagon and buggy wheels and other parts were also made or repaired.

Word filtered in from the "outside world" that this Henry Ford was making a success of that contraption Grandpa and Grandma had ridden in at the 1904 St. Louis World's Fair, a conveyance that did not need horses to pull it. "Handwriting" on the livery stable

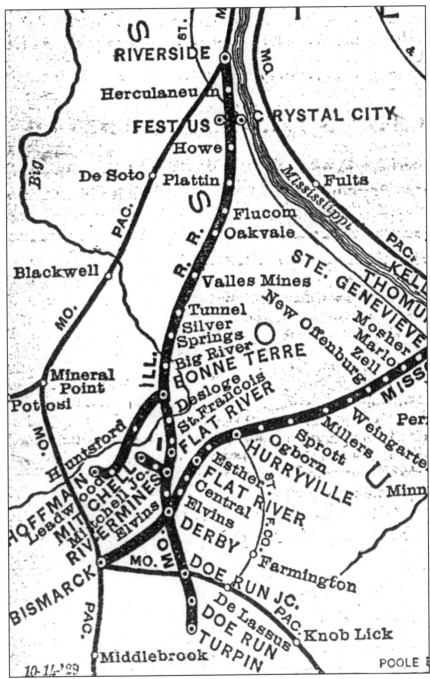

Early railroad map showing the many branch lines. Many of the lines have been abandoned, including the one that ran through the Bell farm and the one that the Bells took to get from Doe Run to Flat River.

and blacksmith shop walls was clearly visible in the minds of Grandpa and Dad.

Too, whisperings of war overseas became louder and louder. Maybe a farm in the St. Francis River bottom, surrounded by thickly forested hills, would be a safe haven away from the vagaries and changing times, and a better place to raise three little girls.

In the aforementioned *History of Southeast Missouri*, Elvins was described as a town with a population of 2,071, which depended on the mines and railroad traffic. Two railroad lines ran through the town, the Illinois Southern and the Mississippi River and Bonne Terre, called M.R. & B.T. for short, which some said stood for Muddy Roads and Bad Tracks.

The Bank of Elvins, so the history says, was organized in 1900 with a capital stock of $15,000. By 1915, perhaps that capital had grown. Anyway, Grandpa et al. borrowed part of that capital to supplement his and Dad's savings to buy the farm.

The move was made. Dad, Mama, Lucille, and I went first in 1915. Grandpa, Grandma, and Lillian followed in 1916. Lillian was in school by this time and stayed on in Elvins with Grandpa and Grandma to finish her second grade there.

My earliest memory of the farmstead was of a colored rubber ball being discovered as a worn back-porch floor was being removed from the farmhouse. As Dad pried the worn boards loose, there was this colorful ball, evidently lost by some other child many years ago. The ball was tossed to me, and I thought it the prettiest thing I'd ever seen, and when dropped, it bounced! Scared me.

The Farmhouse

The farm was known for many years as the Billy Wilbourn Place, since a family by that name had homesteaded it in 1860. A son of John London married a Wilbourn girl, and it then became known for many years as the old London Place. After that, it was ours. After we left, a family by the name of Watson owned it, and then, in the last decade of the twentieth century, the last known owner, at this writing, is Harry Lynn Peterson. He has added much more acreage to the original farm.

This is the way the farm home looked when the Bells lived there. Taken from an early drawing/painting by sister Lillian Bell Wichman who turned out to be an accomplished painter after retiring from 43 years of school teaching. Built sometime in the 1800s.

The original erection of the farmhouse is lost in history, but it could readily be observed that the back part of the house was once a log cabin. The great, hand-hewn logs were put together in the saddle-notched style, chinked with a gray plaster reinforced with some sort of black bristles. A brick and sandstone chimney was at one end. At some point in time, there must have been a partition in the cabin because there were two doors close together on each side, not needed unless there had been a partition between them, making two rooms, or, indeed, maybe a two-family cabin. Before we arrived, the partition had been removed, leaving those funny four doors leading to the outside from one room.

Maybe it was at the same time when the partition was removed that the east side of the cabin was also removed, and a two-storey, wood-sided, four-room addition was added with stairs leading up from the four-doored cabin room which was now our kitchen. The addition made an ell-shaped house, with a roofed back porch partially filling in the lower part of the ell. The upper floor of the

21

room attached to the older cabin part was two steps higher than the original floor of the cabin loft. So, leading out of this upper room was about a six-foot platform with two steps down to the loft floor. The inside walls of this cabin loft, or what we called the attic, were the exposed logs. Many pleasant childhood hours were spent in this attic area, cutting out paper dolls, playing with real dolls, playing house with some of Mama's furniture that was stored there when the two families' furniture was combined. There was always a pile of rags, saved for making rag rugs. This was a good place to nestle into with a good book to read.

The place was kept fairly warm in winter, as the warm bricks of the fireplace chimney coming up from the kitchen were also exposed. There were two small casement windows on either side of the chimney. These windows were kept open in summer, and in winter, although closed, an unreplaced broken windowpane allowed Tabby Cat to enter at will by way of the lean-to pantry roof,

Farm home after subsequent owners enlarged it

to have her family of kittens or just to keep warm if she wasn't already behind the kitchen stove downstairs.

When the two-storey addition was made, it is thought that the outside cabin logs were then covered with wood siding, same as the new front. In the beginning and maybe some time thereafter, the house was painted white with bright green, louvered shutters at all the new windows. But by the time we arrived, it was a faded gray, and the shutters were not so green. That's the way it remained all during our occupancy.

To the left of the stairs, going up, was a place we called the catchall. It was the space created by that six-foot platform leading out of the new upper room and the two steps down to the original cabin loft floor. This catchall was left open on the side facing the stairs. It was a handy place to hide things quickly or store things seldom used. It was dark and rather scary back in the far corners. Grandpa's and Dad's shotguns were kept in the catchall, and whenever old ragdoll Betsy was lost, she could usually be found in the catchall.

Other Log Structures

Another log structure, as big as the one with the fireplace which was now our kitchen, was about twenty feet west of the house. What this was in former years, who knows? We used it as a smokehouse. Every year, at hog-butchering time, the middlins (bacon slabs) were salted and placed to cure on a wide shelf at the rear of the building. Hams and shoulders, salted or sugar-cured, were wrapped and hung from a beam above this shelf. There were no windows in this building, but it wasn't dark inside because some of the chinking had fallen out here and there, which let in light.

In one corner of this building, a corner cabinet had been constructed of rough-sawn boards. To us it seemed a peculiar architectural feature. Perhaps some housewife of long ago had longed for such a folderol, and someone who loved her fulfilled her dream, but where were any windows?

Our hulled walnuts and hickory nuts were also kept in the smokehouse. Hanks of sage that seasoned our sausage were hung from beams to dry. Onions dried on the floor.

About 150 feet north of the house was another log structure which must have been the barn before the big "modern" barn had been built in front of it. A lean-to shed had been built on the north side of this log barn. Here, from time to time, some piece of farm machinery was housed, but in the main, high, log part we kept the surrey, a handsome two-seated carriage, complete with fringed top and kerosene lights on either side of the front seats. It was black, with black leather upholstery. The surrey required a hitch of two horses. It was probably one that Dad rented from the livery stable for special affairs.

Log structures, denoting pioneer days in our locale, were common. A half-mile southeast of our farm home was another one-room log cabin. It stood on about a two-acre, cleared, grassy site. It had long been abandoned. No one remembered anyone's having lived there. The dry dusty floor marked the passage of wildlife, and little inverted cones of the doodle bugs could be found. This structure was always referred to as the Little Log Cabin. It would seem that it would have been a perfect place for a playhouse for little girls, but this building, with its vacant, staring windows, deathly still, was always approached with some timidity. We stepped through the doorway with rapidly beating hearts, half expecting to find some residents. If not residents, surely there must be some unfriendly Indians lurking in the surrounding woods!

Log buildings could be found elsewhere at neighboring homes, especially parts of barns and outbuildings. Neighbor Wallens actually still lived in an ancient log home.

The Blacksmith Shop

The blacksmith shop was rather dilapidated, with a board missing here and there. It was some sort of shed or small barn already in existence when Daddy moved his blacksmithing equipment into it. The fire bin and bellows were installed. The anvil, mounted on a sturdy wooden platform, stood in the middle of the dirt floor. There were tubs to hold water into which were plunged the red-hot horseshoes or wagon-wheel rims to be tempered. There were lots of other tools, including a press drill mounted on a wall. This was operated manually by turning a big wheel. My sister, Lucille, whom I shall hereafter refer to as Lou because that

The smoke house

is what I called her, learned how to change the bits on this piece of equipment, and with both of our arms' strength, we could turn the wheel to make the bit go through pieces of iron or steel. To see the little, curly, silvery bits of metal winding up around the bit was fascinating, although I don't think Daddy approved of our thus dulling his drill bits.

The horse and mule shoes were bought, factory new, in various sizes, then processed by the blacksmith to fit individual hooves. They hung on nails around the walls of the shop. Sparks would fly as the hot iron shoe was hammer-tortured into the proper shape and size. This was as exciting as any Fourth of July sparkler.

There was a distinct odor, not unpleasant, when horseshoeing was going on. It was a combination of the steam rising from the water as the red-hot shoe was plunged into it, the smoke from the coals in the fire bin, the sparks hitting the dust of the floor.

The horse to be shod waited patiently outside under a mulberry tree. The hoof had to be filed off a certain measure. This was done by a long cross-hatched file, somewhat like a finger-nail file that had been on steroids! The little semi-dump pile of hoof filings that mounded

The blacksmith shop and grindstone

25

up on the ground had its own faint odor, too. I always cringed when Daddy, holding the horse's hoof between his knees, did the filing, although he assured me it did not hurt the horse. If the cooled horseshoe did not exactly fit the filed hoof, it was heated and formed again, then nailed on with a special big-headed nail that was driven through holes in the shoe into the thick hoof. This caused me to double cringe, although the horse stood patient, maybe even sleeping.

Sometimes Daddy or even Lou and I would bend the horseshoe nails around a suitably sized chisel to form a "ring" for one of our fingers. The nail head would be the "jewel." We wore them proudly and found them to be much more durable than the paper "rings" taken from Dad's or Grandpa's occasional cigars.

One of our hens, hearing a different drummer, would abandon the neat, straw-lined nests in the chicken house and lay her eggs in a corner of the blacksmith shop amongst some shavings of wood and maybe a few coal ashes or clinkers.

The Chicken House

Since one of our sources of cash was to be chickens and eggs, we built a long, sturdy, airy chicken house. I faintly remember the time of its construction, not so much the actual hammer-and-nailing, but the pride we took in choosing the type of chicken house that was to be built. It was not to be just a dinky, little old coop constructed of scrap lumber. No, this was to be the type shown in our agriculture textbook we studied at school, written by Professor Ghers. Some in our community actually knew Professor Ghers!

The chicken house

Mary Ellen St. Johns Curd (Edward Mosley's grandmother)
Picture taken some time in the first decade of the 20th century from somewhere
deep in the Bootheel.

The architectural feature of this chicken house was the upper row of windows beneath a roof that slanted to the north and a lower level of windows beneath a roof that slanted to the south. Eleven windows with a southern exposure! These windows were sliding, screened windows, which in the winter could be covered with a white, opaque sort of oilcloth tacked over the screens to keep out the cold winds, snow, and sleet, yet let in the light.

There was a long row of about twenty joining, partioned nests about two feet off the ground, supported by a number of two-by-four legs. The ceilings of the nests reached to the rear of the house. Slanting roosts of slender poles, from our own woods, were above the nests' ceiling, from which the droppings could be easily scraped off, a chore with which I was later to become acquainted.

The floor of the chicken house was the ground, covered with straw, replaced at suitable intervals, another learnable chore. The chickens could always find water from the livestock watering trough in the summertime, but inverted half-gallon jars, screwed to a type of lid that released the water gradully as it was consumed, were always kept filled in the winter in the chicken house. These had to be monitored closely on freezing days.

Long metal feeding trays, called hoppers, were always kept filled with cracked corn or other types of chicken feed. There were spaced partitions in these hoppers where the chickens could poke their heads in to feed. These partitions prevented them from walking in the trays and thus fouling the feed.

Setting hen

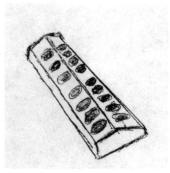

Feeding hopper

watering jar

If I seem to be spending too much time describing such a common thing as a chicken house, it is because I found it a rather pleasant place to be. Time moved slowly and orderly here. The clucking of the hens was a sound of contentment; the crowing of the roosters, a comical announcement of "I'm in charge here!"

Going down the long rows of nests, gathering the eggs, and placing them carefully in big buckets was always a satisfying thing for me. How many eggs might there be in the next nest? Maybe seven? Eight? A dozen! Knowing the eggs were a source of livelihood as well as food, the feel of them in my hand — white, brown, or speckled — gave me a sense of security and well-being. If I found one still warm from the hen's body, I held it in my hand a long time. Even today I tend to hold an egg lovingly in my hand before breaking it for any purpose, maybe even touch it to my cheek, especially if it is a brown speckled egg.

We had Rhode Island Reds and White Leghorns. When the rose-combed breeds came on, we proudly turned to some of them because, as much care as we took in housing our wintertime chickens, some of their combs, big and floppy as were the Leghorns', froze in the bitter cold.

Occasionally we would swap settings of eggs with neighbors and thus get some Buff Orpingtons or White Laced Black Wyandotts. However, we were always "heavy" on Leghorns since these were the best layers. Leghorns were high-strung, and if you entered the chicken house abruptly, they grew hysterical, flying in any direction they were facing, even if it was into your face.

In the beginning we hatched our own chickens, depending on a certain number of hens to become "broody" in the springtime. A setting of eggs was given her, usually twelve, and a special straw-lined box. If she chose her own place, say in the plum thicket, we let her be.

As this industry increased for us, an incubator was purchased. This was a square-like contraption with a pull-out drawer that could hold a certain number of eggs, usually two dozen. A constant heat was provided by an attached kerosene lamp which had to be watched carefully. For that reason, I remember that the incubator was kept in Mama's bedroom so that it could be watched in the night. I wonder how well Mama slept. The faint odor of the kerosene lamp permeated the upstairs bedroom, which was rather pleasant because we knew it meant good things were underway.

The eggs to be put into the incubator had to be candled first to see if they were fertile. A special piece of equipment, called a candler, held an egg in front of a lighted candle. The light, shining through the egg, could determine if the fertilizing element was present. Also, the eggs had to be marked with a dab of shoe polish or blueing so that we could tell if they had been turned over, a thing that had to be done every day to assure proper development of the chick inside. A hen, by her nature, will do this without any benefit of marking.

Then we outgrew the incubator and ordered baby chickens by mail. This way we could control the number of hens and roosters we wanted. A suitable number of roosters were always kept, not only to fertilize the eggs, but for their eternal cockiness, their cheerful morning calls, the shimmering of their beautiful tail feathers.

Maybe a hundred chicks would be ordered at one time. These came by mail to the nearest post office. To go to a post office when everyone's ordered baby chicks were arriving in the spring was an exciting experience. Hearing all those hundreds of chicks cheeping at one time is one of the lost sounds of the twentieth century.

Increasing the flock meant the construction of a brooder house. This we built about a hundred feet west of the smokehouse.

The brooder, a large, round, metal canopy, was placed on the floor. It was supported by short legs raised about three or four inches from the floor. Thus the chicks could wander all over the brooder house if they so desired and come back any time under the metal canopy to get warm. It, too, was heated by a kerosene-type heater in the middle, as well as windows facing south, which captured the heat of whatever sunshine there might be.

One dramatic event in the life of our chickens and chicken house was when Mama discovered some hens were missing. Sometimes their half-eaten carcasses were left inside the chicken house. Tracing the path of the thief, Mama found a dug-out opening at the base of a wall. She set a trap and a few mornings later there was a fine-furred mink in the trap. This creature was sold to a not-too-faraway firm dealing in animal skins. It brought the handsome sum of $6. Ah, bonuses. How rare and welcome they were.

The Barn

Two other buildings necessary to our livelihood were the barn and the cellar. The barn dwarfed all the other buildings. Perhaps it was built when the addition was made to the cabin home. No date of its construction was ever found, although this was a feature of early barns, the date being painted on at the peak of the roof or on the massive crosspiece of the "collar" that arose from the loft floor to support the roof. When we arrived, the whole structure was silvery gray and weather-cured.

Our barn was built in the familiar Western style. Resting on a rock foundation, it had a tall, wide, middle section with an expansive loft. The roof was pitched at about a 45-degree angle, then, lower down, in what is known as the broken gable manner, flared out to cover a machine shed on the right, cow stalls on the left. Through the squinted eyes of imagination, one could from a distance see it as a gargantuan dominecker hen hovering protectingly over her chicks, or a great ship moored on a smoothed-out plain on a mountainside that gently sloped down to the nearby river.

The interior of the barn was constructed by barn raisers who intended it to last. A farmer's barn was the most important building he had. The huge posts and crosspieces that supported the roof were put together with wooden trunnels. Wooden braces extended upwards at an angle from the crosspiece and were fastened to the rafters which, in turn, were fastened to the ridgepole running the length of the barn.

30

Originally the barn roof was of wooden shingles. During our watch, a shiny sheet-iron roof replaced the shingles. It was done with the proud knowledge and much repeated assurances to anyone who would listen that the barn would never have to be re-roofed. It never was, although after a while the sheet iron rusted, and from time to time a severe storm would loosen one of the corrugated sheets and bend it backwards. To Mama's and Grandma's dismay, especially during sleep-disturbed nights, it might flap noisily for many weeks before Dad or Grandpa, much occupied with other pressing chores, would get up on the roof to fasten the loosened sheet down again.

The Bell Family
Taken in front of the farmhouse with the barn in the background. Left to right: Lucille (standing), Wilson (Dad) holding Stephen Wilson (called S.W. for short), Lillian, Jean seated in front of Lillian, Myrtle (Mama).

A perpendicular ladder was nailed to the side wall and loft floor just inside the hallway on the left side. Its side posts were slick as satin from the grasp of many hands over the years.

A hallway ran through the center of the barn, wide enough to accommodate a team-drawn wagon loaded high, wide, and handsome with hay and, many times, two or three laughing, tumbling, little girls on top, reveling in the warm hay, still smelling of sunshine and fragrant grasses.

The hay fork, a big semi-U-shaped piece of equipment with two sharp prongs about three feet long and two feet apart, hung just inside the upper front wall. Through a complicated system of ropes and pulleys running the length of the high ridgepole and down the outside rear of the barn, the fork could be lowered, fastened into the hay, and great bundles of it lifted into the loft.

The rear rope, threaded through yet another pulley system, would be fastened to a singletree which was, in turn, fastened to the harness of a horse, and on signal from the loader in the wagon, the horse was led or ridden about one hundred feet behind the barn, lifting the load into the loft. It could be deposited anywhere in the loft underneath the ridgepole, depending on the loader who tripped the hooks on the hay fork to release the hay by pulling yet another rope. It was an ingenious system, especially for loose hay. Later, when we acquired a hay baler, the bales, which took less storage space, were heaved into the loft by manpower.

Entering the barn from the eastern front, on the right of the wide hallway, partitioned into rooms, were the corn crib, the harness room, another bin for any assorted grains we might choose to raise (rye, barley, oats), and the wheat bin. The corn and wheat bins were constants. On the left were the horse and mule stalls, occupied in our time mostly by Russell, Ned, Bill, Sam, Dobbin, and Raleigh. From openings in the loft floor, hay could be pitched down into v-shaped mangers resting on half walls that separated the stalls. The hay was held loosely in place by thin, spaced slats. Thus, horses in adjoining stalls could feed from the same manger.

Everyone had a sure knowledge of where these openings were in the barn loft floor, so that, if inadvertently camoflauged by loose hay, he would not fall into them. I did not travel that side of the loft very much. Even to get near the openings made my heart beat faster. What if I fell into a manger and old Bill or Sam took a big bite of me before realizing I wasn't hay!

Under the left wing of the broken gable were the cattle stalls. The stalls were separated by an open construction of wooden posts and cross slats so that the cows could have spaces of their own, but the whole wing appeared to be one big sociable cow room. When the cows came in from the pasture, hills, or barn lot, it was always a mystery to me how each one went along the walkway to her own stall, there to be confined by only a sliding rail put into place by the milkers. But in they came—Star, Stella, Cherry, Rose, Jersey, Polly, and Heart, in soldier-like order.

In the front corner of each stall, about cow-head high, was a feed box. At milking time, someone would come down the narrow walkway on that side of the stalls and deposit a certain measure of bran, not only to supplement the cows' forage, but to keep them quiet while milking. The hungry cows would snort, sniff, and generally blow the bran around in their hungry delight. Their moist noses would be covered with it, but soon all would be licked off with their long, grainy-textured tongues, and they'd look toward the doorway to see if more might be coming.

On the opposite side of the barn, where the roof swept low, was the big McCormick reaper, the corn planter, the rake, cultivator, and an assortment of plows, all intertwined and overlapped, making, in the mind's eye, one huge machine that could surely plow, plant, and harvest the whole state of Missouri.

The buggy, too, was kept in this section, and sometimes the big farm wagon. When stored, the buggy top was folded back, resulting in deep, long pockets of canvas. When I knew that Daddy had been to town in the buggy, I hurried to search these folds, for always there would be a little striped sack of stick candy hidden somewhere. Such a simple gesture of love and such utter delight for me and my sisters!

Above the machine shed and cow wings were lower lofts, dropped down about three feet from the main loft. There were short wooden wall barriers to keep one from inadvertently falling from the main loft to these lower floors. These lofts held additional hay when crops were exceedingly good. Sometimes the crops were so stupendously good, hay had to be stacked in tall stacks just inside the orchard fence adjacent to the north barn lot.

In summer the barn was airy and fragrant with the newly stored hay. All doors were left open. The big hallway was breezy, dry, and dusty. Except for calling cows home or going after them at milking time, they were free to roam the barn lot or the big meadow. If they roamed the surrounding hills, they came home smelling of pennyroyal or mountain mint, which their feet had trod upon.

The horses, too, could enjoy such day and night freedom, except those to be used the next day. They were kept in the barn lot for easy access, since a farmer's day started early and was not to be frittered away with capturing horses which might, with flying manes and switching tails, have preferred to stay in the pasture with the others.

Barn swallows, in the gentler months, attached their mud nests to the inside walls of the machine shed and there raised their young. The hard-to-confine Leghorns and some of the other chickens sometimes abandoned the summer-nighttime henhouse roosts and roosted on the big reel of the binder.

In winter the barn became especially cozy when all doors were shut, all bins filled, all stalls occupied. Passing by on a snowy day, unless some cow, suddenly remembering summer pastures, gave a bawl of lament, one would think the barn a forlorn, empty, lifeless thing, but actually it was vibrant with life, almost warm from the heat of the animals' bodies as they rested in their stalls. Up in the dim, dusty, cavernous region of the rafters were the mud daubers' labyrinthine homes, their occupants waiting. Here, too, woolly spiders hung their winter festoons. Often an owl would squeeze in through some loose board and find shelter.

Barn cats rounded out sleeping quarters in the hay, convenient to some pungent mouse hole that led to secret passageways where the beady-eyed creatures made noises with old corncobs and left intricate patterns on dusty floors with their dainty feet.

Going to milk at winter dusk was a tender time. The cows, shaggy with their winter growth of hair, would low gently at our coming, and the horses made soft, throaty, welcome sounds through their velvet nostrils. The barn and all that was in it seemed bound together in some mysterious way, each a part of and dependent on the other.

Sitting on a low stool, made from a leftover wagon-wheel hub of livery stable days, I would warm my hands in the soft, fuzzy hair between the cow's udders and then begin to milk, making little tunes with the streams of milk in the tin bucket until the tune was swallowed up by the warm foam.

Through the cracks in the board walls, I could look out and see the snow swirling and, through the snow, the light from the kitchen windows where I knew Grandma and Mama would be cooking a supper of maybe fried ham, potatoes, and canned green

Rear view of the homestead buildings after the Bells left.

beans, corn, tomatoes, or peas from the cellar. Biscuits or cornbread and maybe a dewberry or apple cobbler would be baking. The ham would be from our smokehouse, vegetables from our garden, apples from our orchard, and dewberries from our fields.

The Bells' farm home after it was remodeled

Woodsmoke from the fireplace and kitchen-range chimney would seep through the barn walls and mingle with the heady odor from the stalls: the hay, harness, corn, bran, and warm sweet milk.

It never occurred to me that there could be any other way of life. Who would want another way? Here was security and love, comfort, and confidence. Splendid simplicity. Although at this early age, I'm sure I never mentally analyzed our way of life in such terms. What did I know about simplicity as opposed to complexity? I lived simplicity. I knew we needed soil, sunshine, water, and seeds. We had them. Did I understand security and confidence? I only knew that I was loved and cared for by parents, grandparents, and sisters, and that I could try anything new, on my own, without crippling derision.

The Cellar

The cellar was a marvel of construction. It was dome-shaped, like an old-fashioned bee skep. The interior brick walls were smooth plastered and whitewashed. Concrete floor. The whitewash made it less dim inside. The only other light was from the opened door or the small round tile pipe protruding to the outside from the center of the ceiling. This was for ventilation. The whole mound was covered with a foot or two of sod. A slanting wooden door, pitched to the slant of the sodded dome, when opened and laid back revealed steps that descended well below the surface of the earth. At the foot of the steps was another wooden door that was kept shut to preserve the warmth in winter or coolness in summer.

A concrete bench about three feet wide and two feet high circled the base of the interior. On this circular platform rested the jars of canned berries, peaches, apples, plums, green beans, beets, corn, mustard and spinach greens, tomatoes, and anything else that was raised on the farm and could be put into glass jars or tin cans. In the early days, tomatoes were put into tin cans and a tin lid sealed on with hot, orange-red sealing wax.

When the County Home Demonstration Agent came to our county, she taught us how to can tomatoes and meat in glass jars. I have never tasted meat as good as those pork chops and sausages, home canned.

Then came Mr. DeLaval. That wasn't his name, but we always called this salesman by that name. Living on a remote farm, with hard-to-travel roads, we did not meet anyone at the door with a curt, "We don't want any and have no time to listen." We usually wanted everything any salesman had to offer, whether we could buy it or not, and time was in plenteous supply.

So when Mr. DeLaval came, he was graciously met at the door by Mama, with Grandma looking over her shoulder, and Lou and Lillian trailing out behind. I had already been sent hopping to the barn or fields to notify Dad and Grandpa that "Company has come!"

"Through some wonder of wonders, a machine has been invented that will separate the cream from the milk instantly, or almost instantly," Mr. DeLaval said and waited for our reaction.

We all just stood silently, staring at this stranger.

"Let me show you," Mr. D. said.

Dad nodded affirmatively, whereupon Mr. D. went to his conveyance, brought in a heavy machine, and placed it on as level a place as he could find on the kitchen floor. He returned to get many more pieces which he identified as the milk container, the floater, the spouts, discs, gasket, screw, etc.

"Works on the centrifugal principle," he told us as he assembled the pieces in a certain order and placed them in the machine.

We stood silently.

"Bring some milk," Mr. D. requested, "and get your cream cans."

Lou and I bumped into each other as we raced to the cellar for some crocks of milk. Mama went after the cream cans.

Mr. D. d the milk into the big container at the top and crank at the side which began to hum gradually lowly picked up speed until we could tell something inside was really moving. He turned the spigot to release the milk from the top container, and in a minute a stream of cream was coming from one spout and "blue john," or thin milk, from the other.

We stood in abject, wide-eyed awe.

Heretofore, the milk had been put into big crocks, allowed to set overnight while the cream rose to the top, then skimmed off and put into two 10-gallon milk cans. When full, these cans were hurried off to the train depot at Elvins, as fast as horse and buggy could take them. From there they went, according to the wired-on, stiff cardboard address tags, to the Blue Valley Creamery in St. Louis, Missouri. In about a week our check came through the mail. We could pick up our empty cans at the Elvins depot, sent back to us by similar address tags described above. Thus for us, four cans were always in use. For other neighboring families it might be only one can, or maybe five or six.

We bought the cream separator! It may have saved time, work, and money, but for Lou and me, who washed and dried the twenty or more different parts two times a day, its glow sometimes grew dim.

Not all our milk was run through the separator. Some was carried up to the kitchen to "clabber." This was then poured into the big cedar churn and churned, by way of a hand-manipulated dasher, to make butter.

A sufficient amount of butter was kept for cooking and table use, the rest molded into pound molds and exchanged at Langdon's Grocery for the things we could not raise, or sold for money we could spend at stores that did not trade for butter.

Another source of security that the cellar provided was that when the severe storms came, we all went down, closing the two doors behind us until the fury was over. Propped against the wall behind the downstairs door were picks, shovels, and axes so that if the house or the big cherry tree blew over on the cellar, we could dig our way out. And if it took several days to do this, there were all the quart jars of canned food, potatoes, and cream cans in various stages of fullness.

Tragedy and Other Events Connected with Milk and Cream

Stephen Wilson, my brother, was born at home on December 20, 1916. I was barely three years old, so I don't remember the event. Nor do I remember much about him, except for photos that seem to call up some dim memories and the things the other family members have told to me.

S.W., as we called him, was fond of somehow getting into a two-gallon bucket and letting Grandpa carry him about in it. Also, learning that Grandma put on a hat and carried a suitcase when she went to visit her daughter, Aunt Luzena Bell Bryan, in Bonne Terre, Missouri, he sometimes put on Grandma's hat and carried the suitcase, evidently pretending he was going on a trip.

Less than two years old, S.W. was playing about the kitchen one day, while churning the milk was under way. Although the churn had a wooden lid with a hole in it through which the handle of the dasher protruded, milk did escape through this hole and also around the lid. It splattered onto the kitchen floor. S.W. picked up a dried bean from somewhere and put it into his mouth, as little ones are prone to do with such objects. He stepped into some of the splattered milk, slid, and fell. The bean went down his windpipe. Mama and Grandma knew instantly that he was choking. No amount of upside down shaking or other methods of trying to dislodge anything that he might have swallowed worked. He was hurried to Elvins to a doctor; hurried, of course, meaning having to harness and hitch a horse to a buggy and drive ten miles.

Since S.W. was still managing to breathe fairly well, the doctor felt that everything would be all right. No

Stephen Wilson Bell (S.W.)
(1916–1918)

X-ray. None recommended. I doubt that there was such a machine available within many miles. He was brought back home to "recuperate." The bean was truly lodged and, surrounded by moisture, began to swell choking off breath entirely. He died. It was a tragic death, something one might expect to happen in early pioneer days. This was 1918.

Stephen Wilson Bell, only son of Wilson and Myrtle Bell, is buried at Bonne Terre, Missouri, not far from where his grandfather and grandmother, Stephen and Josephine, were to be buried later.

Stephen Wilson Bell (S.W.)
(1916–1918)

*   *   *

Not only was it the cream and butter that helped to finance my raising; cream, in an indirect way, launched my later writing career.

When older sister, Lillian, was ready for high school, having finished the eighth grade at rural Loughboro School, she attended Doe Run, Missouri, High School for her ninth grade. This school was about five miles from our home. It proved very difficult to get her back and forth. Therefore, for the remainder of her high-school education, she spent these school years with Grandma Mary Alice Casey at Fredericktown, Missouri, about fifty miles south of our home. Here she was within a short walking distance of the school.

When it came time for her graduation, she wrote a letter to us saying that the graduating girl students were going to wear caps and gowns and black shoes.

We saved enough of the butter, egg, and cream money to buy a pair of black shoes for her graduation and, with a sense of enormous satisfaction that few would understand today, mailed them to her.

Then, as women sometimes do, the girls in her class decided they were going to wear white shoes. What were we to do? The shoe money had been spent. Lillian was to be salutatorian and would be in at least partial limelight.

As mentioned above, we took our cream to Elvins, about ten miles away, by horse and buggy or wagon. There it was put on a train and shipped to the creamery in St. Louis. Naturally, by the time it got there, it was always sour cream. But the one and only time it ever stayed sweet on this long trip was the very time we needed extra money to buy a pair of white shoes. Sweet cream sold for almost double that of sour cream! We bought the white shoes and got them there in time.

In 1947, after a short career of teaching and longer career as a secretary, I wrote about this incident and sold it to *Woman's Day.** My first story sold! More about this later.

The War Years

The first scary thing was the aurora borealis. It happened one clear night, turning the whole sky red, silhouetting Simms and Little Stono Mountains. Someone, I suppose half-jokingly, said, "The Germans are coming!" I had heard about the "terrible" Germans but not about an aurora borealis. I cowered near Mama's skirts, although the red sky was the prettiest thing I'd ever seen. We blew out the lights from the lamps and sat in a dimly lit "red" kitchen. I remember it well, for the red light from the sky fell upon the topknot of the pileated woodpecker pictured on our Arm and Hammer bird chart. It seemed to make the red crested feathers glow. With Mama's arms around me and that woodpecker glowing in the red darkness, I felt I needn't be afraid of anything. Woodpeckers still give me a lingering sense of peace.

Not so scary, but still hung up in my memory, are the brown biscuits we ate instead of Mama's usual white fluffy ones. The brown flour was something like the bran we fed the cows.

Then there was the day when Daddy had to go to town to get shot! That's the way I understood it. I associated being shot with the guns in the catchall, which were used to kill rabbits and squirrels for the cooking pots. Oh, aching heart, why was Daddy going

---

* *Woman's Day,* April 1951.

to be shot? Was that the way war worked? I climbed to the barn loft and hid in the hay where no one could hear me.

They were necessary medical shots before being inducted into the army, of course. Why didn't someone tell me? Probably because everyone was too worried and coming down with influenza. Daddy got it first, then Grandpa, Grandma, Mama—right on down the line to me, the youngest. All of us were in bed at the same time. Tom Alexander, a neighbor who had already recovered from it, came over, about a mile and a half, to milk our cows and feed the livestock.

A message was sent to friends at Fredericktown, and Mrs. Isom Ware came up to try to feed us and give what medicine was available. Something was put into a water with rock candy, which I remember throwing all the way across the room from where I was bedded down on the leather-tufted couch that could be flattened to make a bed. Mrs. Ware then got the flu, but by that time those who caught it first were staggering to their feet and were able to take care of her.

Besides the surrey, buggy, and big wagon, there was another conveyance we had which was called a hack. It had benched seats along the sides. I remember at least one ride in it. When World War I was over, we all went to Elvins to celebrate. Whether we picked up someone on the way, I don't remember. We probably did, for everyone was going to Elvins.

The streets were crowded with joyous young and old, and Kaiser Bill, the German leader, was hanged in effigy. Burned, too, in front of Fatty Klein's Shoe Store. I didn't understand it at all. I was frightfully scared, albeit the hanged thing looked like a scarecrow.

On the Way to School

I entered Loughboro, a one-room rural school in September, 1918. Woodrow Wilson was president. World War I was coming to a close. I was unaware of either of these conditions. My red-backed Big Chief, 5¢ tablet, my penny pencil, and what my first teacher would be like were of more interest.

Out the front door we went: Lillian, Lou, and I, school lunches, tablets, pencils in hand. We followed the old wagon road past the barn lot, down a hill, and across a creek. There we branched off onto a footpath that went up a hill, across a little clearing, down and up a small draw. Here we followed the path that led high up alongside the St. Francis River, until we came to the first potential hazard on our journey: the swinging bridge.

Dad and Grandpa built this bridge, anchoring it, to my dismay, by a buried "dead man"! This was as bad as Daddy getting "shot" preparing for World War I.

Later, much later, I learned that such a "dead man" was something heavy and metal, such as a big wheel from a binder or other big piece of machinery. This "dead man" was buried deep into the ground with two long, heavy, twisted wire cables attached to it. These cables stuck up through the ground, about three feet apart, and were stretched across the river and there anchored again by another "dead man"!

Since the northern bank was much lower, it was necessary to build a tower so that the bridge would be straight. There were steps from this tower descending to the ground, but the cables went on from the top of the tower before being angled down and buried again.

Planks were wired in place across these sturdy cables, stretching about seventy-five feet across the river. There were other cables, hand high on each side to hold on to as we crossed the suspended, swinging affair which always seemed to ripple behind us as we walked across, as if to urge us on. Chicken wire was attached to both sides to keep us from slipping off into the river below, should the bridge be icy or snow-covered, which it certainly was many winter days. Also, sudden floods brought the angry, muddy, boiling water up to the floorboards and sometimes covered them.

After descending the wooden steps of the tower, we continued our journey alongside a field where, in summer, plump dewberries grew. At the end of this field and across a road that ran alongside was the second hazard, a high log footbridge above a creek that flowed into the river. After negotiating this, we left our farm and entered a field belonging to a neighbor, Jess Stacy. Here, still close to the riverbank, we had to make a new path each September which, by that time of the year, was usually full of cockleburs and other scratching, stinging, waist-high weeds. Sometimes, wishing to arrive at school looking as neat as we could, we would take off our shoes and stockings, if the day was warm enough, and put them back on when this field was traversed. We knew a foot-washing creek was coming up.

Through the strands of a wire fence we left that field and came upon this gravelly bottomed, foot-washing creek. It was usually shallow enough so that we could cross it by stepping on suitably placed rocks. It flowed beneath a railroad trestle. Now it was our task to climb a steep chat bank to get up to the railroad tracks. We always paused here to listen for the morning train whistle, coming out of Bismarck and going our way to who knew where. Some of the boxcars had Rock Island, Burlington, Chesapeake, and so on, printed in large black letters on their sides. We decided those places were where the train might be going, wherever in the world they were.

Once on the railroad track, the going was easier, except that the ties were not the right distance apart for us — too far. Later I learned that models learned to walk gracefully by carrying a book on their heads. If I had to give reason for my gait, I would have said that I learned to walk by railroad ties.

The railroad stretch that we covered was about two miles. It wound for some of this stretch alongside the river, between bluffs which we dubbed the Little and Big Bluffs.

On our way home from school, if there was still plenty of daylight, we stopped to play at the Big Bluffs, sometimes making bird

This is a portion of the Bellmont Branch of the Missouri Pacific Railroad the Bells traveled by foot to school and early church. Here it winds through the Big Bluffs. This branch of the railroad has now been abandoned.

nests of dried grass and sticking them way back into the crevices, just to see what would happen to them. Once, Lou, wishing to make them more realistic, put some little round rabbit droppings into a nest! Her sense of the ridiculous, her good humor, practicality, patience, and this-is-what-we-must-do-now manner compensated somewhat for her lame right leg, caused by polio when she was an infant. Numerous operations and a myriad of braces helped some, but she always had a decided limp. She made the three-mile daily walk and crossed that swinging bridge and foot log as well as any of us.

Mama and Dad could not caution us enough about getting off the tracks the minute we heard the train coming and waiting for its passage. Sometimes we could hear the whistle miles away, and dutifully got off and waited, spending the time to more thoroughly learn the multiplication tables or our spelling lessons for the day.

Sometimes — oh, trembling heart — we saw a hobo coming toward us. Those were the days of such "bums" and their chosen way of life. Today they are on welfare. "Just speak and walk on by," Mama said. And that really was all we had to do. Not one, no, not one, ever so much as asked for our lunches. Still, we had a certain amount of fear, just because it was a stranger and we were far from home. Mornings, we might see a little thin column of smoke arising from a hidden cliff shelter somewhere on the riverbank, could smell coffee and maybe even bacon frying, but we ceased our talking and tiptoed on the railroad ties until we were far past the smoke. That the bacon may have come from our own smokehouse, in the dead of some night, was brought to our attention later.

When we came to the cattle guards, a gated place along the tracks where a short strip of ties were set far apart with deep spaces beneath so that it would be impossible for four-footed animals to negotiate, we had the choice of departing the tracks and walking down a lane alongside a goat pasture or continuing on the tracks. If we continued on the tracks, we had to pass a gravestone. A *gravestone*, miles away from any cemetery. It had been there many years, a concrete slab, the name on it so worn we couldn't read it. No one remembered who was buried there. Rumor had it that it was someone who got killed working on the railroad and, there being no one to claim the body, was buried right there beside the tracks. We grew quiet when we passed the gravestone. We were sad to think there had been no family to claim the dead person. Who then had put up the slab stone? Later, when studying Gray's "Elegy Written in a Country Churchyard," my thoughts always wandered back to that lonesome grave.

Perhaps I have a childish conception of heaven, but it is satisfactory. Sometime I may round a corner in that dimension and, meeting someone, intuitively know the person or spirit I encounter to be the one that was buried by the railroad tracks.

A little farther along the tracks, we came to the switchyard. This is where boxcars were left on a side track to pick up railroad ties the local tie cutters furnished. Here we would pick up little squares of green tissue paper, wadded up and discarded from bills of sales. We had never seen such green tissue paper. But more exotic than that were the little squares of carbon paper we found along with the green tissue. It was our first encounter with that marvel of marvels. You could write on something with it beneath, and the writing would come out on a second piece of paper beneath it. Glory be!

There was fear encountered at the switchyard, too. Our cousin, Collar Bell, had once gotten his foot caught in a switch. Some workman had thrown it the wrong way and an oncoming train had cut his leg off at the hip. We stepped widely around those places where the rails came together in a V, even though there was no switchman around anywhere nor a train within miles.

Sometimes, at the cattle guards, we chose to take the goat lane. In the autumn months it was beautifully bordered by goldenrod, wild asters, and sumac. Where such growth was sparse, the goats, white and silky-looking in the morning or afternoon sunshine, noted our passing and came over to stand and stare at us, even walk along for a while beside the fence, their odor opening our heads of any stuffiness we may have been feeling. The lane eventually made a sharp left turn, and we could see the white schoolhouse ahead, perched up on a steep hill. Yet there was another creek to cross. Again, this was usually done by friendly rock placements, but when it was flooding, we had to go through nearby Mr. West's barnlot and cross on another foot log.

After this long journey, encumbered with lunch buckets and school paraphernalia, we felt it was some kind of cruel joke that the schoolhouse had to be placed up on that high hill. If the song had been written and we knew the tune then, we would have gone in singing in breathless voices, "Climb every mountain. Cross every stream."

The five-minute bell, rung by the teacher at the door, sounded at five minutes to nine o' clock. We were always at or near the foot of this hill by this time. I don't ever remember being tardy. There was the County Truant Officer to deal with tardiness!

When the nine o'clock bell rang, all those outside lined up in two rows, the boys in one, the girls in another, and marched into the schoolhouse. There was no pushing, jostling, shoving. All was quiet and orderly. We were embarking upon an education—an education which we knew was necessary to get on in the world.

1920–1930

School Days at Loughboro

Someday a definitive paen of praise will be written to the one-room rural school. They were cozy little nests of learning. The pupils were almost family. We knew each others' homes intimately, the names of their cows, horses, dogs, and cats, where the closets were and what was in them, the layout of their outbuildings, what they had for breakfast, and whether they prayed aloud or silently before meals and at bedtime. One of our biggest adventures during the school year was to be allowed to stay all night at each others' homes. We stayed mostly with the McFarlands or Stacys, since their homes were closer to our home.

The Loughboro school was typical of the early twentieth-century rural school. A big, metal, round-hooded stove was placed in one corner with racks of good dried wood behind it. The hood was ornamental bas-relief. The teacher, or one of the bigger eighth-grade boys, kept it stoked all day and banked the fire for the night. A wood house, separate but nearby, was filled sometime during the year by the parents of the pupils, the wood being from someone's timbered hills.

Desks, graduating in size to accomodate the length of the first graders' legs up to those of the eighth graders', faced forward toward the teacher's desk. These desks were seats and desks combined, the seat in front with a desk attached to the back for the use of the pupil seated behind. Ornamental black iron legs bolted them to the floor. The slanting top of the desk had a groove to hold pencils and pens and a hole to hold an ink bottle so that its contents would not be inadvertently spilled when in use. Underneath the desktop was a compartment to hold books, tablets, pencils, rulers, crayons, or any other objects the pupil wished to have, provided it didn't take up too much room. Such desks now are considered antiques.

Sometime before leaving school for work or higher education, some pupils, knowing their possible punishment days were over, would carve their initials somewhere in their desktop, a thing much frowned on by teachers, school-board members, and the more fastidious pupils. Such carvers were seldom ever caught in the act. It was a sort of valedictory rite for those ending their school years at the little schoolhouse atop the hill.

Rows of small-paned windows were on each side of the schoolhouse. There were no blinds, drapes, curtains, or screens. Wasps, mud daubers, and sometimes even butterflies wandered in and out of the opened windows before cold weather demanded they be closed. If a grasshopper made a huge arc and landed somewhere inside, it was caught and either put down the back of someone's dress or shirt or into a box for the nature-study class. I suppose those windows were washed before school started each year, but I don't think they were ever washed after school started.

It was good to have a desk by a window, even though it might be a cold spot in winter. There wasn't much to see going on outside, though, because the schoolhouse was in a little clearing in the woods. But one could see the woods softly filling up with snow in winter or dripping with rain in the spring and fall. Maybe someone's hound passed by occasionally or even a foraging pig or two.

Once a man on a horse rode rapidly around the schoolhouse shouting, "Vote for Coolidge! Vote for Coolidge!" The horse and rider were so close to the windows, I could have reached out and touched the horse's flying tail. But we all drew back toward the center of the room in surprise and almost fear. No one recognized the horse or rider. Elva Russell, the biggest boy, got up and locked the door for fear on his next journey around, the horse might come right up the front steps and down the center aisle.

After the horse and rider had disappeared, his voice receding in the distance toward the river, Miss Mary, our teacher, explained that it was the year when our country was to elect a new president and that this fellow on the horse had chosen to campaign in this manner. This was 1924. I was in the fifth grade and, of course, knew that the head of our country was a president, but this was my first experience with campaigning methods. That's what Miss Mary laughingly told us it was: "Just someone's enthusiasm to get folks to vote for Coolidge." Since none of us except the teacher was old enough to vote, I assimilated it all as more of a modern-day Paul Revere's Ride: *T'was in the year of twenty-four. Horse and rider came shoutin' by. Scared us to the very core. Vote for Coolidge was his cry!*

In the corner opposite the big stove was a small walled-off space. One side was shelved to hold the lunch buckets; the other side was studded with rows of nails upon which to hang coats and sweaters. Winter overshoes, smelling much of barnyards, were all piled in a congenial heap on the floor at the back of this space.

Just inside the door, on a small homemade table, was the galvanized two-gallon water bucket and communal granite dipper. Some more squeamish pupils used the dipper to fill their collapsible tin drinking cups which they carried in their pockets or kept in their desks. Some drank directly from the dipper and put it back into the bucket.

Water came from a cistern a few feet away from the right front of the building. Filling the empty water bucket from the pump, dusting the erasers (beating them together outside to remove most of the chalk dust), washing the blackboard were all little chores that somehow were regarded as being given to the best-behaved children.

In addition to the windows being washed before school started, the wooden, narrow-planked floor was oiled to keep down the dust.

At this time of advertising for Lifebuoy Soap, little sample bars were provided for the pupils. There was a wall chart accompanying the samples. The teacher inspected our hands upon arriving at school, to see if they were Lifebuoy clean, and if they were, we got a gold star put on the chart beside our name. I believe that Lifebuoy provided the gold stars, too. This was the first Lifebuoy soap made, and it smelled strongly of carbolic acid. Not an altogether unpleasant odor, just clean. It was probably the first time any of the pupils got a gold star for anything, although they had milked hundreds of cows, hoed miles of corn, or put up 500 loads of hay into the barn loft.

48

The combined odor of all the little boxes of crayons, the oiled floors, filled lunch boxes, chalk dust, little, middle-sized, and big bodies, and cedar penny pencils combined to produce an odor that could only be called one-room rural schoolhouse.

Reading!

Learning to read and having more books available were two of the best things to come out of Loughboro school days.

I had a head start, not in the sense of government-sponsored Headstart programs at the last of the century, but we had a funny collection of books at home from which Mama read aloud to anyone who wanted to listen.

My first book, given to me before I could read, was *Little Boy Blue*. This was an expanded version of the Little Boy Blue who was urged to "come blow his horn." The book had a blue hardback cover and the indented title was in black. The black eventually wore off from my tracing the lettering with my finger. Before I knew an A from a B or the word "cow" from "horn," Mama, Lillian, Lou, anyone I could babyishly beg, read this slender book to me, over and over and over.

The book mysteriously disappeared! But it was too late for any relief its disappearance may have afforded. I had, unknowingly, learned it by heart, could recite it exactly, and did so over and over and over without it being in my hands, could even turn the absent pages at the right word. So I knew what the words "boy," "blue," "horn," "meadow," "cow," "little," etc., looked like and could identify them on sight long before I started school. However, when I started school, the word "little" was introduced to me in a box at the top of the new lesson page as "lit-tle," with a strange marking over the first "t." It threw me off a "lit-tle," but still I had a good head start.

The most elegant piece of furniture we had was the combination bookcase and desk. On one side were the bookshelves behind a long, outward-curved glass, wood-framed door, complete with keyhole and key. On the right side, about halfway down, was an inward slanting door that could be dropped down to form a writing board. Behind this writing-board door, also with keyhole and key, were a number of interesting little pigeonholes of varying sizes. Below the slanting door were more open shelves for books—a truly antique piece of furniture today.

It was the books behind that glass door that were of interest to me, although the curved glass and key and keyholes were always a marvel for me. There were no other keys anywhere around, except those to wind the clocks.

To a perceptive adult reader, the little collection of books would have seemed odd, perhaps even comical. Titles were *The San Francisco Earthquake*, *The Great Chicago Theater Disaster*, a gloomy volume entitled *Night Scenes from the Bible*, agriculture books, *Romola*, two Waverly Novels with gold thistles on their green covers, a softly padded black leather volume of *Longfellow's Poems*, *The Poems and Dramas of Lord Byron*, an old *Missouri Blue Book*, and Douglass' *History of Southeast Missouri*. This must have been the original collection that was brought to the farm. How did that curved glass door ever make it intact, in the bed of the wagon, over those rocky hillsides and rocky-bottomed river to the farm?

In the San Francisco and Chicago disaster books (How did we come by them?), there were many pictures of those who had lost their lives. Their names and ages were given. Lou and I seemed morbidly interested and could, eventually, recite the names of everyone pictured without benefit of looking at the caption. We affectionately shortened their names. A little blond Rebecca became Becky to us. A distinguished looking Peter became Pete.

As we girls grew, a few more books began to be added, mostly gifts. They were the Five Little Peppers series, *The Girl of the Limberlost*, *Georgina of the Rainbow*, and *Laddie*.

We subscribed to the magazine *Comfort*. Maybe it was this magazine that contained Thornton Burgess' little animal stories. I could hardly wait for the next issue to come so that Mama could read another such story about Old Granny Fox, Jerry Muskrat, or Sammy Jay. In addition, there were adult continuing stories. Mama read these aloud too, primarily for Grandma's benefit, whose eyesight was failing. I listened to these stories as avidly as I did to those about Bowser the Hound or Reddy Fox.

There was one I shall never forget, "The Unseeing Eye." It was my first exposure to mystery stories. Such listened-to reading acquainted me, by some peculiar literary osmosis, with plot, characterization, and climax, all unintentional and all with profound unawareness on anyone's part.

When Mama began to read *Evangeline* to us after supper, and all chores and homework were done, the words fell from her lips, again unintentionally, like some beautiful but somber notes of music. "This is the forest primeval. The murmuring pines and the hemlocks, bearded with moss . . . indistinct in the twilight . . . voices sad and prophetic . . . the deep-voiced neighboring ocean . . . answers the wail of the forest. . . ."

It seemed that the lamps in this enchanting winter kitchen suddenly burned lower, the fireplace light dimmed, and the tea-kettle on the back of the kitchen range sighed. Something bitter-sweet was going to come about in the poem that lasted for several evenings of reading.

Mama would pause often to see if there were any questions. There were, but we seldom interrupted. Once I ventured, "Let me see that word, 'murmuring'." Mama showed it to me. It even looked like it sounded. We pronounced it slowly together, which precluded any explanation of what it meant. It made me think of the river where it "murmured" over the rocks between the Big and Little Bluffs on our way to school.

"Primeval," "Druids," "disconsolate," "prophetic," could go by the way to be attended to later. I had picked out my glimmering, emerald jewel, "murmuring." It was sweet and sad, yet comforting. No doubt I went about for days, murmuring.

As Mama continued, I also, without any scholastic lesson, imbibed cadence and rhythm, adding them unconsciously to my sense of mood, plot, characterization, and climax. In later life when these concepts were presented to me scholastically, how was it I already seemed to know about them?

If this account of Mama's reading sounds just too literary, let me say that when she opened the beautifully bound *The Poems and Dramas of Lord Byron* and read from the very first page a poem entitled, "To E_____," all of us were as puzzled as one of Grandpa's hounds who had lost the trail.

When Mama caught Lou and me thumbing through that gloomy, darkly illustrated book *Night Scenes from the Bible* and identifying pictures as, "That's Nick with Jesus," "Here's Pete, Jim, and Johnny asleep in the Garden," she, flashy-eyed and tight-lipped, took it from our hands and put us to bed without even a teaspoonful of chamomile tea. We were glad she didn't turn the fascinating key in that fascinating keyhole and put it out of our reach.

The following Christmas, a new book was put into our hands. It was highly illustrated and the title was *Bible Stories for Children*.

Early Christmases

Our early Christmases were very simple, but the best. Childhood wonderment, expectancy, and fulfillment made them so.

There were no parties. No one went caroling or a-wassailing. Homes were too far apart. Except for the school and church programs, Christmas was largely a family affair. But with seven of us—eight for a very short while when S.W. was with us—that was just the right size.

We had things at Christmas we didn't have the rest of the year—divinity, molasses candy, oranges, and popcorn balls. There was the smell of the cedar tree, too. We could smell cedar anytime we wanted to with two such trees in our front yard and hundreds of them in the surrounding woods. But to bring a cut cedar tree into the warmth of the fireplace-heated parlor, or even kitchen, was to smell cedar.

Mama and Grandma had brought with them to the farm some tinseled tree ornaments, mostly green glass pinecones and some tinsel-edged, holly-printed, basket-like cones with hanging loops so that they could be hung on the tree branches. I don't remember them ever holding anything as they were designed to do, but they made the tree sparkly. Lou, Lillian, and I made the paper chains, and always there were garlands of popcorn. We raised popcorn.

We had some glass windchimes which were never hung outside to blow in the wind. They were small, different-sized pieces of hand-painted glass suspended by varying lengths of string from a red hoop with a centralized hanger so the strings would hang straight. Did someone make them? Mama? Grandma? Some aunt? Brought from Virginia? They were the cherished ornaments, above all others, of our tree trimmings. It was a joy to brush by the tree every chance one had, to set off the enchanting, tinkling, fairy-like music. The whole tree seemed to shiver with gladness.

In the early years, it was Santa Claus who brought the presents, but later, one gift to each one was the custom. From me, Grandpa and Dad might receive little cloth bags of tobacco with yellow drawstring closings, for Grandma a new dust cap, a package of needles for Mama, and handkerchiefs for Lillian and Lou.

The earliest gift I remember was a pair of red felt, bead-trimmed Indian moccasins. Then there was the monkey-on-a-string. By some pulling on the string at the bottom, the metal monkey actually climbed the string. When Dad wound up a metal ladybug and it started crawling across the floor toward me, I frantically climbed to the top of Grandpa's head by way of watch fob, shirt pocket, moustache, and ears.

The year I received a can of violet-scented talcum powder was memorable. Sweet violet has been my favorite scent since then, and so hard to find.

One year, Lou and I decided to have our very own Christmas in the attic. The attic has been earlier described — exposed interior log walls, fireplace chimney coming up through to keep it fairly warm, casement window with missing pane so that Tabby Cat could come in when sleet and snow swirled outside.

Lou and I often used the same route of entrance into the attic as did Tabby Cat. We, of course, had another entrance by way of stairs and doors, but it was much more challenging and secretive to hop up onto the outside washbench, throw one leg up over the nearby lean-to pantry roof, scramble on, crawl up the slanting shingles to the pane-missing window, reach inside to unlatch it, and, with enormous effort, pull our bodies up and over the sill.

That winter we had a secret tree of our own in the attic. At least we thought it secret. If others knew about it, they never let on.

Trudging through the surrounding snowy woods, hatchet in hand, we selected a small cedar we judged we could manipulate from the washbench to the pantry roof and through the casement window.

We trimmed our tree with crayon-colored paper chains. From ads and greetings in the pre-Christmas weekly newspaper, we cut out a suitable number of figures for the nativity scene (this was after Mama gave us the book of Bible stories), pasted them on cardboard, and tried to make them stand up.

The manger was the exciting thing that particular Christmas. It was a doll bed Dad had, some years ago, made for us. It was enormously out of proportion to our paper people and animals. Dad had attached four slat legs to the corners of a wooden box. Painted red, it was a treasured possession.

It was easy to bring straw from the straw stack through the casement window to make the "manger" look like the one pictured in our book of Bible stories.

"I wish we had something live," Lou would say nearly every day after we had attended the school Christmas program at which one of the school "shepherds" had surprisingly brought a real live lamb for the nativity tableau.

"Well, we sure can't get old Star" (our big red cow) "up here, nor Ned, Raleigh, nor Russell" (some of our horses).

We continued to sort through our few dolls to decide which one to put into the manger.

"None of them even look like a baby," Lou complained.

"Nor alive," I added.

On the last Friday before Christmas, it was near dark, snowing, and sleeting when we got home from school. Without going through the downstairs first, we climbed up the pantry roof way to place three paper wise men and camels we'd made at school. It was late, and with no lights in the attic, we could hardly see anything.

From the direction of the crib, there came a faint "meow." We bent over the straw-lined crib, and there was Tabby Cat with four newborn kittens. Soft and warm, all curled up together. Five things, alive!

After a while I asked Lou, "What'll we do?" feeling, vaguely, that something wasn't quite right here, but not exactly wrong either.

After another long while, Lou said, "Nothing. Something alive and warm is better than a cold doll."

And that's the way it was that Christmas.*

And God Talked Back**

Loughboro school days now seem so far away, yet so near and dear. Each day brought something new to my mind. I read about "The Spider and the Fly," "The Leak in the Dike," "The Song of Hiawatha," "Pandora's Box." Oh, how I could relate to Browning's lines from "Pippa Passes":

> *The hillside's dew-pearled;*
> *The lark's on the wing;*

---

* A portion of this appeared in the *Southeast Missourian*, December 24, 1995.
** *Daily Word*, November 1985.

The snail's on the thorn:
God's in his Heaven. . . ."

My lark was the meadowlark which, with seemingly dozens
of others, rang out its silvery cheer over the wide meadows as
I passed through. There were thorn trees and dew. As for God,
Browning said God was in His heaven. To me that sounded as if
He resided in a fixed place, way off. My little brother had gone
to heaven, so they said, and I never saw him again. I would have
liked God nearer. Although I knew from early teaching at home
and Sunday school that God couldn't be seen, I would have liked
to think He was walking through the meadows with me, up old
woods' roads, down along the spring branch, much like an imaginary playmate I'd had when Lou wasn't around. I talked to her,
waited for her to come through gates behind me before closing
them, pushed her in the empty swing. I would have liked to talk
to God as familiarly as I did to her or Lou and to hear, feel, or see
some words as He would talk back to me.

Some have a real jolting spiritual experience, such as St. Paul
on the road to Damascus, C.S. Lewis on his way to the zoo, John
Wesley at a small meeting at Aldersgate. Mine was as soft as an
autumn breeze, as gentle as a falling leaf, and took me several
years to get the full import of it. Some would say, cynically, that it
was wishful thinking, creating something that was not and is not
there. They would be wrong.

My conversations with God seemed one-way. Simple now-
I-lay-me-down-to-sleep prayers were said as soon as we could
master the words. I had, one glorious spring day, even before I
had begun going to school, climbed to the barn loft, crawled over
that low, protective wall, and dropped down to a lower loft. From
there I looked, through some missing boards, over the countryside. The nearby wild-plum thicket was in bloom, sending its
spicy fragrance into the loft. Chickens were cackling. Trees in the
adjoining orchard were in bloom. In the meadow I saw our cows,
heard their bells ringing, and, for some reason, I wanted to talk
with God. So I did, in this manner: "God bless Mama. God bless
Daddy. God bless Lillian and Lucille. God bless Grandpa and
Grandma." I then ventured into unlearned petitions, "God bless
our horses, cows, and chickens." It was the only way I knew to
pray. A voice from below said, "I hear you up there saying your
prayers." It scared me. I thought that if God ever spoke to me in

audible words, it would be from above. When I realized it was Lou, I was somehow embarrassed.

But later on, when I was about ten years old, this happened: I was walking home from school. I cannot now remember why I was alone. It was October, and October at its best: blue skies, crickets' songs, and poplar trees shimmying in slow motion, losing scraps of their clothing.

Rays from the lowering sun were full in my face, warm and autumn tender. The world seemed to have a heartbeat, and I had found its rhythm. It pulsated with a beauty and a joy. All things around me seemed to say, "Well, hello!" It was as if, heretofore, things, although lovely and wonderful, had been slightly off-center and now they, or I, had suddenly slid into place. There was a sweet foreverness about it, a quality I now, years later, can put into words and call *divine contentment.*

I had not yet read Thoreau's passage, "This is a delicious evening, when the whole body is one sense, and imbibes delight through every pore." However, when I did so, my mind went swiftly back to that afternoon, and I whispered to myself. "Yes, that's the way it was for me too. *But there was more.*"

When I read the Psalm: "He makes me lie down in green pastures. He leads me beside still waters; he restores my soul," I am back walking that woodsy path again. I remember the liquid murmuring of the nearby river, the sweet-sad odor of dying grasses, and all the other things that had curiously stormed my senses, especially that indefinable *something more.*

I sat on a tree stump by the side of the path that afternoon, not to critically examine these new feelings — at ten, one hardly does that — but rather just to let them flow over and through me. It was new and different. I had walked this path hundreds of times, but never had I felt so full of such beautiful emotions. The main one, as I am now able to describe it, was that, for the first time, I felt that the river, the colorful trees, the crickets, the asters, the weeds, the tree stump, all things, including me, especially me, were a warm and comfortable whole, each a part of the other, a part of the world's heartbeat.

I had not yet read Jacob's exclamation, "Surely the Lord is in this place." In following years when I did so, I smiled at the additional meaning it had for me.

While sitting there on the tree stump, I heard a bullfrog sound its primordial call. A far-off cow's bawl and a dog's bark told me that evening chores had begun somewhere. I knew I must move on and attend to mine, but had no desire to do so. Enchantment had afflicted me. And *something more.*

A Virginia creeper, climbing halfway up the hickories, never looked so red. A blue-tailed lizard crossed the path, its irridescence such as I had never before noticed. I was reluctant to move for fear that some mysterious spell would be broken.

I felt as though someone else were with me; however, no one was visible. I thought about God. Of course, He was with me all the time, I had been told. We spoke of Him much at home, at church, at school. I said prayers, but they were one-way conversations. I did all the talking.

I had not yet read Samuel's plea, "Speak, for thy servant hears." When I did, and still do, over and over, because I feel such a kinship with it, I laughed aloud. And a joyous feeling shivered over my body.

The shadows lengthened and still I stayed, seeing with new eyes that which was to be my particular rich inheritance and wishing that God could or would talk to me. I closed my eyes and said something like this: "Dear God, I feel so good now. I wish it would last forever. Is it just the pretty things around me? I'm going to look for them and notice them always. Are you around here somewhere, God? When I open my eyes again, I wish I'd get some kind of plain answer from you."

Several moments passed before I opened my eyes. When I did, a dazzling light met my gaze. It was brilliant. Soon I saw the light was coming from a clump of grasses beside the path, about twenty feet ahead of me. Forgetting all else, I ran to see what it was. The sun was striking against the reflector of a small brass carbide light, the kind railroad men and some hunters wore on their caps at night. I remember saying, "Maybe Dad or Grandpa can use this." The spell was broken. Here was a shiny bit of earthly treasure I could take home.

When I passed the spot the next day, nothing special happened, nor the next, nor ever again there, because I moved on to other schools, other paths. But I never forgot that time. I hung onto it, not knowing exactly what it was, feeling as if I had had a great chance at something and muffed it, and hoping maybe, just maybe, it would come again.

From time to time in the remaining growing-up years, I thought with great concentration of the incident and would have liked to discuss it with someone, but I was too timid. People might have said, "Who did you think you were? Paul on the road to Damascus? Moses at the burning bush?" The moment had been too precious to have anyone laugh at it or rationalize it.

There is always God, I would think just as I did at ten, but my thinking was tinged with the thought that I did all the talking. No plain answering back.

The carbide light

This was my frame of mind, years later, when I was again walking a woodland path. It was spring. Wood thrushes were calling; chipmunks were scattering among the trillium and violets. "God," I whispered, "are you talking back and I don't hear?" I closed my eyes but did not ask again for a plain answer. However, when I opened them again,

there was light shining in my eyes, just as it had that afternoon of sunshine reflecting on the brass carbide light. Ahead was an oak tree, a post oak with broad leaves. Everything was still and wet with morning dew, but there was one single leaf out of the thousands around me, reflecting sunshine into my eyes so that all else was pushed from sight.

A piercing sense of joy shot through my body, calling me back into the sweet rhythm of the universe. Now it was even better, for I realized that God *was talking back* in one of His ways in response to my heart's longing.

God had used a carbide light reflector lying in the sun at the right angle and the right time to reflect into my eyes, as if to say, "Here I am," and I had not understood the language — one of the many which I now know He speaks. The arrangement of circumstances was a silent voice, but it was plain. Plain to me. That was the *something more*.

Jean Bell Mosley in the grassy knoll where she found the carbide light

Self-creating indulgence, you think? I don't. I grabbed it, and it has made all the difference.

What two-way conversations we have had since! Two little rosy-breasted finches are blown by a gust of wind on a bleak day and perch momentarily on a limb outside my kitchen window. An arrangement of circumstance? Part of the Plan. "Hello, God!" A wild rabbit hops up my back steps, turns around, and sits down on the very step where I am sitting motionless. "You've made a good day, God." My car slides on the ice and finds sudden traction on a discarded tow sack. "Thank you, God." A butterfly alights on my shoulder and rides along. "Good day for a walk, isn't it, God?" I look up; suddenly and unexpectedly, there is a single blue morning glory, perfectly framed in a square of the white trellis. "That's good, God. That's good."

And the divine contentment goes on.

Do You Notice?

Later on, when it became apparent that my role would be to use the written word in an attempt to hold up before readers a gentler way of life, to make them aware of the little things they might miss if they aren't looking and that these things are His arrangements, His silent speech to us, I wrote the following article. It is a sample of my continuing conversation with God:

The heavens were molded. The sun and moon and stars arranged in proper place. Everything polished, shining, glowing. Sparkling waters of seas and rivers and little singing creeks reflected this ceiling of beauty. Wide grassy fields were laid down, covered with carpets, now green, now brown, now white, sometimes patterned with patches of bluets or splashes of buttercups. Rocks and trees and shrubbery made a sort of furniture. Clever little pantries of food were established — food in perpetuity whose seed is within itself. Sweet singing birds and furry animals and bright flowers were scattered about for accessories, little extra touches that feed the soul's hunger for beauty.

Reminded me, God, of how Mama used to ready her house when expecting company — cleaning, cooking, making everything as pretty as possible. The company came and many times didn't notice the crisp curtains, the polished lamps, the freshness of the home-baked loaves. Just came and went and didn't notice.

So has it been with your house, God, and the company you invited to come. Some miss so much. But that old roadbank there, the one sloping up to the field where green corn soldiers with tasseled helmets march in measured ranks across the field; that bank, it is covered with creamy white honeysuckle and clover, and a froth of white daisy lace washes like ocean foam down to the road's edge, over-embroidered with black-eyed Susans; I see it, God!

Those two little killdeers, long-legged, pert-tailed, full of new life, new voice — those little killdeers ran ahead of me down between the bean rows, stopped, looked around, ran again. God, I had to laugh at their freshness. They were so clean, so neat, each feather in measured place, their cry a tiny replica of their mother's. I saw them, God!

That dragonfly that lit on my toe the other day, just lit there like it was a fishing cork or lily pad. I bet he had a six-inch wingspan. He looked so comically fierce with those out-sized eyes. But those iridescent wings! Now blue, now green, now purple, glowing and shimmering as if from some inner light, some colorful sunset going on inside. I saw it, God.

Old Black Silk the cat curls up in my lap. I gently spread her toes apart. The hair that grows in between is so silky soft, just like milkweed floss. It is for a purpose, keeps down rubbing irritation. I know all that, but so pretty, more silky really than the rest of her. So seldom seen, but I see it, God.

A black and white cow came up to the fence where I was just standing, staring. She just stared, too. At me. She'd been cropping grass, and a field daisy was clinging to her mouth. She stopped chewing as if to let me notice. I noticed, God.

The summer symphony! Bee hum. Cricket chatter. Insect drone. Frog plop! Quail flurry. Children's laughter. Above all, the serenade of the mockingbird. He perches in the wild cherry tree at eventide and pours out an ecstasy of song, now soft and muted like chimes in some faraway cathedral, now growing in intensity until the notes storm the ears, and changing, ever changing, as if he cannot stand the thought of boresome repetition. I heard it all, God.

The morning glory bud is tightly twisted at dawn. Slowly, slowly it unfolds as the invisible fingers of the sun probe at strategic places here and there. In less than an hour, it is a blue trumpet heralding the gladness of a new day, inviting its company. And soon they come — the butterfly, the bumblebee, the hummingbird. I watch it all, God.

The odors! The green smell of fresh-cut grass, the perfume of the phlox, the faint detection of sun-warmed clover! In special places, the damp ferny smell of cool woods. Woodsmoke of campfires. Corn pollen. Hay smell, essence of summer itself with a touch of yarrow and wild mint and a trace of fennel. I smell it, God.

I linger at the children's wading pool, and eventually they will come running to me, wet and dripping, eyelashes matted, eyes bright. While they speak of some delight, I look into their eyes, and what is there? Two tiny reflections of all the surrounding beauty — the rose hedge, the oak trees, the blooming trumpet vines, the grass, the spraying water. I see it all, God. And thus I see it thrice!*

Snakes

One other incident during Loughboro school days will not be forgotten. It was again an October day. Long, silken spiderwebs floated in the air. Falling leaves, woodsmoke, cricket song. Indian Summer.

Lou and I (by this time Lillian had gone on to high school) did not follow our usual path home from school but decided to take a shortcut, which meant leaving the railroad tracks at the Big Bluffs, crossing the river on nature-placed rocks, and proceeding up a densely forested mountain on the other side of which we knew was home.

The way was only faintly marked by an old road where, in time past, someone had come to cut and haul firewood.

Dry leaves were thick on the ground, and like all children, we loved kicking them up as we walked along.

Something sharp scratched my ankle. At first I thought it to be a sawbrier, but as my foot went up, a long dangling thing went with it, and there was blood on my stocking.

It was a copperhead snake, and I had to shake my foot several times to get it loose, for its fangs had caught in my stocking.

"Cooperhead!" Lou shouted. Country children are well versed in the markings of snakes, especially the poisonous ones.

"Did it bite you?" Lou demanded.

"Yes," I replied calmly, not knowing the danger. After all, I had been stung by wasps and hornets, and such stings had hurt much worse than this bite.

Natural instincts are to get rid of your enemy, so I threw my books and lunch pail down on the snake. Lou had already pelted a

* Expanded from "Do You Notice?," *Southeast Missourian*, Oct. 26, 1997.

62

few rocks at it, and I soon joined in. Rocks are always plentiful in the Ozark hills.

The snake slithered away, apparently unharmed.

Gingerly, Lou went back after my books and pail, and we started the rest of the journey home, which was about two more miles. Lou, to my bewilderment, cried all the way.

Mama was seen first, out in a garden patch. Lou cried out to her. Mama came running.

After that came such a flurry of community activity to "save my life"; it made me feel very important.

The whole community could be summoned at once by one long ring on the party-line telephone. One long ring was like a fire bell in the night.

Someone killed a chicken, split it open, and put the warm body over my foot. Others brought wet clay and wet, chewed tobacco poultices — anything that had drawing-out effect as it cooled. The one poultice we never understood was cockleburs boiled in sweet milk.

When word reached Uncle Ross McGee, from way up north (twenty-five miles), he brought a jug of homemade elderberry wine.

Tourniquets were employed, even though it was late for them after the long walk. A knife slash was made across the wound, even though it was late for that, too. Prayers were said.

Many years later, I read that although poisonous, copperhead bites seldom killed anyone. This comment was made after serum for such bites had been discovered. My snakebite was pre-serum, and I had walked two miles after the bite, which gave the poison time to spread. Where the tourniquets were applied, great green blisters appeared. What caused them, nobody knew. My leg swelled to about the proportions of our kitchen range stovepipe and became about as black. Were the late tourniquets too tight, some of the poultices too pointless? Who knows?

I don't know why it was thought a "swig" of the elderberry wine would be helpful, but with a "swig" of that and other feverish effects from the poison, I became dreamily confused and thought for a while I was a little lamb on a tombstone with which I was familiar.

This tombstone was in a little German graveyard we passed on our way to Doe Run. The tombstone was near the roadway, very visible, and I was always fascinated by that little lying-down lamb atop the white marble. Fascinated and sad.

Many years later, I went to examine the name on that stone, which still, at this writing, stands. Alas, there was none, or perhaps time and the elements had erased it. I put the one buried there in the same category as the one buried by the railroad track.

I lost about six weeks of school, but Mama saw to it that I kept up-to-date with my schoolwork, and if the classmates at school had moved up to mixed fractions when I was away, I had, too.

My next encounter with one of our Ozark poisonous reptiles was not quite so dramatic, but the thought of how near I came to being bit by the big rattlesnake still sends little prickles down my spine.

Large patches of sweet williams and bluebells grew at the edge of our big meadow bordering the river. I loved to walk amongst them, bend down to smell them, pick some for bouquets, just hug them where they were.

One spring day, not many years after the copperhead, I was strolling dreamily through the bluebells. I should have been warned by the rattle. Perhaps the rippling sound of the nearby river overrode the dry, short, sharp sounds, or perhaps I wasn't expecting a rattlesnake to be in a patch of bluebells. They're supposed to be up in the hills. This was outrageous juxtaposition.

When I reached down to pick from a clump of the fragrant flowers, there he was, already coiled, ready to strike, his rattlers sticking up and wagging warningly, evil eyes upon me like black beams of death. Was it a guardian angel that snatched me backward in time to avert the ugly fangs? "Thank you, God."

I didn't stop running until I was home with the kitchen screen door slammed shut behind me. Mama gave me a glass of buttermilk and brushed my hair back lovingly. I stayed in the house the rest of the day, didn't even go to milk my quota of cows or help Lou with the carrying in of the firewood. No one quarreled with me.

I suppose that sometime there will be, maybe even is, a movement to save the endangered species of the Ozark copperheads and rattlesnakes. I will not be a charter member.

Even the old, lazy, fat, harmless blacksnakes tormented me terribly. They were to be found most anywhere, but especially around the barn and chicken house. They loved eggs.

We had a mis-bred hen that was determined to be as different as her pedigree, which must have been a cross between a stubborn barred rock and an upside-down black bat. Instead of laying her eggs in the neat, straw-lined compartments of our well-built henhouse of which we were so proud, she had to go to the far corner of a dark crawl space underneath the harness room of the barn.

I don't know who discovered her errant behavior. Maybe Grandma or Dad, passing down the barn hallway, heard her proud cackle emanating from that ghoulish place and suspected an egg. I do know who had to crawl back into that far corner and see. Me. I was the smallest and only one who could navigate the course. There were several eggs there when I first made the journey. That whole, dim, dusty, ten-by-twenty feet of space could have been completely covered with eggs, and remained that way, if I'd been boss. But eggs meant money, and money meant shoes or sugar, tablets, and pencils. "Everyone has to help" was the constant reminder. "Black snakes are harmless, probably scared of you," I was told.

In retrospect it seems that hen could have made a good Sunday-company dinner. Dumplings, green beans, slaw. Or a board could have been taken up in the harness room floor where one could just reach down and get the daily egg. Given her disposition, though, she would have changed her place of production.

This was my first experience with planning my own potential escape route if necessary, eye-measuring distances, calculating angles, speed, and the shortest distance between two points. It sharpened my mind, stretched my alertness to the limit. There would be no one in there to help me if one of the slithering, black, barn snakes was in there at the same time.

This was the procedure. I stuck my head into the entry hole (Why wasn't it stopped up?) and waited for my eyes to become accustomed to the darkness. With my head in the hole, it was darker than ever, for the hole was the only source of light. Then I wiggled in, being careful to stay as flat as I could so as not to bump my head on the harness room floor and thus addle my brain, when such addlement would not be advantageous. Then I would scramble, lightning-fast, to the nest, grab the egg, turn as fast as any competitive swimmer at the end of a pool, and get back out again, leaving a cloud of dry dust behind me.

My fears materialized. One day when I made my quick turn and started for the entry hole, there, silhouetted against the dim light from the hole was old Black Snake himself, between me and the exit. My prearranged plans were of no use. I waited for him to move on, saying to myself the words I'd often heard, "Black snakes are not dangerous."

He did not move. I edged closer to the foundation wall, thinking I could get around him. He edged too, seemingly being careful to keep his crooked length between me and the point of escape.

There was nothing to fight with. No stick, no corncob to throw at him—except the egg! If I can hit him in the eyes, he won't be able to see me, I thought. I took deadly aim and hit him, as best as I could see, square on the head. A sense of victory surged through me. I scrambled toward the hole, smiling a bit inwardly that maybe the egg yolk would impair his vision for many years to come. It was many years later that I learned snakes have a protective covering over their eyes that is all-in-one with their skin.

"You didn't forget the under-the-harness-room egg, did you?" Mama asked.

"No, Mama."

Symphony on the Farm

Visiting town and city cousins—accustomed to the sound of motors running, squeak of tires and brakes, factory whistles, and voices seemingly everywhere—must have thought it very quiet on the farm, but we had our own symphony of sounds. Even on a still, winter night, when snow was deep and ice covered everything, should one step outside and be inclined to climb Strawstack Hill behind the house, there was something to be heard. A crackle of falling ice told of a squirrel stirring in its high-up leafy nest or an owl settling on some limb that seemed cozier than the one it had just abandoned.

Far off, someone's dog would bark, and farther off, another one would respond. And there might be a long, loud, "Yippee" from a 'coon hunter who just had to release his feelings on the snowy wonderland of his world. If anyone else was out on such a night and heard the call, he usually responded in like manner, agreeing that it was a great, wide, wonderful world.

Year-round, the day's sounds, for me, and I suppose the rest of the family, always started with the crowing of the two or three roosters. Seems as if they knew they had to crow louder in wintertime to be heard from behind closed doors and windows. In summer, they didn't need to expend so much effort, but they did.

Soon after the roosters' alarms came the rattling of the stove lids on the kitchen range downstairs, opening of the firebox door, shove of wood, closing of the firebox door. Then there would be the gravelly crunching of the coffee grinder accompanied by the scraping of the bread board where Mama would have just cut out the big buttermilk biscuits.

Mama didn't need to come to the foot of the stairs and yell, "All right, children," for we would already be at least half-dressed. Farm children, with inexorable chores and school to get to on time or the Truant Officer would getcha, didn't dawdle.

The perking of the coffeepot, steam song of the teakettle, splash of water in the wash pan all mingled together to agree with the chanticleers that here, indeed, was another day. What we did with it was up to us, but whatever we did, we had the sweet knowledge that we would be corrected or protected by the others.

The only motor that ever disturbed the air around us was that of a lone airplane that might have flown over once a year, perhaps off-course. It was such a rare occurrence that everyone, if not already outside, would run there to see it and yell loudly, "Airplane!" to alert anyone within hearing distance.

In spring and summer, most familiar were the creaking, metallic sounds of the cultivator, corn planter, rake, and wagon, as Dad and Grandpa plowed and harvested the fields of grain. Mostly, corn and wheat. Occasionally, oats. At harvesttime came the big, noisy McCormick reaper and the hired, steam-engined, threshing machine.

There was always the busy cackling of hens as they rejoiced over laying yet another egg, or their contented clucking as they scratched for bugs or overlooked grain.

Occasionally there would be a loud squeal from the pigpen where some unknown dispute was suddenly underway, although usually the hogs were quiet until feeding time when a cacophony of grunts and snorts revealed their piggishness.

A sloping wooden chute between the boards of the fenced pen ended in a long trough. Slop, as the kitchen wastes were called, mixed with skimmed milk and assorted supplements, was poured into the chute. Ten or twelve hogs would want to have first choice as this mixture came flooding down the chute.

This sort of feeding was wintertime hog activity. In the summertime, there being open range then, the hogs were turned loose to "Root, hog, or die." With the plethora of acorns and other such food in the woods, they never died but may have grown a bit skinny, rooting.

In the fall the hogs were rounded up, fed all the corn they could eat, and a certain number of them were butchered for our meat. We had some form of pork year-round, sugar- or salt-cured.

Before I leave the swine section of the symphony, let me speak of Betsy, our best brood sow. She was a big red New Hampshire. One time when money was in very short supply, she came forth with fourteen pigs in one litter, ten of which were raised, fattened, and sold to fill the cash gap which always seemed to come about the time the mortgage interest was due.

In the summertime, there was the constant droning of insects. In locust years, it reached a crescendo. From sunup to sundown and even thereafter, there was birdsong, including bluebirds, whippoorwills, and chuck-will's-widows, sounds the towns-people didn't hear. Early mornings we could hear the wild turkeys up on Gillman's Hill, which rose up in front of our house.

Dad and Grandpa never hunted the wild turkeys. Nor did they hunt deer, quails, or 'coons. They were foxhunters, not to kill the foxes, but to listen to the voices of their hounds mingling with those of other farmers in the river-valley community. It was pure music to them.

The river had its own set of sounds, like a special section in an orchestra, different and inimitable. There were several shallow places as it wound its way through our fields and forests. According to the amount of water it had gathered from tributaries to the northwest, it made little liquid rippling sounds over the rocks, like fairies at play, or splashed vigorously against the rocks, spraying white lace into the air. In places, it murmured with the cadence of Mama's reading *Evangeline* — "This is the forest primeval, the murmuring pines and the hemlocks," or the soul-stirring vibrations of a bow being drawn slowly across the strings of a cello.

In summer, fish leaped up in the river, causing a small splash, and frogs plunged from the bank, making a splash as if to properly end some compound word.

Surprisingly and almost humorously, in the middle of an afternoon, a bullfrog might sound his "Belly-deep," but mostly they were heard at night along with the myriad of tree frogs with their continuous minor tones telling lonesome tales.

Then there was the cowbell section of this great country orchestra, the bang of gates, the opening and closing of doors, each one having its own note, the buzz of saw, the whine of the grindstone, hammer against nail, hens calling chicks to safety beneath their wings as the hawks flew over, hiss of steam as the butchered hogs were slid into slanting tubs of boiling water to make the scraping of hair easy, the fox horns, the feisty trains, whistling at every crossover road — all joining in at their appropriate time.

School Dresses

There was another sound, not exclusively a country sound, but very sweet to the ears of three little girls, and that was Mama's sewing machine.

The younger children in a family wore the hand-me-downs unless they were hopelessly worn out. Mama was clever enough to redecorate them in some way or make combinations of two or more garments into one to make them seem new and different.

One particular garment of hard-twist, black and white, shepherd-checked wool had been a full dress at first when Lillian had it. It was a jumper when Lou inherited it, worn with a dark red blouse. By the time I got it, it was a pleated skirt. "It sure pays to get good material," Mama would say from time to time and there was a tinge of sadness in her voice, denoting, perhaps, that she was not always able to buy the best. However, our clothes were of durable material — gingham, Indianhead linen, serge, organdy, or, later on, rayon and ratine.

The first experience any of us ever had with a money-back guarantee was with green ratine. Ratine was a loosely woven cloth with a nubby texture. Lillian had a dress of the material. The green faded to an ugly color. To revive it and change the color, we attempted to follow the instructions on the box of Rit, a dye. The instructions were to dip the material into boiling water to which the Rit bleach had been added, then stir until the material became white. Then repeat the process using, instead of the bleach added to the boiling water, the Rit color you had chosen which, in this case was a lovely pink, according to the described hue on the little box.

We did just that, and it came out a color that has never been seen before or since. Ugly!

Wondering about the money-back guarantee, we sent the dress to the Rit Company to show them what had happened. Back came the loveliest pink dress we'd ever seen.

"Well, I swan!" Mama said.

White middy blouses were the style then. These had large sailor collars with navy blue stars in the back corners and navy blue soutache braid outlining a border. Worn with a navy pleated skirt and long red tie, it was almost a uniform in the 1920s.

While her three daughters were still rather shapeless, Mama needed no patterns. We'd pick a dress we liked in the Sears, Roebuck Catalogue, and Mama could duplicate it.

Once, some avant-garde fashion designer bravely departed from the age-old button-down-the-front styled dresses to button-down-the-side. I was proud to be the first to flaunt this style among my peers at Loughboro. The skirt was of orange and white checked gingham, the top of white Indianhead linen, both remnants. Collar and cuffs were of the checked material, the collar not opening in the front as usual but where this new side opening reached the shoulder. I felt like a butterfly when I floated off to school in that dress.

I was wearing that dress when one of the Loughboro schoolboys decided to call me "his girl."

It was the custom on pretty, warm days to take our lunch pails or boxes outside, find a comfortable place to sit with some friends in the shade of a tree, and proceed to eat. To my immense surprise, and a little embarrassment, Delbert McFarland detached himself from the group of boys and came over to sit beside me. Merciless was the ensuing teasing Delbert received, to which he calmly replied that he guessed he could sit by "his girl" and eat lunch if he wanted to. This was such a surprise to me, I must have blushed as red as the comb on one of our white Leghorns.

A navy blue bengaline, with gathered panels at the side waist, set Lou aside as a fashion leader. Dark red picoted ribbons about a half-inch wide were tied over the gathered panels at the waist, with a bow in the middle. Short streamers were allowed to flutter in the breeze if there was any.

Except for the green-then-pink ratine, Lillian's most memorable dress was of yellow and orange organdy with loose, gathered, lace-edged panels about eight inches wide hanging all around the waist as a sort of overskirt.

Then we learned to cross-stitch on checked gingham. Lou and I picked and sold enough dewberries to buy small black and white checked gingham yardage. Using the checks as one would a stamped pattern, we cross-stitched borders of red rabbits and deer around the top of the hem, following directions from some embroidery thread company. It was a departure from the mundane.

Someone, somewhere, discovered that the ultra-crisp organdy could be cut into a petal shape which, with moistened fingers, could be rolled up around the edge to make a pretty petal. Several of these petals, in graduated sizes, could be tacked together at the middle and result in a very handsome flower. Such an outbreak of organdy dresses! It was epidemic! Mine was the then-new color, aqua blue. Some, being complimentary said the dress made my eyes seem even bluer. I was glad they could even see my eyes because they are small. But I still *see* everything I look at, for fear I might miss some precious conversation that started with the carbide light.

Mama's sister, Minnie, had migrated to California and set up a milliner's shop. She made hats for some of the movie stars, particularly Marion Davies.

Being in such a business, Aunt Minnie accumulated lengths of ribbons she could not use. Scraps. Yet some might be a yard long. These scraps she sent to us. Plaid, checked, and plain, taffeta, picoted satin, grossgrain — oh, they were treasures. Some were embroidered with tiny roses, violets, and lilies of the valley. It was the day of the bow-clasped ribbons worn atop the head or at the nape of the neck if your hair was long. We were rich in ribbons, as rich as Hollywood stars.

Leaving Loughboro

Our halcyon days at the Loughboro School ended in the spring of 1925 when Lou had finished all the grades there. Lillian, having finished two years earlier, had gone to Doe Run High School for her freshman year, then on to Fredericktown to stay with Grandma Casey, who was then a widow, to finish high school. At Fredericktown she was only a short walking distance from the high school, while on the farm she had to walk about a mile to the nearest neighbor and catch a ride, or drive herself back and forth from the farm in the horse-drawn buggy. It was much easier for her at Fredericktown, but we missed her.

Making the change from the Loughboro School to that at Doe Run was a sad-happy time for me. I liked permanency, roots, familiar surroundings, yet realized that circumstances sometimes demanded that you move on. There still was the family, the farm, the brown speckled eggs, the hay loft—anchors to cling to—and I knew that God was everywhere, ready to talk back to me through his handiwork, particularly through the shimmering of every drop of sun-struck dew, the call of every bird, the fall of every leaf. But entering this new school, I felt like a new child in a new family. Most of my Loughboro schoolmates would go to Elvins High School. I don't remember why. Maybe high-school districts were different from grade-school districts at that time.

The old closeness of knowing everyone, their homes, barns, cellars, dogs, cats, cows, horses, goats, who made thick biscuits and who made thin, had to be started all over again, or possibly never again.

Whereas at Loughboro, my friends who lived on scattered farms had last names of McFarland, Russell, Stacy, Ritter, Aldrich, Britt, and Gillman, now all was new—Schmidt, Zimmer, Henrich, Zolman, Haynes, Hughes, Cromer, Hahn, Burch, Williams, Wichman, Kassabaum, Matthews, Wallace, etc.

Doe Run had a population of about four hundred, counting the outlying families. It had a post office, three general stores, and five churches.

I was in a classroom almost as large as the whole Loughboro School itself, and it had only two grades: fifth and sixth. There was unfamiliar slate for blackboard, unfamiliar water fountains. No pull-down maps, no big-hooded stove, no smell of woodsmoke and Lifebuoy Soap. There was a coal furnace in some underneath region and strange, noisy, hot-water registers in every room. Windows were on one side of the room only. They had tan-colored shades that could be lowered from the top to the center or raised from the bottom to the center. They never seemed to be lined up neatly.

I was in the sixth grade, the farthest row from the windows—I, who always liked to see what was going on outside. Coats were hung in a hallway separating the four downstairs classrooms, and lunch packages brought by those, like us, who lived too far away to go home at noon, were deposited there on shelves built for that purpose.

The way to school lost some of its charm. There were no trains with friendly engineers to wave to us, no hobos to wonder about, no swinging bridge nor footlogs to cross, no goat pastures to pass, no wild strawberry patches.

We still had a mile to walk. The road, part dirt, part gravel, wound around between two steep hills. At an appointed place we met someone Dad had hired to drive us back and forth to school for $1 a day. We had agreed to walk the mile because the road descending to our house was so rocky and rough. These drivers were Freeman Zimmer and Leemon Gillman, a boy also making the school change, who had a rickety Ford he could drive. Others, from time to time, were Mike Thurman and Chester Boswell, men from Doe Run.

At this time, we changed the location of our mailbox, since it was along our new school route and we could easily pick up the mail each school day. It no longer stood at the shady fork in the road, under a spreading white oak tree, next to Alexander's companion box. At this new mailbox location is where we waited for our rides. There was no nearby murmuring river to listen to, but there was a hill rearing up behind us, thickly wooded, and here lived wild turkeys, squirrels, chipmunks, and all manner of Missouri wildlife. Maybe even a black panther! In front of us stretched Zimmers' and Schmidts' broad fields where horses and cows roamed. I didn't know their names.

The journey to school in the wintertime was almost as cold as the long trek to Loughboro, since we still had the mile to walk and maybe a long wait for the car to come. There were no heaters in the cars. If some of them had canvas side curtains with isinglass windows, no one bothered to put them on for they weren't easily attached. Little movable long metal buttons had to go through just the right slots and then be turned crossways so as to fasten. Quite often the curtains came open and flapped in the wind, rain, snow, or sleet. To be wrapped in an old blanket was just about as effective as the canvas side curtains.

The sixth grade was a blur for me. I suppose I learned whatever it was I was supposed to learn. I always made good grades, always wanted to make good grades. Mama and Dad insisted on thorough homework, spent time helping us. If anything, those of us coming from the Loughboro School were scholastically ahead of those at Doe Run. After all, we had those wonderful Books of Knowledge at Loughboro.

The next year I moved across the hall to the seventh- and eighth-grade classroom. Things were beginning to get a little more interesting, although my seat in the seventh grade was next to the wall again, away from the windows. By this time I knew everyone, even those in the four high-school classes upstairs, and the whole physical layout of the school—where the furnace was, how the separate well house, run by a Delco system, could get the water into those strange inside fountains. The wide stairways, one at the front and one at the rear of the first-floor hallway, led to the three classrooms, study hall, and library/office upstairs.

A new gymnasium was underway. There would be an indoor basketball and volleyball court, bleachers on one side, and a raised stage with dressing rooms and showers on each side. Doe Run was going "uptown." On the playground there were three swings, one see-saw, a dirt basketball court, a baseball diamond, and, later on, a girls' softball diamond.

When I moved to the eighth-grade side of the room, I was closer to the windows, but still one row of seats away. However, I had a wider view of what was going on outside. Not much. No neighbors' hogs rummaging around, no woods to fill up with snow. There were the woods beyond the baseball diamond and a row of houses. I could tell whether Mrs. Ratley washed clothes on Monday, Tuesday, or Wednesday. If her laundry wasn't flapping on the line by the middle of the week, someone went to see if there was someone sick. Nearly every family washed on Monday, ironed on Tuesday, mended on Wednesday, and so on, as the old cross-stitched samplers advised.

Dad's Horrible Accident

Two months into the eighth grade, something happened in our family that was going to require a profound readjustment in our lives.

A few years before we made the change to the Doe Run School, Dad had gone to work at the Iron Mountain mines in the southwestern part of the county to supplement our farm income and maybe be able to put some money aside for *when times got hard!*

The iron ore had been quarried out at that location, but much rock slag had been cast aside. Dad got an independent contract with a railroad company to supply riprap for their track beds and banks. It was still pre-depression. Financial affairs for our family were improving.

We were impressed and proud when Dad came home with some stationery that said at the top in bold black letters, "Wilson L. Bell, mining contractor." Furthermore, there was a black silhouette of a dump truck and a loading derrick placed like bookends around the contractor's name. Along with this bold venture came a portable Burroughs adding machine that said in gold lettering that it was protected by U.S. and foreign patents. You pressed on certain numbered buttons, pulled a lever and, behold, up came the numbers you had pressed, printed onto a roll of paper. Then, if you had brought up a column of numbers and wanted to add them, you pressed the button marked "total," pulled the lever, and there it was, always and always correct. We tested it over and over by doing our own pencil and paper additions. Although we didn't understand it, we concluded that Burroughs had invented a marvelous machine.

We kept it well dusted, in between all the little buttons and around the paper roll, over the gold lettering and lever handle. Burroughs and DeLaval!

This machine was not to add up the dollars Daddy was going to make but to add numbers for payroll checks. Workers had to be employed to load the dump trucks, drive the trucks to the rock crusher, run the crushing mill, transport the riprap to delivery vehicles. The location and operation was amusingly called "The Redworm" on account of the red clay soil and the red-painted buildings.

Daddy installed his little office in his and Mama's bedroom, the same room where little S.W. had died, the same room where the incubator had hatched the chicks. I got to either read out the number of hours of work for each employee while Dad operated the Burroughs adding machine, or vice versa. There was also an Oliver typewriter on which we pecked out necessary letters on that important-looking stationery.

Rock was hauled by truck to a crusher where it was ground into suitably sized stones for the railroad's use. Great, wide, unprotected belts ran from rotating wheels to rotating wheels to operate the crusher.

Everything was going well. So, on a beautiful October day with monarch butterflies fluttering southward and thistledown drifting, as Lou and I walked the last stretch of our way home from school, things seemingly couldn't be better.

We had not been home long before there came a knock at our front door.

"Well, Mr. Holly! Come in," Mama said, surprised at this visit, but secretly maybe a little alarmed because Mr. Holly worked at the same place Dad did. He evidently had come home. Dad had not. We all crowded around.

"There's been an accident, Mrs. Bell."

"Wilson?"

"Yes."

The big, fast-moving belt at the rock crusher had caught Dad's sleeve as he was passing by and snarled his arm up into it, tearing it away below the shoulder to where it was just hanging by a few shreds of muscle.

The Iron Mountain fast train, running to St. Louis, was due to come by shortly after the accident. A "fast train" did not make stops at small towns but just whistled on through. But someone, evidently standing between the rails and waving wildly, got it to stop. As fast as it could travel, the train arrived in St. Louis and Dad was whisked away to Baptist Memorial Hospital.

Nothing could be done to save the arm. The surgeon saved as much of the shoulder stub as he could so that Dad might be able

Wilson Bell after the loss of his right arm. Lucille Bell in window.

to manipulate an artificial arm by shoulder muscles and leather straps that embraced his body and encircled his other arm.

With today's technology and sufficient speed to the surgeon, completely detached arms can be restored to a certain degree of usefulness. But we were years back of such technology.

Polio in infancy before vaccine, a bean in a throat before widespread X-ray machines in rural areas, poisonous snakebite before serum, a severed arm too early for possible present-day reattachment — it was hard.

Our heritage from way back, of contending with wild, dark moors of Scotland and the Irish pugnacity of facing fights head-on, prevented any knock-out blows.

Life went on. Different. We had to patch the holes of grief, sew up splitting seams of sorrow. Dad's big, muscled blacksmith arm was gone.

I climbed to the hayloft. "God?" There were no shining leaves. No birdsong. Eventually I smelled the sweet, dry fragrance of fleabane and meadow daisies deep within the hay, and whispered, "All right, God. All right."

Eighth-grade Graduation

In the spring of 1927 there was Eighth-grade Graduation, a much-looked-forward-to event. Right after Christmas of 1926, the girls in my class began to talk of the dresses they would wear, all made at home, of course, although times were getting better and better for everyone. We discussed crepe de chine, georgette, voile, dimity. No two dresses were to be alike, but all would be white. Thelma Ross said, to our amazement and envy, that her dress was going to be trimmed with bugle beads. I'd never heard of them, but they sounded beautiful. When I, full of hope, relayed this information to Mama, she said there would be no bugle beads on my dress. But she did begin to finger the silks when we went to the fabric stores, or dry-goods stores, as they were then called. Eventually we decided on white crepe de chine, a sort of non-shiny, crinkled silk. The yardage was brought home months in advance of the graduation ceremony, so I could have the joy of anticipation. Many times I folded and unfolded it, pressed it to my cheek, decided, poetically, that it looked like moonlight on white ice.

The final pattern we chose from a picture, naturally. The dress had two box pleats from shoulder to hem, both front and back. They were sewn like big tucks and then flattened out equally over the seams and pressed. No pulling apart with these pleats/tucks. They stayed in place. A Buster Brown collar, short sleeves, and the belt of self fabric to pull in a waistline formed the utter simplicity of it, contrasting sharply with the bugle-beaded trim of Thelma's. No one saw my nainsook bloomers with lace insertions about two inches above the elastic casing and the ruffle-and-lace-trimmed slip. I was clothed more fancy underneath than on the outside. Maybe this was Mama's subtle way of saying that dressings, either in clothes or in personality, shouldn't be just a facade for what's underneath.

We had a rosebush with early blossoms, pink, very fragrant, the name of which I never discovered, so I just call it the May Rose or the Graduation Rose. It grew beside and drooped over the woven-wire fence between the front yard and the garden. I made corsages of these roses for all my girl classmates.

We marched down the steps of the new gym, boys in one row, girls in the other, perfuming the air around us with this inimitable old-fashioned fragrance.

The high-school graduation class shared the same ceremony, the older ones being seated across an aisle from us "upstarts."

I'm sure the speaker tried to make his message suit both classes, not over our eighth-grade heads but yet not "dumbed down" to the older graduates. I don't remember any part of it, being much more interested in Thelma's bugle beads, my own crepe de chine, and the heady fragrance of the old roses.

Maybe the speaker talked about opportunities and what a wonderful world it was waiting for us "out there." "Out there" didn't interest me much. The here and now was pretty wonderful for me. There were Mama and Dad, Lou and Lillian, Grandma and Grandpa, the dogs, cats, chickens, cows, horses, bluebells, wild pansies, the woods, the river, the land, a silk dress, and high school coming up in the near future.

When I review what was happening nationally at that time, I think maybe the speaker might have talked about the Kellogg-Briand Pact, a pact that nations were then signing, promising they would use peaceful means instead of war to settle quarrels among themselves.

That wouldn't have interested me much either. We had already fought the war to end all wars. No more Daddy getting "shot." No more Germans coming over Simms Mountain in a red glare. No more brown biscuits.

Maybe the speaker quoted Coolidge's advice given during his administration: "Spend less than you make and make more than you spend." Since it would be several years before I would start making money, that wouldn't have impressed me either. Even if he'd added, "But people are spending more than they make," I'd probably have just readjusted my mock box pleats and smelled the roses. "Let the good times roll," was the attitude of most everyone. Yes, sir, let 'em roll.

They did "roll" for two more years. Even longer than that for us, for we had no money in the stock market which crashed. We read in the newspapers that in New York, financiers had jumped out of windows to their death. Mama and Grandma clucked their tongues. Dad and Grandpa read aloud in ominous tones that something bad was coming. That something was to be called the Great Depression.

If a meadow full of daisies, a nest of robin's eggs, chimney swifts diving down the chimneys had interested me more than any national or international events I could have read about, something did happen in that arena not long after eighth-grade graduation that caught my attention. Not only mine, but everyone else's. Charles Augustus Lindbergh had flown an airplane, by himself, across the Atlantic Ocean! An airplane, like the ones that used to make us go outside and shout, "Airplane!" to alert everyone to the sight!

Neighbors talked about the feat at mailboxes and stores, in the fields, before and after church services. Sunday editions of the *St. Louis Globe-Democrat* were purchased and brought home to be read. Charles Augustus Lindbergh had flown from New York to Paris, 3,600 miles in 33½ hours. Alone! And the people of my state, Missouri, had bought the plane for him and named it the *Spirit of St. Louis*. How proud I was to be a citizen of Missouri.

In order to keep up with such fast-moving events, we subscribed to the metropolitan daily. I kept up with Andy Gump, Mutt and Jeff, Little Orphan Annie, and other comic-strip characters, including Winnie Winkle, she of the pretty dresses.

The rotogravure section interested me, too. This was a chocolate-brown reproduction of pictures, most especially of movie stars and actresses who were on the stage at the St. Louis Municipal Opera in Forest Park, St. Louis. Once there was a picture of Laura LaPlant. I thought she was so beautiful and tried to wave my hair to look like hers and mimic her expression. Yes, yes, I was Laura LaPlant, and after her, Janet Gaynor, Clara Bow, Billie Burke, etc. My hairstyle changed often but very temporarily, always falling back into the part in the middle with bangs across my forehead.

Always, somewhere in the paper, there were little nagging articles about a bank failing here, there, yonder. Dad and Grandpa read these aloud as if they thought we ought to know.

Gaslights at the Atwater Kent

Daddy's artificial arm worked fairly well. He could screw in a hook or a hand at the end and manipulate both by a twist of his shoulder muscles, which would set in motion certain leather straps that embraced his upper body and other arm. He preferred the hook which he could open and close to clasp anything he wanted. The first thing he learned to do quite well was hold his pipe in the clasped hook, fill it with the live hand, transfer it to his mouth, light it, and smoke. A glimmer of pride shone in his blue eyes when he had accomplished this — he who had made wagon wheels, hammered horeseshoes on the anvil, operated a diamond drill at the mines, drilled boulders out of a granite quarry. A flash of pride over lighting a pipe. What class! Sometimes, at a fork in the road, one had to take the one less traveled.

The rock-crushing business continued and thrived. When Dad had, much earlier, gone to work at the Diamond Drills in the lead mines, as the new procedure was called, he had purchased a 1916 Model T Ford, brass radiator and all. When he lifted and folded back the side of the louvered hood to show me the workings of the motor, all the little things jumping up and down scared me so that I ran to climb into the bed of the big wagon, a haven of safety from this strange, noisy thing that might take a notion to run after me.

From the Ford, Dad moved to a Chevrolet coupe, a Baby Overland with red-spoked wheels, and by my high-school time to a long, low, sleek, gray Chrysler touring car. Oh, if only the roads had been better.

Coolidge was nearing the end of his second term as president, the same Coolidge the strange rider at Loughboro had urged the pupils to vote for, or maybe just the teacher. Times were good for everyone but the farmers, so they said.

Grandpa and Dad were, in a way, hedging their bets: Grandpa largely operating the farm and Dad going into business.

At home, things moved along. Cows were milked, the cream separator with its many parts was operated, dismantled, the parts meticulously washed and dried for the next twelve-hour shift. Hogs were butchered, corn planted, eggs gathered, the payment on the mortgage made.

Cousins came from the cities to visit and stayed for long stretches during the summer months. It was their vacation, I suppose.

We ate good meals at the same kitchen table we had used since moving to the farm. Hounds chased foxes and wild turkeys called from Gillman's Hill. Nothing in the kitchen had changed, except the wood-plank floor was covered with blue-and-white-checked linoleum. It seemed to perk up everything in that big comfortable room, including the Arm and Hammer bird chart, the same chart upon which the pileated woodpecker's crest had glowed more red in that wartime aurora borealis.

I feel more indebted to Arm and Hammer for my accumulated knowledge of birds than I do for the many biscuits and cakes it helped to rise. At that early time, this company put into their yellow boxes (they are still the same yellow) of baking soda a little colored picture of a bird with the bird's description and habits on the back.

Then, suddenly, came a forward leap. Gaslights! Dad, always the innovator, never let the loss of an arm get him down. He installed a carbide-light system in the old farmhouse.

The system worked much as did the little, brass carbide light I had found that wonderful, turning-point day.

In the nearby smokehouse, two tanks were placed, one to hold the granular carbide, the other to hold water which was arranged to drip into the carbide. This, of course, formed a gas which was piped, underground, into the house. With the turn of a switch and the scratch of a match, we had wonderful gaslights with pretty glass fixtures in both the kitchen and parlor, a great improvement over the kerosene lamps which had to be filled weekly, the chimneys washed and dried, wicks to buy and keep properly trimmed. We didn't discard them, though, for sometimes we would run out of carbide before we could get another supply.

I should mention that this gaslight project was interrupted and delayed for a year or more because one of our neighbors had fallen upon hard times, and "light" funds were funneled in that direction for a while.

The first night we sat in the glow of the gaslights, a family conference was held—a serious conference. We never, never, were to all go away from the house unless the last one out turned off the lights before shutting the door. This ordinance supplemented the old one to never leave without blowing out the lamps.

The gaslights paled into insignificance when Dad brought home the Atwater-Kent radio, powered by batteries in what was known as the Delco System. On Saturday nights especially, we all sat near the round speaker and listened to the Grand Ole Opry. I loved it when Bradley Kincaid sang, "The Trail of the Lonesome Pine." I ordered the sheet music from Sears, Roebuck and pecked out the melody on our piano.

DeLaval cream separator, Burroughs adding machine, gaslights, Atwater-Kent radio! Boy, were we moving up through the twentieth century!

On to High School

In September 1927, I felt very grown up as I left the "little kids" downstairs and climbed one of the wide stairways to settle in as a freshman in high school. Three classrooms, library, and a study hall! Each of the ensuing years I got to move closer and closer to the windows. By my senior year I was right beside them. Things hadn't changed much, except that in high school there was movement. No staying in the same room all day. Thus, on one day I could still see if Mrs. Ratley was hanging out her clothes and, moving to an opposite room, see whether Mrs. Burch was washing her clothes the same day.

In addition to the required courses, by the time I was a junior, the high school had introduced a business course into its curriculum—typing, shorthand, accounting, bookkeeping. While learning to type to the music of "Stars and Stripes Forever," it never occurred to me how large this new discipline would loom in my later life.

Doe Run Public School
As it was when Jean Bell Mosley attended from 6th to 12th grades. She gradu-
ated in 1931. The school is now consolidated with the Farmington schools in
Farmington, Missouri.

Original Doe Run High School

It was girls' basketball that interested me the most. High-school enrollment was so small that it didn't take a lot of athletic ability to make the team. Most anyone who wanted to play could be on the roster. I was fast and quick, having been honed for such by those snakes, hysterical chickens, the mythical black panther, and cows that didn't want to conform with the rest of the herd when being driven home out of the hills.

Basketball widened the scope of my life physically and so-cially. We went to compete with all the schools in the Lead Belt, in addition to DeSoto, Herculaneum, and Ste. Genevieve. I became acquainted with girls and boys beyond my own schoolmates. I was most impressed when the girls at Ste. Genevieve served us hot chocolate and doughnuts after the game. I think it was my first realization that social graces extended even beyond hard-fought games.

We didn't win very many games, since all the other schools were much larger in enrollment, hence more to choose from. At that time, the girls' court was divided into three equal sections. The jumping center and receiving center, as they were called, played in the middle section, the forwards and guards in the end sections. Only the forwards could shoot for the goals.

My initiation to basketball was at the exact time when girl bas-ketball players were moving from black bloomers and white mid-dies as sports costumes to the sleeveless jersey tops that tucked into flannel shorts. Scandalous, some thought. The first two years of my basketball career, the outfits were white trimmed with blue; the second two years, we had blue suits trimmed in white, blue and white being our school colors. My number throughout the four years was seven, and I've always considered that my lucky number.

The Green Fountain Pen

The great fashion, when I got to high school, was for the girls to wear a fountain pen suspended from a black ribbon worn around their necks. The ribbon was threaded through a ring at the top of the pen and was long enough so that writing with the pen could be accomplished without removing it from the neck. Gone were the old ink wells and scratchy ink pens of Loughboro days, although bottles of ink were still necessary because the fountain pen ran dry and had to be refilled. You dipped the point of the pen into the bottle, pulled down a little lever which squeezed air out of a rubber tube inside the pen. When the lever was released, ink was sucked up into the rubber tube.

I wanted one.

Although times were better for us, Mama said I could have one if I earned the money to buy one myself. Earn money myself! The only money I had earned to date was picking dewberries and digging sassafras roots to sell to the drugstores. There was that two dollars I earned from the Blue Valley Creamery Company, but it was long gone.

There were several creameries in St. Louis where all the local farmers sent their cream. They all paid about the same. Blue Valley offered a dollar reward to anyone who could get them a new customer. I had persuaded two neighbors to switch to Blue Valley.

No berries were ripe at the time of my passionate desire, and it was off-season for digging sassafras roots. There was another avenue. There always seemed to be another avenue if one would only put one's mind to it.

On a visit with Grandpa to the Farm Bureau Store, I learned that you could return good feed sacks to the store and receive a nickel for them. Trouble was, all barns had mice, and mice loved what was in these feed sacks too, so a good non-holey sack was hard to find.

"Can they be patched?" I asked.

"Yes."

So, up and down the river valley I went, asking for holey sacks that would otherwise be thrown away.

The green marbled fountain pen I wanted, in Tetley's Jewelry Store window at Farmington, was $3.95. No tax. That meant sixty-nine sacks — really about seventy-five, for some had to be used to cut the material for patches. The twine and darning needle, Mama furnished.

My sack enterprise was carried out in the smokehouse after school and on Saturdays. I cut nice square patches, turned under edges, and whipped them down over the holes. It was a long, dusty task. Hardest $3.95 I ever earned.

Princess-style dresses had come into fashion. Mama, still with no pattern, made me one of red calico print with white organdy collars and cuffs delicately trimmed with narrow ruffles. This was my favorite dress to wear with the green fountain pen. I think I must have preened like a peacock. Perhaps I was Clara Bow, by that time. No lipstick, though, to change the shape of my lips, which took on a rather hard and determined line during all that sack patching.

Leaving the Farm

I had no notion that there was an undercurrent in the family, an undercurrent that whispered of such a thing that it might be best if Dad, Mama, Lillian, Lou, and I were to move to Doe Run.

Looking back, I can understand how much easier it would be for us girls to get to school and Daddy to his work, if we made the move.

The thought had never crossed my mind that we would leave the land. The Land! It is described as real estate, as if everything else is artificial. How would anyone ever have any security without land? Land to raise food? Land to raise cattle, hogs, chickens. Woods for firewood and wild turkeys and foxes. I had even fantasized where on the farm I would have a future home built. Me and who? Jay? George? Arley? Dink? Willie? Chesley? — boys I had met at school.

Never to go out with Grandpa in the spring to see if the ground crumbled enough for plowing? Never to follow him around the furrows as the plowshare laid back the great, brown, satin layers of soil? Never to clean out the wet-weather spring to let it run free, handle the fuzzy new chicks, find candy in the buggy top? I was leaving childhood literally and chronologically.

But Coolidge continued to make it better for business, worse for the farmers, so they said. Finally, in 1929, we made the move and the separation.

One of the saddest days of my life was when the last load of furniture departed from the farm, and I with it, sitting on top of Mama's dresser and waving goodbye to Grandma, standing in the doorway, waving. I turned to look at myself in the dresser's mirror. I didn't look at all like Janet Gaynor nor Laura LaPlant, Clara Bow, Billie Burke. I could see Grandma in the mirror, still waving. As I waved back, facing the mirror, some kind of butterfly or leaf or bird passed in the space between us. It was vague. "Was it a comforting message from you, God?"

If someone had told me it was the overall plan for Grandpa and Grandma to sell the farm and come to Doe Run later, I would not have suffered so much from the lumps in my throat, the lying awake at night thinking of Grandma and Grandpa out there alone with that lonesome call of the tree frogs in the night.

We moved into a big, interesting, three-storey house that a family by the name of Neal had vacated. It had originally been built for a Dr. Graves. There were many floor levels, closets, and stairways in unexpected places. Two big bay windows on either side of the first floor added architectural grace. There were eight large rooms and two hallways big as rooms at the bottom and top of the stairway. The stairway had a little twist at the top. There was also a stairway off a side porch leading to floors a little lower than the main second storey, and then another short flight up to the main second storey. These middle-level rooms were for servants, so they said. I was unacquainted with servants except those I had read about.

Then there was a stairway leading from the second storey to the third storey. This third storey had a skylight. This was new to me.

A long, brick walk bordered by maple trees on both sides led from the street to a wide flight of stairs that ascended to the front porch. This porch spanned the entire front of the house. Swiss chauteau-like banisters bordered the stairs and the porch and the roof of the porch. There was a large, concrete-floored back porch. Double doors, level with the porch floor, opened to steps that led down to the cellar.

A detached summer kitchen, which we used as a laundry room, bordered the west side of the back porch and a few feet in front of it was the well pump. The furnace under the front porch that had once heated the house was no longer operable. We erected our trusty heating stoves, fueled now by coal.

The expansiveness of the new home seemed to represent the new dimensions of life I was entering into. I did not go back to visit Grandma and Grandpa as often as I had promised. School and church activities took much time. And I was on that basketball team, and could now stay and practice after school along with the rest of the team.

1930–1940

Turning Point

Sometimes, after most of a century has passed before you, you can look back and see turning points in your life, some big or little thing that determined the road you would take.

The first and dominant one for me was that moment when I realized that God was talking back to me in a manner I chose to believe. Another one happened in high school. The Depression was gathering force. I knew that my chances of going on to college would depend upon a partial scholarship, gained by being valedictorian of my graduating class. Flat River Junior College offered such scholarships to local graduates. Although I was always a good student, Birdie Matthews continually nipped at my heels scholastically.

I had to figure out some way to inch ahead in grades and stay there. In an English class, we had come to that section on "Giving a Speech." Fortunately, many of the students, including Birdie, gave their speeches before I did. Everyone used notes. Aha, I thought. I'll give my speech without notes.

My subject matter was inconsequential. It was about a haunted house somewhere in California. Certainly not a dissertation nor a thesis, but given without notes and with eye contact with my fellow classmates, it was effective.

The speech put a plus sign after my grade. And the thin, hanging-by-a-thread plus held up and made me valedictorian.

I entered Flat River Junior College, September 1931.

The scholarship meant I could work in Dean Wesley Deneke's office, typing this, that, and the other for part of my tuition. Also, I could work in the school's cafeteria during the lunch hour and then, when everyone was served, get a free lunch myself.

The MR & BT Railroad had a terminal spur at Doe Run. Often, after spending the weekend at home, I took that train to Flat River, about a twenty-mile ride. Along with enough clean clothes for the week went a sack of potatoes from Mama's garden (Mama always and always had a garden), some slices of bacon, ham, and cold fried chicken, a jar of kraut, some apples, and my purse containing a one-dollar bill and lipstick! Yes, by this time I could use lipstick, purchased at Woolworth's. If I was careful with my lipstick money, I could occasionally buy a tiny bottle of Radio Girl perfume or Mavis talcum powder. I juggled these things down Cochran Street and up Field Street to the home of the Upchurch family where I rented a tiny room and had the privilege of using the kitchen after that family was through with it for the day.

Myrtle Casey Bell in her garden

Essie Waltman Upchurch, the mother of this family, was a daughter of the Waltman family, our nearest neighbors in Doe Run. So I had a sort of "in" with them. We all helped each other as best we could to get through the Depression, which grew worse and worse.

Although I was invited to mingle with the family in the evenings, I seldom did so. The two Upchurch sons, Clelle and Byron, had homework to do. David was just a baby. Mr. Upchurch, a teacher, had papers to grade and lesson plans to make. Essie tended the baby or went endlessly through the Sears, Roebuck catalog.

Flat River, now incorporated with other Lead Belt towns, the whole of them known as Park Hills, is a very hilly town, and my walk of about a mile from where I stayed wasn't as easy as going down that old railroad track beside the murmuring river.

My free hours were mostly spent in the dean's office, typing. If there was nothing to do there, I joined my new friends in the girls' lounge where we played auction bridge, a forerunner to contract bridge.

The scholastic honorary society at Flat River Junior College was Phi Theta Kappa. Such societies were new to me, and I didn't give it much thought, but when the first semester's grades came out, there were three S's and an M+ on my card. We graded by

Excellent, Superior, Medium, Inferior, and Failing. The M+ was in the class taught by Wesley Deneke, the Dean for whom I worked. Perhaps he was afraid he would have shown favoritism if he'd given me a better grade, since I was his office girl.

A boy, whose last name was Stracky, sat next to me in this particular class. He had seen all my test scores and heard my class performance. He "hit the ceiling" when he learned of the M+ and advised me to "take it up with the Dean." I was too timid. Besides, I might lose my job. "Well," said Stracky, "I'm going to." And he did.

Flat River Junior College

Jean Bell Mosley worked in the office of Dean Wesley Deneke as a stenographer to help pay for books and tuition. The college has been relocated and renamed Mineral Area Community College.

Dean Deneke never changed my grade, but he did mumble some sort of apology that he thought my responses were too "memorized" and "not thought out."

That M+ haunted me for two years. Thereafter, my grades were all Superior and Excellent except for another M+ in Introduction to Art. But now, instead of a Birdie Matthews nipping at my scholastic heels, it was a Helen Estes, and the Estes and Deneke families were good friends.

Once again I was faced with the fact that if I couldn't be valedictorian and earn a partial scholarship to Southeast Missouri State College, my formal education might come to a sudden halt.

There's always a way out if you think hard enough. I knew that if I could "overload," that is, take more five-hour classes my last semester and make E's in all of them, I could beat Helen. I did.

Still, the talk on campus around graduation time was that Helen was going to be valedictorian.

After the last semester's grades were posted, I walked into the dean's office and requested him to compare the grade-point average of the two of us.

Wonderingly, he did so as I sat nearby watching. When he was through adding and dividing, he looked at me, stunned.

"I'm valedictorian, aren't I?"

"By six-tenths," he replied.

So I got to go on to Southeast Missouri State College with the partial scholarship providing a job, again in the dean's office, typing. The dean was Vest Myers.

Of course when I transferred to SEMO, as it was later to be called, my grades were transferred as C's, a custom I do not think entirely fair, but I understand the point.

The scholarship game was up. If there was to be more college after this third year, I'd have to pay for all of it.

At the end of the first season, 1933–34 at SEMO, I applied for a teaching position so that I could earn tuition money to continue my education in the summer semesters.

But before I leave Flat River Junior College days, let me tell about a few other experiences.

I fell "in love" with Henry Bolen, Joe Underwood, Ray Crabdree. I can't remember why I didn't fall in love with Stracky who went to bat for me over the M+.

At the same time, I was "in love" with my high school sweetheart, Jay Wallace. He had gone off to Boliver College in the southwest part of the state. And then there was this lad from Farmington, Lawrence Cleek.

At Christmas 1934, I received a Dubarry compact each from Jay, Joe, and Lawrence. I had to be careful how I switched those compacts about on various occasions.

The boys all managed to get little odd jobs at filling stations or hamburger joints to make enough money for a gallon or two of gasoline a week and enough to take their "girls" to a picture show and stop somewhere for a Coke afterwards. The "girls," cognizant of the financial situation, often pretended they really didn't want a Coke.

Still battling the Depression, it came my time to entertain Phi Theta Kappa members. (I made Phi Theta Kappa the second semester after that M+.) My roommate, Mildred Mitchell from Belleview, Missouri, was my co-hostess. This was the second year at Flat River, and I had co-rented a room with her at the home of Alice Board, a home much nearer the college. However, Alice never heated her house in the wintertime unless it was a fire in her fireplace. We had a King Heater in our room, but when we were away at school all day, the room got miserably cold.

We decided to serve a square of Jell-O, cut from two 9x13 pans. Not having access to a refrigerator and it being wintertime, we set the Jell-O outside to gel. When we came home from classes, there was a layer of black soot on top of the Jell-O. Someone nearby had stoked their furnace vigorously.

We tried to blow it off. It wouldn't blow. We scraped it as best we could, but knew we couldn't serve it in such scraggly looking blocks. In a fit of temper we thrust a spoon into it and began to stir. It came out beautifully. Red whipped Jell-O with just a tinge of black served in the cafeteria glass dessert dishes.

After I made Phi Theta Kappa the second semester, a teacher, Miss Bloom, wanted to take some of us girls to the state convention, which was going to be in her hometown of Fulton, Missouri. "Now we'll all be wearing formals at the banquet," she said matter-of-factly.

A formal!

I knew my landlady, Alice, had a formal. I'd seen it hanging in her closet. Would she let me borrow it? First, would it fit? While she was away one night I slipped into her room to try it on. No full-length mirror. So up onto a chair to look into a dresser mirror. The skirt was of ruffled georgette, white with red roses in it. In stepping up onto the chair I stepped on one of the ruffles. The undeserved M+, the darkened Jello, faded into the Land of Inconsequential.

I put the formal back in the closet. This was a matter to take up with Mama. Precious Mama.

"You must tell her, of course," Mama said, and I nodded dumbly, thinking of the hog carcasses I'd seen hanging from the pole down by the maple tree.

"I can get white georgette, have it picoted like the other ruffles and insert a white one alternately with the rosy ones," Mama said. Her eyes seemed to glisten with her own ingenuity.

I had to go through a whole weekend and a whole Monday before I saw Alice Board. There was no easy way to do it.

"I was trying on your formal and I ripped a ruffle," I blurted. Any tears leaked were dried up instantly on my red-hot face.

The dictionary defines the word "embarrassment" as to feel "ill at ease." That isn't strong enough.

I went to the convention, but I did not enjoy it.

In my second year at Flat River, I had "Practice Teaching." Sounds like measles or mumps, doesn't it? Those who were aiming for a sixty-hour teaching certificate went to various schools in the community and taught classes under the watchful eye of the regular teacher.

I practiced teaching in the first grade at the Eugene Field School, and who was in my class but Dean Wesley Deneke's little daughter! Hmmmmmmmm.

She was a beautiful, blond, curly haired, intelligent little girl. Sometimes the afternoon sunshine coming through the windows caught and tangled in those curls, sending off glints like those of the sunshine on the carbide light and the shiny oak leaves. I gave little Miss Deneke my best attention.

The mode of teaching reading then was by the "flash card" method. You held up a word printed in manuscript letters on a white cardboard card and the pupils learned what it was, the size, the shape, the pronunciation, the meaning, etc. No phonetics like I had at Loughboro long ago, and which I still think is the best. But somehow the children learned to read, and it was the method I used when two years later I began to teach the first three grades in a small-town school, Graniteville.

The first floor of the college was like a long capital "I." At each end were classrooms and a flight of stairs going to the second floor. Down the long hallway between the ends of the "I" were the students' lockers.

When we were enrolled, we were issued the number of our locker. They were metal upright affairs connected with all the others up and down the hallway so that they seemed all of one piece. We were to furnish our own locks and keys. That is, of course, if we felt it necessary. No one did, for we were still in an age of innocence and enjoyed the high moral values of the Midwest.

Nevertheless, we thought it looked "uptown" to have a lock, so I used one we had around the house for a long time as a sort of novelty. It was a combination lock. One could pick a number, set the lock to open at that combination, and when the "hand" was turned backward and forward to the combination one had chosen, it would open. Innocently, I set the lock to coincide with my locker number lest I forget. Who wouldn't have guessed that? Most times, locks were not snapped shut. They just hung there as a device to keep the locker door from inadvertently swinging open. We hung our coats and sweaters there, placed textbooks not in use on the top shelf, our tennis shoes on the bottom. It was a sort of micro-combination of the old Loughboro desks and cloak room. Marijuana, cocaine, cigarettes, condoms, guns had not come to the locker scene yet.

The Frog

When I first entered Dr. Laura Nahm's zoology class during my second term at Flat River, I did so with much trepidation. I had heard she was a no-nonsense teacher who expected her students to reach, reach, reach to the apex of their mental capacity. I was prepared to do that. I needed an E in this five-hour course. The textbooks, lectures, and workbooks were "a piece of cake." But—The Frog!

About the second week into the class, each student was presented with a whole frog, preserved in formaldehyde or some combination of formaldehyde and water in a glass pint jar, with lid, of course.

That frog, even closed-eyed, seemed to peer accusingly at me through the fluid and glass even before I opened the lid and removed him as per instructions.

With about thirty students opening thirty jars of that preserving fluid and taking out a dripping frog to deposit on absorbent paper, it was, well, heady. Not only heady, but stomach-ey, when we were further instructed to take the sharp knife, also provided, and make the first slit all the way down the underneath side from throat to tail.

These, I thought, were the same kind of frogs which had delighted me, sitting on a lily pad in the St. Francis River, underneath the swinging bridge or making their sudden plopping sounds from bank to river as Lou and I sat on the Flat Rock fishing for perch. Dragonflies with their beautiful irridescent wings would light on our poles. Scarlet tanagers would move in and out of the riverside thickets. Cowbells could be heard. I'll keep my mind on these things, I thought, as my head seemed too light for my body, and my stomach too unsteady for its purposes. *And you have to make an E in this subject too, remember*, I reminded myself.

Day by day we got deeper and deeper into the frog, and I grew more unstable by the day, but my drawings of the frog's insides in my workbook were meticulous and came back weekly with an excellent grade.

Dr. Nahm, not only a demanding teacher but an observant one, no doubt noticed my dilemma and quite often just casually came to stand close by my spot at the long table. I imagined she wanted to be on hand if I fainted and fell forward, spilling the preserving fluid.

At the close of this second semester of my second year, I stopped by her room when she was straightening things and said, "Thank you for the E."

She replied, "Don't thank me. You deserved it." We exchanged knowing glances. I walked away quickly, hoping I'd never again have to smell formaldehyde.

Conceited?

One other incident of junior-college days rambles around in the recesses of my mind. There was another Jean in the enrollment—Jean Murphy, a very lovely, dark-haired girl, descendant of the pioneer Murphy family that had settled Farmington, the County seat. I admired her very much.

Jean Murphy and I were mutual members of a class wherein we were studying genes—the dominant gene and the recessive gene that determine our personas. My then-boyfriend, Joe Underwood, was also a member. We had spent much class time on these two kinds of genes.

One day at an off-hour gathering of friends in one of the lounges, someone stuck his head in the door and called for Jean.

With our recent classwork in mind, I asked, smartalecky, I suppose, "Do you want the dominant Jean or the recessive Jean?" I was making a sort of pun, but my friend Joe took what he described as a superior glint in my eye to mean that perhaps I was the "dominant" one the caller wanted. Such are the trials and tribulations of one trying to show off with newly acquired learning.

On our next date, in discussing the incident, Joe told me in no uncertain terms that he thought I was conceited. That hurt. Down deep. I started to protest and explain, but the lump in my throat told me to remain quiet. I knew I was innocent, but I also knew I was losing a good friend. Later on, a bottle of Evening in Paris perfume from Joe did not close the rift. I loved the perfume in the pretty blue bottle, but thereafter its fragrance always made me wonder if I did have such a character flaw and was unaware of it. Not the innocent "gene" remark, but had there been other occasions when Joe had seen or thought he'd seen this flaw? Oh, Murmuring River and Hemlocks, I'd have to watch this.

Grandma Dies

During the winter of my first year at Flat River, Grandma became ill. At home on weekends, I'd walk the short distance over to her house. She and Grandpa had sold the farm and moved to Doe Run about a year after we had left. I would try to read to her as in the old days on the farm, but I could see her mind was not on the story. She would suddenly interrupt to ask me to look down her throat and try to see what was there she couldn't get up.

"Grandma, I just can't see a thing," I'd report.

"Well," she begged, "just reach down and see if you can get anything."

I did that, too, among much gagging and coughing and spitting on her part.

"Just let it go," she said with sad resignation.

After my last try, I went into the kitchen and pretended to busy myself at the old kitchen range, same one we'd used on the farm. I picked up the stovelid lifter Grandma had used thousands of times, and rearranged the lids, inspected the reservoir for water, opened the warming oven.

When Grandpa heard a tear sizzle on the warm stovetop, he walked over and put a hand on my shoulder. "It's all right," he said.

It was a small gesture, but comforting. He had accepted that life moves on and we have to move with it.

When I saw Grandma's old hands, gnarled by too much rheumatism, clasped in death, I thought of the doll dresses those hands had made, the little pieces of biscuit dough she had pinched off to let me "bake" on top of the stove, the only hands that old Star would let milk her. I'll think of these things, I said to myself, although "these things" could not stop the tears.

Grandma's death certificate reads: Date of death, February 9, 1932; cause of death, perinephritis abcess; contributing interstitial nephritis and arterio sclorosis. Age at death, seventy-seven years, one month.

She was buried in the Bonne Terre, Missouri, cemetery, the town to which she had come from Virginia fifty years earlier.

Eternity as Seen Through an Apple Orchard*

In addition to the above-mentioned things about Grandma, I will remember her for her concept of Eternity.

On a lazy summer afternoon, Grandma would tie on a big, white, starched apron, get her basket of quilt scraps, and head for the orchard. "A person could get a breath of air there," she explained. She would find a comfortable spot to sit, probably on the shady side of the Maiden Blush apple tree, and soon the click of needle against thimble would blend with other busy sounds—insects droning, chickens clucking up in the barn lot.

I usually accompanied Grandma, hoping a ripe apple would fall at my feet or that Grandma might have a peppermint in the bottom of her basket.

The orchard fell away gently toward the meadow where we could see our cows lying in the shade of the river trees. Across the river were fields rising toward the hills that folded into each other higher and higher, blue deepening to indigo and then purple.

It was not a setting where one's thoughts would often take a dolorous turn, yet it was there in our orchard that I learned about Grandma's concept of Eternity.

Someone had recently died in our community. I had noticed that the folks roundabout skirted the word "died." They would say "passed away" or "gone home." Our minister had said Tim had entered Eternity. Grandma took issue with this. On a day in the orchard, I asked her why. "Nobody can enter Eternity," she said with conviction. "They're already there."

---

* "I Learned about Eternity" *Farm Journal*, October 1958.

This map, hand-drawn by Jean Bell Mosley, shows the places that were important to her when she was growing up on the farm.

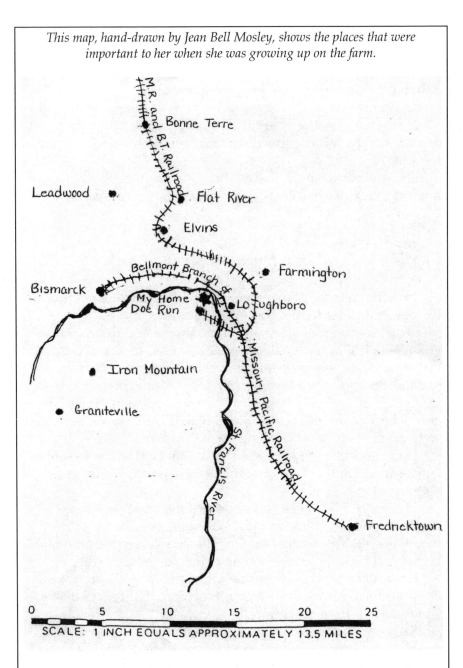

SCALE: 1 INCH EQUALS APPROXIMATELY 13.5 MILES

Bonne Terre: Where Wilson Bell was born and lived during his youth. He was treated at the Bonne Terre Hospital several times for heart attacks. Stephen Bell, Josephine Lyons Bell, and Stephen Wilson Bell, together with other kin, are buried in Bonne Terre. Also the headquarters of St. Joe Lead Company were located here after it was removed from Doe Run.

Flat River: Where Jean Bell Mosley attended Flat River Junior College. The Bells shopped here at Christmas in the new Woolworth 5¢ and 10¢ store, which was the first such store in the country.

Elvins: Birthplace of Jean. The Bells took eggs and butter to exchange for groceries, shopped for shoes and dress material, got haircuts and occasionally ice cream sodas. Jean saw her first movie here. Kaiser Bill was burned in effigy here after WWI. The Bells took cream to the railroad station to be shipped to St. Louis. Wilson Bell's livery stable and blacksmith shop were here. Elvins had several mine shafts and large chat piles.

Leadwood: Where Stephen Bell and Josephine Lyons Bell and three of their youngest children lived for a while when Stephen was needed to establish a lead-mining endeavor. Leadwood was formerly called Owl Creek. There is a street named for Stephen Bell in Leadwood.

Bismarck: A busy train junction where the Bells went to catch a train to St. Louis or anywhere else in the U.S.

Farmington: The county seat. The Bells went here to pay taxes and the mortgage on the farm. Gradually they began to trade here for clothing and other goods, and they transferred medical and dental service from Elvins to Farmington. Jean was married here. Her mother and father worked here in the state hospital No. 4 after Wilson ceased his rock-crushing business. Farmington and Doe Run were great rivals in athletics.

Doe Run: Small town where the Bells moved when they left the farm. Jean attended school here from 6th to 12th grade.

Loughboro: Where Jean attended grade school from 1st to 5th grade. Also where she attended Sunday school and church for these years.

Iron Mountain: Where Wilson had his rock-crushing business and lost his right arm. Jean spent many hours swimming in Iron Mountain Lake.

Graniteville: Where Jean taught school from 1934–1936 and where she spent time with friends exploring Elephant Rocks.

Fredericktown: Where Myrtle Casey lived.

Bellmont Branch Railroad: Jean walked a portion of the way to Loughboro along this railroad track.

St. Francis River: The river Jean fished from, swam in, and skated on.

Star: This shows the location of the Bells' farm home.

She took off her glasses and wiped them thoughtfully. "Eternity began a long time ago. No one can say for sure how long, but for a starting point let us say it began on the first page of Genesis. You know about that, don't you?" she asked, focusing her pale blue eyes on me.

I nodded that I did, then quoted what I'd learned in Sunday school, "In the beginning, God created the heavens and the earth."

"That's right," she said. "Heaven and earth and all of time. That's Eternity."

She sewed a couple more patches together. Then, "Look," she said, pointing, "there's the barn lot up there. Here, next to it, is the orchard, and there, over the fence, are the pastures and fields and hills. Let's say the barn lot is that part of Eternity which was here before you were born. This orchard is the place where you are this minute. The pastures and fields and those high, mysterious hills are part of Eternity you'll learn about when you leave the orchard. It's all connected, see?"

I thought that over while the insects droned and the grasshoppers made high jumps. "But, Grandma, that means we're in Eternity now!"

"Exactly!" How pleased she was at my childish logic. I got a peppermint for it.

Grandma was not the first to reflect that Eternity is here and now. But she was the one who first told me about its immediateness and its endlessness. The picture she gave me of eternal change and progress brings me serenity. Why count the passing of my days in one place any more than in another? I feel so sure that life is all of a whole, a forever-continuing chain of place and circumstance.

Sometimes I wish Grandma could have been buried right there under the Maiden Blush apple tree, but the time for little family graveyards had passed.

And Then Came Edward

Although I applied for a schoolteaching position in the spring of 1933, having secured my Sixty-Hour Teacher's Certificate from Flat River Junior College, I did not get one. Anyone who had a job in 1933 held onto it tenaciously. Dust storms clouded the Midwest,

CCC (Civilian Conservation Corps) camps appeared around the country. My "old friend" Coolidge had departed the White House. No one had paid much attention to his advice about "Make more money than you spend. Spend less money than you make."

Herbert Hoover won the presidency in 1924, and he was one of the many who thought, "Just let things alone and they'll eventually work out." Economically speaking, that is.

It didn't work out that way. Things got worse. For a while it looked as if America was just going to spiral away, upward into a dust storm. The barren fields with no cover crops to keep the topsoil down were just left "swinging in the wind," an expression that was to be made popular in another coming crisis.

Thousands of families in the Midwest packed their pitifully few belongings into and onto old jalopies and headed west. This sad era in American history was depicted in a best-selling novel by John Steinbeck, *The Grapes of Wrath*.

One night I overheard a bedtime conversation between Mama and Dad. I didn't mean to eavesdrop, but when I became aware they were talking about me, I listened.

"If we just let her stay around here, she'll end up marrying some no-account and getting nowhere."

In the darkness, I blushed at this assessment of my future. Gee Whiz! Hadn't I already perfectly dissected a frog and given a speech without notes!

Mama said, "Well, she does have the partial scholarship. Do you think we can swing the rest?"

"We will," Dad replied stoutly. After that there was silence. They had gone to sleep, and I did too, smiling.

Going as a junior into a four-year college with no one else from your hometown attending was not easy. Campus friendships had already been formed.

The other girls staying at 383 N. Henderson helped, although we seldom had the same classes. I was "that girl who worked in the dean's office, typing."

During the first term I was introduced to Sorosis "rushing." There were social societies for girls: Clio, Sorosis, and Hesperian; and for the boys: Websters, Bentons, and Mark Twains.

I had not experienced anything like this at Flat River. There were no social sororities there, only Phi Theta Kappa, the honorary scholastic society which held social parties occasionally. Remember the red, soot-covered Jell-O?

I was chosen by Sorosis and attended their meetings, learning for the first time what blackballing was. I did not like that. In fact, I did not enjoy Sorosis much at all. They had dances and I didn't dance. They had parties. I seldom went. Once, the girls in Sorosis were assigned a boy from the Mark Twain fraternity to ask for a date for some party, maybe Valentine's. I did not ask my assigned date. Also, I failed to notify anyone that I was not going to ask, so this boy, a popular boy on campus, Jimmy Wax, was not at the party. I had made a faux pas.

Before the school year was over, though, I had made many friends who at the end of the year wrote warm, encouraging messages in my *Sagamore*, our college yearbook. Most of those who had written referred to my basketball and swimming abilities. I had led Sorosis to an inter-society championship and earned a letter in swimming, was even nominated in the first of several eliminations as the Sagamore Queen. The nomination was made by someone whom I had helped write a thesis!

Since the boys who lived in town knew there was always a number of girls staying at 383 North Henderson, they made it their business to come by in the early evenings and sit on the porch or in the porch swings, which were at either end of the long porch that spanned the front of the house. Mrs. Rosena Perry, the landlady, who was otherwise rather strict with "her girls," seeing that they signed out and in when on a date, didn't seem to mind these town boys stopping to visit on the porch. One or two at a time, of course.

One evening, after dark (no girl was afraid to walk anywhere on the campus after dark at that time), returning from the library to my home-away-from-home, there were the girls on the porch along with two boys. Dim light came through the two front windows, and I didn't really get a very good look at the two boys who introduced themselves as John Hirsch and John Mosley. I stayed to chat awhile with them and the other girls, then went upstairs to my studies.

About a week later I was called to the telephone. It was John. For some reason, I did not ask "John who?" Instantly, for some weird reason, it popped into my head that it was the one who had called himself John Hirsch. He wanted a date. I told him I would think about it and for him to call back in a few days.

There was only one other person in town that I knew besides those I had recently met, someone who had lived in Cape Girardeau a long time. It was Alene Sadler. She had taught school

102

at Doe Run, my hometown. I called her to ask if she knew a John Hirsch, and if so, what kind of fellow was he? She said she knew no one called John Hirsch but that the Hirsch family was highly respected, well known, and she thought it would be all right for me to accept a date with this John Hirsch.

So when John called again, I did accept the date. When he came to the door, I realized it was not the one I had expected, although I had seen both of them only in dim light.

After I had called him John a few times, he admitted that his name wasn't really John but Edward, Edward Mosley.

Edward and Ralph Hirsch were best friends, and, through who knows what boyish ritual, custom, or habit, they had been calling each other John. They did all their lives. Ralph went on to marry LaVerne Moore, and after about four children, they had another child whom they, at last, called John.

Well, the Mosley family was well-thought-of too. Edward lived with his mother and father at 501 Themis Street. Two older brothers, Sylvester and Juel, and a sister, Bernice, had already married and had homes of their own.

Edward had gone to college for a few semesters, but dropped out to take a job at the Southeast Missouri Printing and Stationery Company. That old Depression again. He had a car and a little more money to spend, and seemed so much more mature than the boys I had been accustomed to dating. He was intelligent, too.

Because he had liked his Shakespeare teacher, he knew the old bard and his works, which always seemed such a funny combination with his other occupations and recreations. He was a printing pressman, a hunter, a fisherman, and baseball player. I bet no one in the outfield of the Capahas, his baseball team, knew he could repeat at the drop of a ball, "Out, out damned spot," and many other well-known quotes. If there was ever one who

Edward Price Mosley (1910–1977)

believed in the work ethic, he was at the top of the class, always leaving for work earlier than necessary and having his press going half an hour before it was necessary.

Teaching School at Graniteville

When I had completed the 1933–34 fall and winter terms at SEMO, I went right on into the summer term in order to get my B.S. degree as soon as possible.

That spring, 1934, I again applied for a schoolteaching position and got one. I could look forward to paying some of my further educational expenses.

The country was still in deep Depression. There were many, many applications for a schoolteaching position—any old school.

At that time, to put in a serious application for a country-school position, one traipsed through plowed fields, across streams, into grocery stores, mining offices, etc., to get an interview with a school-board member.

You needed to look your best on these trips. Lillian had already been teaching school for several years. She secured a teaching position right out of high school by passing a County Teachers Examination. So Lillian could afford some nice clothes. And she was generous in lending them. She had a new, black spring coat which she let me borrow when I went interviewing.

A school-board member I wanted to talk to was plowing a field with a team of horses. A barbed wire fence was around the field. I crawled through the strands and hooked the underneath sleeve area of Lillian's new coat on a barb which made an ugly tear. But on I went across the plowed ground to interview the board member, who was kind enough to stop his plowing and listen to my pleading. The horses, grateful for a brief rest, stood patiently, tails switching flies from their backs. The sun glinted on some of the brass ornaments of their harness. It shone right into my eyes, reminding me of that long ago carbide light reflector and the wonderful convictions that followed. Heartened by this reminder of His presence, I made my case and was curiously confident that I would get the position.

Back home, I told Mama about the tear in the coat. She placed a finger over her lips to indicate this would be our secret.

Mama had long, black hair—black as the coat. She pulled out one of the hairs, maybe two or three, and did such a masterful job of reweaving the tear together that no one ever knew about it until years and years later when it didn't matter anymore. But it has always mattered to me.

I got the teaching position.

Graniteville was a small town that had grown up around a red, granite quarry where most of

Elephant Rocks State Park

the men of the families worked. There was a nearby area known as Elephant Rocks, a huge upheaveal of granite boulders big as elephants, some of them balanced on the granite mountain with no more than three square feet underneath them. Most peculiar formation. At that time, it was just a unique, rather wild place to go and marvel. Later it was made into a state park, especially for the blind. Trails wind around through the gargantuan rocks. Guiding ropes are beside the pathway, and at intervals there are metal plaques printed in Braille, which the blind can stop to read and see with their minds' eyes what is all around them.

At Graniteville I taught the first two grades for two years; forty-two pupils the first year, fifty-two the second, far too many. Some of my little pupils could not even afford underwear, and sometimes I could see their bare skin through the worn seats of their overalls, even in the depth of winter.

We had the same type of round hooded stove as had been at Loughboro. Although Mr. Frank Phillips and a Mr. Berry, who taught the other four grades successively in the adjoining room, usually got the fires started in the mornings, it was up to me to stoke the stove in my room during the day with chunks of dry wood stored behind the stove.

There was an old, beat-up piano which hadn't been tuned in possibly twenty years and of which maybe one-third of the notes didn't sound at all. But, once a week, the whole school would

Graniteville, Missouri, Grade School
Picture taken in 1935. Jean (far right) taught the first two grades. Mr. Berry (far left) taught the other grades.

meet in a third room, which was a sort of all-purpose room for coats, lunchboxes, and indoor play on rainy days, and sing lustily the songs we knew, drowning out the old piano which I attempted to play.

The first year I taught school, I stayed at the Tim McCabe home. They were farmers. In addition to the parents, there were seven children. All but two of them were in the same school where I taught. Three of them were my pupils.

My bed was the couch in the living room. With the noisy family, my lack of privacy, and the new experience of teaching, in which I wanted to succeed, it was a difficult year. One night, after everyone else was asleep, my head throbbed with pain so severe I thought I would die. I never even thought then of carrying a supply of aspirins. I awakened Mrs. McCabe as gently as I could, asked her for an aspirin. She had none. Seven children in the middle of the Depression and no aspirins!

I returned to my couch in the living room, fell to my knees, and asked the Lord to relieve my pain and see me through the night. In the midst of the awful pounding pain, I tried to center my thoughts on that wonderful experience of feeling that God was talking back to me. Next morning I awoke, still kneeling, my head still resting on the couch.

I paid four dollars per week for that couch, breakfast, supper and a paper-wrapped sandwich for lunch. This sixteen dollars a month, subtracted from my fifty dollars per month salary, left thirty-four dollars for me to save to get on with my college degree and buy a little tin box of Bayer's aspirins!

As soon as school was out in the spring, I immediately entered SEMO for the spring and summer terms. I was getting closer.

All the time since I met Edward, we were dating. During the Christmas holidays of 1934, we became engaged to be married and made plans for a future together at Cape Girardeau.

Edward was still working at the Southeast Missourian Printing Company. The newspaper-publishing company and the printing company were in the same building at 301 Broadway, a handsome Spanish-style building. Both companies were owned at the time by George and Fred Naeter. Much later, the printing company moved to a building on William Street.

We did not move quickly, Edward and I. I was saving part of my meager schoolteacher's money and he was saving his meager pressman's money so that we could buy a lot where we would, someday, build a home.

My second year of teaching at Graniteville was a bit easier. With a year-end bonus, I made sixty dollars per month. This teaching year I stayed at the home of Ethel and Edward Sheahan, co-owners of the local Sheahan Granite Quarry. I had a lovely, comfortable bedroom and had learned to carry a supply of aspirins!

As soon as school was out in the spring, Edward and I were to be married and would build a new home. I paid eight dollars a week for room and board which, deducted from my now sixty dollars per month salary, left even less money to save than my first year. But the wonderful private bedroom was worth it. Also, it was closer to the school.

With our small savings, Edward and I were able to buy a lot soon after we were married. Lot 6, Block 3 of the Rodney Vista sub-division owned by Mrs. Iska Carmack became ours for $400. Full of corn stubble, no trees, gravel road in front, we knew it would take much work and planning to make it an attractive place to live.

The subdivision was originally part of a Spanish Land Grant given to Don Louis Lorimier, founder of Cape Girardeau, but was long known at the time of our purchase as the Old Haman Farm. The French Creole-style house on this farm, constructed of brick made by slave labor on the spot, was built in 1842. Renovated, it still stands about 300 yards from where, in 1936, we chose to build our home. At the time, the Aven Kinder family occupied the gracious old home. They were our nearest neighbors.

April 11, 1936

I arose early, bathed, ate breakfast, helped Mama with the refreshments which were to be served at our home after our marriage ceremony. I noticed some tears in Mama's eyes which she surreptitiously tried to wipe away. Her last child was moving out.

I dressed with care — a gray suit, trimmed with fur on the upper arms, the style of the day. My blouse was gray; hat, shoes, and purse, navy blue. I limped a little. The last week of school I had sprained an ankle while playing with the children at recess.

Edward arrived, dressed in a gray suit with a shadow check in it, a gray hat, and new shoes.

Mama, Dad, Lillian, Edward, and I started to Farmington about 10:30 AM. It was about a five-mile drive. The ceremony was to be at 11:00 AM. Lucille was pregnant and chose not to go.

We were married at the Methodist minister's home in Farmington. Edward's brother, Juel, was best man. Lillian was my matron of honor. Juel's wife, Clara, was also present.

The ceremoney was brief, and we were soon on our way back to Doe Run.

After the reception, Edward and I departed in a Model-A Ford roadster for St. Louis for one of the shortest honeymoons ever. Some of Edward's pals had seen fit to put a skunk in the back area of the roadster. It had been removed, of course, and Edward had done his best to scrub and spray and douse with perfume. But. . .

We stayed overnight at the Mayfair Hotel, went to see Charlie Chaplin in the movie *Modern Times*.

The next morning was Easter Sunday. I awoke to the sound of what seemed like a bunch of hogs grunting. Briefly, I thought I was back on the farm and this marriage bit was all a dream. But when I walked to the window and looked down three storeys, there was a truckload of hogs. I supposed they called them swine in the city.

My school had been out on Friday. We were married on Saturday, returned from St. Louis on Sunday, and I enrolled at SEMO on Monday for the spring and summer terms, the last legs of my B.S. degree.

That summer of 1936 was one of the hottest of the century. I was again doing practice teaching, this time at the SEMO's Training School. Ninth grade. My supervisor was a Mr. Boucher. He was very ill at the time. About midterm, "Cyclone" Jones took over. It was upsetting to me.

I was also writing my required thesis, the title of which was "The Social Effect of Addison and Steele." Edward and I stayed in a hot upstairs bedroom at the Mosley residence at 501 Themis St., now the site of a car wash.

The bright spot of the summer was that Edward and I had secured an FHA loan, and our house was going up at what one day would be 703 E. Rodney Drive, but then, outside the city limits, our address was merely known as Rodney Vista.

It was so nice after school to come out at evenings and sit in the rooms that were, so far, only divided by two-by-fours. Sometimes a late evening breeze came through the skeleton house. I sat looking out of all the walls and windows to be, embroidering a luncheon cloth—colorful lazy daisy motifs on unbleached muslin. All the perplexities and complications of Boucher, Jones, Addison, and Steele slipped away. Even the war events going on in faraway places didn't occupy a lot of my thoughts, although, on the backroads of my mind, I knew they were going on. Mentally placing the stove here, the table there, the bed yonder was more pleasant to think about than what was going on in Manchuria, Ethiopia, and the Rhineland. I felt as if I had suddenly matriculated from the fence corner playhouse of my childhood directly to this place. Life had been simple, basic, and good in that fence corner with wagon-wheel-hub chairs, wagon-wheel-hub tables, wagon-wheel-hub stove. I expected life to be simple, basic, and good in this new home with real tables, chairs, and stove.

It was still Depression days. Would they never end? Talk about Uncle Remus's Tar Baby! Or Scheherazade's unending stories!

Edward's father, Edgar Scott Mosley, was a carpenter, and he, along with out-of-work brother-in-law Oliver Hope, built the house. That is, they did the carpentry work. Subcontracts were let to Lear Brothers for excavation, Stoval and Co. for the brick and concrete work, Drury for the plastering, A.E. Birk for plumbing, Missouri Utilities for wiring and fixtures.

It is a sturdily built house. No one was in a hurry to finish a job, for there was seldom another one in sight. Sometimes three nails were used when one would have done. There are two layers of brick for the walls with dead airspace in between. The builders said it would be the best of insulations, but twenty-two windows seem to defeat that theory.

I, being a farm girl, and Edward, probably always wanting to live on a farm, had a very large garden. I loved that garden. Setting out the tomato and pepper plants in spring, and the long row of onion sets, planting the lettuce, radish, bean, and corn seed made me feel like a magician, for I knew what those little green plants and dry brown seeds could become. With April's blue skies above, wind in my hair, a cat rubbing against my legs, all the birds singing, and an ongoing conversation with God, it was good to be in that place. "You did good with seeds, God."

Very soon a big chicken house went up, and then another one. I still loved to gather those eggs, especially the brown speckled ones. As in the days when Mama and I took the eggs to Langdon's Store and exchanged them for groceries, I took eggs to Horn's Grocery Store and exchanged them for sugar, flour, coffee, and other staples.

We constructed a budget box so that we could "make it" financially. This was a shoebox, divided into compartments labeled: House Loan Payment, Electricity, Furniture payments, Groceries, Insurance, Coal, Gasoline, and Entertainment.

The Entertainment section was always very empty.

We were subsisting and very happy with our new home in the cornfield. But it soon became apparent that, say, if we wanted to go to St. Louis to see a major-league baseball game or to a hometown movie, we needed more money.

I applied for a teaching position at several local schools, without luck. I did substitute teaching at Central High School. Then there appeared in

Jean in front of home, built in 1936.
Photo taken in 1998.

110

the paper an ad stating that a secretary was needed by the Equitable Life Insurance Company, headquartered in the Himmelberger-Harrison Building, commonly called the
H & H Building.

I made a navy blue, dotted-Swiss dress, the white dots being in the shape of small butterflies. I bought a turned-back-brimmed navy straw hat, and with my navy purse and wedding shoes intact, I went to the H & H Building, got in the elevator at the end of the long marble-floored hall, and traveled upward, determined, but with more butterflies in my stomach than on the dotted Swiss.

I got the job!

Although I had my B.S. in Education degree with a major in English, the only formal office training I had was that high-school course in typing, shorthand, and bookkeeping, and a summer term at a private business school in Farmington. But with a résumé stating that I had taught school for two years and had worked in the dean's office as a typist at both Flat River Junior College and SEMO, I got the job! It was 1938.

We were able to go to Jones' Coney Island Hot Dog Parlor on Broadway about once a week in addition to a picture show. A small increase was made on our church pledge. I had moved my church membership from Doe Run Methodist Church to Centenary United Methodist Church in 1937. Edward was already a member of the congregation.

A real treat for us was to board the Frisco train at the depot on Water Street at 4 AM, arrive in St. Louis some hours later, and walk down to the Forum to get waffles with maple syrup for breakfast. We would ramble around through Stix, Baer and Fuller, and Famous-Barr Department Stores, then catch a streetcar to Sportsman's Park to see a Cardinal baseball game. Late night we would arrive back in Cape by train and get into our car, a Chevrolet by that time, and come home. We could have left that car parked there for a month or more, and no one would have ever touched it.

1940–1950

The War Years Again

By 1940, the Depression was receding, but something worse was asserting itself into our lives. Hitler! We had been vaguely aware of far-off things going on. Even as I was graduating from high school, Japan had seized Manchuria. While I was teaching school at Graniteville, Mussolini, dictator of Italy, invaded Ethiopia, and Japan invaded China. But as an old song goes, these were faraway places with strange-sounding names. However, when the fighting came to Britain, France, Belgium, and other places where we had fought before, it was different.

Then came December 7, 1941, Pearl Harbor Day, when the Japanese made a sneak attack on our Pacific naval fleet stationed there and practically destroyed it. Next day we sat close to our radio and heard President Franklin Delano Roosevelt speak in somber tones, "Yesterday, December 7, 1941, a date which will live in infamy, the United States of America was suddenly and deliberately attacked by naval and air forces of the Empire of Japan." Things looked bleak.

The German army was invading all neighboring nations and annexing them as German territory. The general cry in Europe was "Stop Hitler."

On the homefront, the Equitable Life Insurance Company, probably because of the Depression plus the war, determined that no married women would be employed by them, just as I was getting well-adjusted to my work.

Ethel Long, an unmarried secretary, was working for the Arnold Roth Insurance Company and getting slightly less salary than I. Together, with our bosses, we struck a deal to exchange jobs since Arnold Roth, being an independent insurance agent, had no such rules about married women.

Arnold Roth and Benson Hardesty, a lawyer, had their offices on the second floor of the First National Bank Building in the 200 block of North Main Street. A room separated the offices, and this room was for the secretaries—Roth's and Hardesty's.

My workload was increased. Mr. Roth represented about a dozen insurance companies, and I had to keep separate books for each company as well as take dictation for ten to twelve letters a day, make appointments, deliver policies, etc., etc.

Arnold Roth was a very civic-minded person, a war hero of WWI, and involved in Veterans' affairs, such affairs adding to my dictation and typing work.

Fortunately, when he dictated, I had a good ear for the message he was aiming at and a good memory, so that if my Gregg shorthand fell behind, I could just mentally fill in the gaps, and I don't think my inexact translations were ever noticed. Maybe it was thought to be better, since before long, Mr. Roth would hand me letters from his companies or clients and say, "Answer these."

A few minimal raises in both our salaries enabled us to "eat up" our FHA loan more quickly. It was our aim to have it paid before we started a family.

Always, though, there was that thorn of Hitler in our sides, and the war that was now raging in Europe. Some days I walked from my office to Woolworth's, a block and a half away south on Main Street, for lunch. I would hear snippets of radio news and sidewalk conversation along the way, such as, "Well, what country has Hitler invaded today?" Or, "Isn't anyone going to stop him?" "He says the Germans are a superior race and they're out to rule the world."

Although the street talk, the newspaper articles, and radio announcers and commentators bombarded us with war news, I didn't yet realize that it was going to be us, the United States, who would pay a dear price for stopping Hitler and would unleash on the world the first atom bomb.

Many young, single, and childless married men began volunteering for the Army, Navy, and Air Force. Edward thought he would fit into the Air Force better than anywhere else, so he enrolled in the flying school at the local Cape Girardeau airport.

He learned the mechanics of flying, but never did overcome the sickness that occurred every time his plane flew high, purposely stalled, and spiraled downward to be pulled out and upward at what seemed to me the last few seconds before hitting the ground. The maneuver was a requirement. Therefore, he did not pass.

Edward then tried to volunteer for the Navy, but failed a physical test on some seemingly small defect—a pronounced overbite and some enlarged leg veins. So we awaited the draft.

Selective Service headquarters, that body established in September 1948, for drafting young men into the military for service, was set up at the H & H Building. Edward received orders to report January 13, 1943, at Legion Hall, Jackson, Missouri, to be inducted into the army and transferred to St. Louis for physical examination.

It had been twenty-five years since the time Daddy had gone to Elvins to "be shot," as I childishly thought, for WWI.

It was a hair-trigger tense time. We had made arrangements to rent our house, furnished, to a married couple. I was going to take my desk and move back to stay with my mother- and father-in-law while Edward would be away.

Edward telephoned me as soon as he could to say that, once again, he had not passed the physical test. Minor things. I think if the war had gone on much longer, he would have been taken.

As it was, we "dug in" and continued the war years with all the rations of gasoline, tires, sugar, soap, shoes, etc., etc. We bought Savings Stamps, saved metal, and did all the things we could on the homefront. We thought that maybe we had "dodged a bullet" as far as starting a family, so, with my biological clock ticking on and on, we did so right away, enduring the scornful looks of some acquaintances who thought it was a war-evasive act, not knowing the true situation.

Arnold Roth, my boss, re-entered the army as a captain and was promptly sent overseas. His son John was already overseas in the army and was subsequently killed in the Battle of the Bulge.

I had made an agreement with Mr. Roth that I would run the insurance agency for a percentage of the profits. This lifted my salary immensely, and, on a late winter day of 1944, I went down-stairs at the First National Bank, the building in which I worked. With a check for $135 and $10.95 in cash, I paid off the principal of the loan without any further interest, a feature of wartime FHA loans.

I was pregnant, but I told Mrs. Roth, who came to the office once in a while, that I would stay on until we could break in an-other secretary. This took a long time, and I worked practically up to the very week of the baby's arrival.

Grandpa Dies

In the midst of all the war turmoil, Grandpa died. He had lived on alone for about ten years after Grandma's death, in the little house in Doe Run about a quarter of a mile from us. I'm sure he missed the farm fields and his fox hunting, but he maintained a great garden until the end of his life. He spent more and more time with his daughter, Luzena Bell Bryan, at Bonne Terre, the town where he had first lived when coming to Missouri from Virginia.

When Grandpa became terminally ill, Dad went to stay with him at Aunt Luzena's, for Grandpa was still a strong man at the age of 85, and it was hard for Aunt Luzena to manage him. He died November 19, 1942, of chronic myocarditis plus bronchopneumonia at Aunt Luzena's home and was buried alongside Grandma at the Bonne Terre Cemetery.

At the funeral site, a chill November rain was pouring. Many people had to sit in their cars. My thoughts at the bleak scene went back to the time he had tried to comfort me when Grandma was dying. I remembered he had said, "It's all right," meaning that death, however sad, is the order of things. It's all right. Go on.

I don't remember what songs were sung at the funeral, but I wouldn't have found it altogether improper if one of them had been, "Oh! Susanna." That was the only song I'd ever heard Grandpa sing. He particularly liked the nonsensical parody, "It rained all day the day I died, the weather was cool and dry. The sun, it shone so very hot, I thought that I would die."

I don't remember Grandpa when he was Captain at the St. Joe Lead Company mines, only when he was a farmer and a fox hunter. My mental picture of him is a strong, well-built man with white hair and flowing white mustache, dressed in a faded-blue denim shirt and blue bib overalls with a big silver watch in the bib pocket that always sagged from the weight of it.

Sometimes when he felt the need, or thought I felt the need, he would take the watch out, remove the leather thong fastener, pry off the back lid with his pocketknife and show me all the busily turning big and little cogwheels.*

This usually took place when I'd taken Grandpa a bucket of cool well-water to where he would be working in some far field. I was usually barefoot and would be as thirsty as he was when I arrived. Many times he would be way over on the far side of the field when I arrived, but I always waited until he came around before I would take a drink. He'd drive the horses into the clos-

---

* *Southeast Missourian*, August 20, 1995.

est shade, and we'd find a shady place ourselves to sit and drink, long and thirstily, always ending with long "Aaahhhs."

I never tired of seeing the insides of the watch. There seemed to be such a maze of those big and little wheels, all circulating at different speeds and in different directions. I think there were some we couldn't see way down in the watch but which we knew were there.

"Where's the belts?" I once asked, being used to belts running some of the farm machinery.

"No belts. Just needs a spring to start unwinding to set one little wheel turning, and that little wheel starts all the others, and if even one of them doesn't work, all the rest lay down on the job."

"Even if that little one down there quits?" I asked, pointing to the smallest one I could see.

"Each one is of equal importance, no matter its size. If it didn't turn, the one its cogs fit into wouldn't turn and if that one didn't turn, the one its cogs fit into wouldn't turn, and so on and on."

"What's a cog?"

"See those little teeth-like things at the edge of the wheel? Those are called cogs."

I wanted to test by sticking a timothy stalk into a turning cog to see if it really would stop the whole works, but knew better.

"Don't they ever stop?" I asked.

"Oh, yes, you have to wind the watch up every now and then." I'd seen him do that many times, but didn't know exactly what he was doing.

"You're a cogwheel," Grandpa said, patting my head. "If you didn't bring me this water, I'd plum run down."

"And the horses would stop?"

"Yep."

"And there would be no corn?"

"Yep."

We went on and on, laughingly, from corncob to pigs and chickens, groceries to money for the mortgage, whatever that was.

Finally, we either tired of the game or Grandpa, having to go back to work, summed it all up, "We're all cogwheels and we'd better do our part."

For a long time after that, he called me Little Cog and I called him Big Wheel. No one in the rest of the family ever knew the source of our affectionate nicknames.

The watch and a garnet ring, which he seldom wore, plus his clothes, seemed to be his only personal possessions. I don't remember him having even a wallet. He wore long underwear summer and winter. There was some theory about it being cooler that way.

Like a kaleidoscope of ever-changing scenes, I can see Grandpa guiding the horse-drawn plow down long furrows, riding the cultivator, the hay rake, the reaper, the corn planter, the big wagon. Especially can I remember him driving the big wagon when it was loaded with hay. Having loaded it to capacity, he would help Lou and me up to the top of the fragrant hay, position his pitchfork safely, then, "Giddyup," we'd be off to the barn, all of us singing, "Oh! Susanna."

Perhaps the clearest picture of Grandpa is when he was preparing to go fox hunting. He would fill the hand-carried lantern, maybe put a cornbread and sausage sandwich in his pocket, take his hunting horn from the peg on the back porch, and give a couple of short toots. This would announce to the foxhounds that he was going hunting, and they would respond with eager barks.

If he was going a far way up into the mountains, he would saddle a horse and ride. Other times he would walk. Dad, too, went along on many of these chases. There was a usual meeting place in the hills for other hunters who enjoyed listening to the chase.

In warm weather, Grandpa always took a bar of soap to the river and did his bathing there. Except for that 1918 flu and his final illness, I don't remember him ever being sick.

One tender remembrance I have is the time I was sick with something or other, had completely lost my appetite, refused to eat anything, was ready to die, dramatically. In the middle of an afternoon he brought to my bed some toasted, buttered crackers, tied with a bright string as one would a package. I ate everyone of them and decided to live!

April 20, 1944

After supper on Wednesday, April 19, 1944, Edward and I and Queenie, the bird dog, walked northward on the gravel street to the top of the East Rodney hill. There were no houses on the east side of East Rodney then. The hilltop lots were owned by Aven Kinder and were lush with lespedeza. Queenie had a great time thrashing around through it. I had earlier called the Wednesday Night Bridge Club hostess to say that I wouldn't be there that evening. There were little telltale signs that something was about to happen—the miracle of a new life.

By midnight I was in Southeast Missouri Hospital, and Dr. John Cochran, my obstetrician, had been notified. He came and went back home, determining the birth was not imminent. It did not occur until 12:52 PM on Thursday, a 7¾-pound baby boy. My first look at him revealed what I thought to be the prettiest little nose I'd ever seen. His hands and feet seemed big. There was a red mark on his forehead when he cried, which Edward and I thought resembled a baseball bat. This eventually faded away after a few weeks.

I had decided, previous to Stephen Price Mosley's birth, that I would bottle-feed the baby, for I felt a vague commitment to Mrs. Roth and the management of the insurance agency while Mr. Roth was still in the war in Europe. A new secretary had been hired and Mrs. Roth was trying to run the agency, but I felt that I should keep myself available for any problems or questions that might come up.

I was called on several times during the transition and hired Mrs. George Spence, a mature neighbor lady, to take care of Stephen while I was gone.

This period did not last long, and I felt free at last from public work. How beautiful and satisfying to stay home and enjoy our new son and the things I had dreamed of while taking dictation, tapping away on the manually operated typewriter in that hot second-storey office. Such simple things as baking a cake, working in a garden, walking in the woods were huge enjoyments.

The long leisurely hours at home brought back, almost, the same deep, childhood joy that I had felt when Lou and I had our little playhouse homes in a rail-fence corner where there was sweet order, no hurry, and time everlasting. But there was still the war.

WWII Ends

Sixty-seven days after Stephen was born, United States forces landed on Normandy Beach in France. It has been known ever

118

since as D-Day. Some of the men who had accompanied Edward to St. Louis that bleak induction day were killed on Normandy Beach.

We knew things were dreadful in Europe, but we actually didn't know that the Holocaust was going on at the rate that it was. Little dribbles of information reached our ears, but it was not until the war was over that we learned the enormity of the death camps at Dachau, Auschwitz, and other concentration camps to which Hitler had Jews and others sent to be killed, mostly in gas chambers.

Each evening we sat huddled before the radio, as if under a dark, damp umbrella, listening to the solemn tones of H.V. Kaltenborn, Edward R. Murrow, William Shirer, and others telling us as best they could what was going on, on both our war fronts — Europe and the Pacific. As in WWI, places we'd never heard of became very familiar on our tongues — Dunkerque, Iwo Jima, Bastogne, Anzio Beach. Audie Murphy, the lad from Texas, was showing the world what a soldier was. The faces of Eisenhower, MacArthur, Churchill, Stalin, Chiang Kai-shek, Mussolini, Tojo, Hitler, and de Gaulle became very familiar to us.

All the time, unknown to us, the common people, the Manhattan Project was underway — the making of the atomic bomb.

Slowly, slowly, things began to look better for us in Europe. We were winning more and more battles, marching steadily eastward toward Berlin, Germany's capital. The Soviet Union was coming at the Germans from the east. It looked as if Hitler was going to be stopped.

In 1944, President Franklin Roosevelt was elected to a fourth term, an unprecedented event in United States history, but the feeling was that to bring in a new president at this stage of the war would not be wise. He won by a big majority, but died eighty-three days later, April 12, 1945, before he got to see the end of the war in Europe, which was twenty-six days later, May 8, 1945.

Our own Missourian, then Vice President Harry Truman, a no-nonsense, pragmatic sort of man, became president.

The war in the Pacific seemed unending. We gained. We lost. We gained. When Truman weighed the probable number of deaths and amount of destruction if the seemingly unending war continued, against the death and destruction the fall of the atomic bomb on Japan could cause, he straightaway, and typically Midwestern, said something like, "Do it."

119

It was done. Hiroshima received the horrible bomb first, on August 6, 1945. When the Japanese didn't surrender immediately, another such bomb was dropped on Nagasaki. This was the end of the war.

Ever since then, some of the leading powers of the world have been trying to stop the making of such a bomb and other nuclear weapons. I keep track of the movement, hoping to see the day when weapons become plowshares.

So the long, weary war was over. I was almost 32. With each birthday, I kept multiplying the accumulated years by two to see if that time had been reached when I could reasonably consider my life was half over. 64? No, surely not. There was so much more to do. I had a son to raise, cookies to bake, flowers to tend, beans to can, and maybe something more. Something more? What?

Getting back to normal life, having rations removed and the "black umbrella" folded, seemed slow. But life was good. To break a couple of speckled brown eggs on the edge of the old blue crock and whip up Grandma's famous Sunday coconut cake without worrying about sugar, to make a meal from our garden, to arrange a bouquet, even if only of wildflowers, and other such simple things was enormously satisfying. God still spoke to me in every beam of sunshine, the silvery slant of rain, the uncurling of a Heavenly Blue morning glory, the unexpected winter cardinal alighting on a twig of the cedar tree when all else seemed dull and lifeless.

Stephen had begun to talk rather glibly in complete sentences. Later, as a history teacher in the Sikeston, Missouri, High School, he taught his students all about WWI and WWII, and probably accumulated more knowledge about them than we who had lived through them.

Changes Going On Around Us

When we moved into our new home in 1936, the property across the street a little to the southeast was a wooded area. I walked there often. When President Roosevelt instituted the Works Progress Administration (WPA) to provide jobs to try to work our way out of the Depression, it was decided by the City of Cape Girardeau to clear part of the area and construct a building to accommodate large meetings, a basketball court, etc.

The building was made of concrete and became known simply as the Arena Building. Later the name was changed to the A.C. Brase Arena Building to honor Mr. Brase who had a great deal to do with construction and redecorating from time to time. But it is still usually just called the Arena Building, and the site, Arena Park.

Much of the underbrush was cut, leaving large oak trees. At the south end of the park ran, and still runs, Cape LaCroix Creek. Also, the south end of the park was lower, and for years it was used as a city dump. Seemed as if there was always a smoldering fire going on at the dump, and smoke wafted toward our house for years. Eventually the area was filled, covered over with soil and sowed with grass. It is now level and a suitable place for several Little League baseball diamonds. There was a half-mile racetrack to the east of the building in front of concrete bleachers. For many years, the Southeast Missouri District Fair has been held at Arena Park. Horse races, small-car races, and old-car demolitions were held on the racetrack, but the track is gone now. In the interior of the oval, more Little League baseball diamonds have been constructed.

In 1947, the Rodney Vista area was taken into the City of Cape Girardeau. Edward, getting very weary of getting stuck up in the mud on the still gravel and dirt roads, especially as he backed out of our driveway, spearheaded a petition to have our street black-topped. This disturbed some of the roots of the large maple trees that had bordered our street. Later came the water line, doing more damage, then the gas line and the sewer, all nibbling at the maple roots until the trees finally gave up. We planted Chinese elms farther back in the yard. One very icy winter practically stripped those trees of their limbs. Then, too, every summer the leaves of these trees were skeletonized by some insect or disease. Soon they were gone too. These were replaced by two pin oaks and a sweet gum.

At the rear of our lot, along a fencerow, volunteer American elms were allowed to grow, some of them growing to great heights. The Dutch elm disease took many of them, although some, in late 1990s, still tower toward the sky. A volunteer wild cherry tree in the backyard, used for third base when Stephen and his pals got old enough to play baseball, was allowed to grow. After the demise of the Westlane elm — an American elm growing near a spring on the original Rodney homesite — the wild cherry tree became the biggest tree in the neighborhood. One summer day as I was turning the ignition on my car, preparing to go to town, lightning struck the tree. I momentarily thought the car had been rigged for bombing. It was a shock. The tree had to be removed.

Some time in the early 1950s, I discovered some maple seedlings growing in a north corner of the house. I said, "Steve, pull these up and plant them somewhere down there." I waved toward the southwest part of our backyard. He did so, and the trees thrived. They are sugar maples, lighting up that corner of the yard in autumn with their beautiful red-gold foliage. Two pink dogwoods were also planted in this area. They sit like gargantuan pink bouquets in the spring.

Our house had been built ell-shaped, the ell extending northward from the front of the house. I felt that it would be more attractive if a porch, the size of the ell, would be built on the south front of the house. It was. An attractive wooden banister, painted white, was placed around the flat rooftop. This addition gave the house a more balanced look.

Later, this banister was changed to fancy iron grillwork, and such grillwork was put around the front porch and down the sides of the steps.

When Steve became of college age, he felt the urge to have a room for himself with an outside entrance so his pals could come and go. The porch was then made into a room. Redwood siding, painted white at first, then brick color to match the rest of the house, enclosed the porch.

A Bridal Wreath hedge adorned the base of the front of the house, along with assorted evergreens which succumbed to bagworms over the years. Finally, a eunymous hedge was planted all along the front to cover the concrete base. This proved to be more attractive, tying the house more effectively into the yard.

A white painted frame garage that was never wide enough to keep our opened car doors from banging against the walls was built. Also, Steve, growing up, practiced his baseball pitching against the rear, aiming at certain drawn-on spots. This was not good for the boards. Eventually the garage was torn down and a concrete-block, wider garage was built. It was just the concrete-gray color for a long time until I decided to have it, too, painted the same brick color as the enclosed porch.

Not long after the building of the garage, we had the graveled driveway blacktopped, and concrete walks replaced granite stepping stones—such stones having been gathered from the Graniteville quarries, the place where I had taught school.

The backyard, as late as the 1950s, was still part garden, part baseball diamond. The garden part gradually shrunk until now; it is only big enough for four tomato plants and a couple of pepper plants.

Buildings went up all around us. Irvin Huff built many of them, and the specifications for such buildings were not very grand, the plotting and specifications having been done when money was scarce. For a long time, now, there has not been a vacant lot anywhere on either side of the East and West Rodney horseshoe-shaped drive. But the town skipped over the Rodney Vista area and moved westward, with prettier and more modern houses after the Depression.

When Interstate Highway 55 was constructed to the west, businesses also moved in that direction. The Drury Brothers, descendants of the Drury who plastered our house, built many hotels and the great retail center, Westpark Mall. St. Francis Hospital also moved to that area and built a large new medical center. First National Bank, where I worked for years on Main Street downtown, moved to Mt. Auburn Road, near all the hotel complexes. The bank's name was changed to Centerre and, later, to Boatmen's. Many other banks were established in Cape Girardeau as the town grew.

Before I realized what was going on, I sat on the back porch many days, wondering what all the hammering was about.

The Town Plaza first took away much of the downtown business, then the Westpark Mall and other businesses took away more, including much of the Town Plaza business. Now, in this last decade of the century, downtown merchants think that a riverboat gambling casino at the foot of Broadway will bring business back to their area. Time will tell.

Journal Entries

Despite the usual childhood illnesses and accidents, and the death or disappearance of two pet dogs, Stephen's preschool days were normal and, I hope, happy ones for him. Just the two of us had many backyard picnics under the weeping willow tree, the pear tree, or one of the apple trees. We walked much in the developing Arena Park. Dressed in his fuzzy brown teddy-bear suit, he loved to walk the low, white fence railing around the racetrack, especially if there was a layer of snow on it. I could not help but keep a hand on him, but he always wanted to do it alone.

At least once a week we dressed up, went to Woolworth's on Main Street, had ice cream or a ham-salad sandwich and large Cherry Coke, then bought a Little Golden Book. He was not tall enough to see the books on the counter, so I lifted him to see the display and let him choose one. I had to read it to him immediately when we got home. After that came the Thornton Burgess Books, the Bobbsey Twin Books, and on up the reading ladder.

Quite often, after supper, the three of us went for rides in the farming country to the west or down to the Mississippi River to watch boats go by. No floodwall then.

I had kept daily journals for a number of years, and, although on the national scene President Harry Truman was forming the North America Treaty Organization, breaking a Russian blockade of West Berlin, keeping an eye on the Korean situation, most of my entries consisted of home and gardening notations and what Stephen was doing, such as:

> *Stephen got first haircut today at the barbershop in the lower floor of the First National Bank Building. Gone are the curls.*

> *Mickey, Judy, and Butch were over to play with Stephen today.*

> *Stephen got his first puppy today, a black cocker spaniel.*

> *Took Stephen to see Dr. Reynolds. Doctor suggested removal of tonsils in spring.*

> *Edward and Stephen went to races.* (Miniature car races at Arena Park.)

> *Stephen has the mumps.*

> *Stephen has the measles.*

Stephen has the chicken pox.

Went fishing at Horseshoe Lake with Edward and Stephen. Had picnic lunch at the spillway.

Had Olan Mills take a picture of Stephen in his cowboy shirt and hat.

Stephen brought home from kindergarten the much talked about recipe book. He had such a triumphant look as he walked up through the yard as if, at last, it was his time to have it. We made peanut butter cookies and "yummy" eggs.

Birthday party for Stephen today. Mickey, Judy, Janet, Sharon, Jimmy came. Judy brought Stephen two bantam chickens!

Stephen got a bicycle for Christmas. Started riding right away without any help. Remarkable balance.

Raked leaves on south side of yard, with Stephen's help.

Stephen had his sled out yesterday going down the front yard slope.

The best thing Stephen likes about Sunday school is the "candy lady" (Mrs. B.F. Johnson), who stands in the hallway after classes to pass out candy to the children.

Stephen has an imaginary playmate he calls Honey Jamban.

Stephen and I went to the Fair today. Ate dinner there and played nearly all the carnival games. Rode the Merry-go-round and Ferris Wheel.

Edward, Stephen, and I got on the 3:00 AM train to St. Louis. Arrived there about 8:30 AM. Ate breakfast at the Forum, then went over to Famous-Barr. Stephen liked the escalators. Bought him a Cardinal sweatshirt which he put on immediately. Got a cab and went to zoo. First time for Stephen. We walked miles. Got a cab and went to the Golden Ivy Restaurant near Sportsman ballpark.

It turned suddenly cold. I went to a neighboring store and bought myself a sweater. After we got in the ball-park, Edward had to go buy himself a sweatshirt. The Browns played the Yankees. We bought cushions to wrap Stephen in. Went back to Famous-Barr for more shopping. Ate supper nearby and then went to Lowe's Theater to see Girl Crazy *and* The Sailor Surprises His Wife. *After show, took a cab to Union Station and got a hotel room for the three-hour wait for our train to leave. We left at 11:00 PM and Stephen slept all the way back home. Got home about 2:30 AM. Got a taxi home and it was to bed for three tired people. Big outing!*

As mentioned above, the Rodney Vista area was not taken into the city limits until 1947. Therefore, in order not to have to pay tuition outside our school district, which was the Kage District, the school being about two miles away, we enrolled Stephen in the Campus Training School when he was but two years old. The Campus school of Southeast Missouri State University was often called the Lab School or the Training School, for that is where a lot of the candidates for an education degree did their practice teaching, as did I.

By the time Stephen was ready for kindergarten, we had been taken

Stephen and Edward Mosley

126

into the city limits, but the Campus School kindergarten had a good reputation, so we kept the enrollment in effect. Four-year-olds went in the morning; five-year-olds in the afternoon. He entered in September 1948. There was a carpool of mothers to transport the little ones back and forth.

Stephen did not get off to the best of starts under Louise Gross, the teacher. For some mistaken reason, she was calling him Edward instead of Stephen. Edward was, of course, his father's name. Stephen did not respond when Miss Gross commanded "Edward" to do something. She called me in for observation and I saw right away what the trouble was. After that, he was off to a good scholastic education, not only academically but to a brilliant sports career in both basketball and baseball all through his remaining twelve grades. His high-school baseball team won the Southeast Missouri Conference championship in 1961 and 1962, and the baseball state championship in 1962.

Stephen Price Mosley

Although many of his classmates changed from the Campus School to the Louis J. Schultz School after the sixth grade, Stephen stayed at Campus through the seventh grade, changing to Schultz in the eighth grade. After graduating there, he entered Central High School. Although much taken up by sports, he nevertheless became a member of the National Honor Society.

At graduation from Central High, he obtained a partial scholarship (baseball) to the University of Missouri, but it was only for books and tuition. Since living expenses were high, he enrolled at Southeast Missouri State University. Here he got down to serious studying, joined Sigma Chi, had a string of girlfriends, and graduated in 1966, *magna cum laude*.

Just out of college, he went to New Athens, Illinois, to teach in the high school there. After one year, he returned to work on his Master's degree. After that he went to Sikeston, Missouri, to teach, first in the middle school for a few years, then to the Sikeston High School where he became a much loved and respected teacher. Loved and respected in the community, too.

127

Life Takes a New Turn

When Stephen was off to kindergarten, I began to wonder if there was any way I could supplement our income while staying at home. I did not ever want to go back to the public workplace.

An A&P store had opened on North Spanish Street, and I was buying groceries there now, always picking up, along with the groceries, a magazine A&P sold for 2¢ per copy, *Woman's Day*.

Della Lutes, a writer who had grown up in southern Michigan, published monthly articles in this magazine about things that were so familiar to me—haylofts, pastures, root cellars, etc.

I wondered—hmmm—could I write something like that? How did one go about sending a story to a publication? Did you have to inquire? Did you have to know someone? Was there a fee for consideration? What would I write about?

At the same time, *Reader's Digest* was running articles in categories called First Person Award and Drama In Real Life. I had never forgotten the "carbide light" incident nor the time the cream stayed sweet on its trip to St. Louis, enabling us to buy those two pairs of shoes at the same time for one person.

It seemed, at that time, that the "light incident" was a secret between me and God, and I did not think I could call up the just-right words to tell about it without sounding, well—pious?

I settled on the sweet-cream shoes, writing only one draft, single-spaced, rubbed-out errors corrected in ink. I thought I would send it around Christmastime, first to my parents and sisters to see how they would like it. I didn't. I put it into a desk drawer where it remained for some time. Edward read it and said, "Why don't you send it somewhere?" So back to the question: how did one go about it? I folded it three times and stuffed it into a 4 x 9 envelope. I looked at the list of editors on an inside page of *Woman's Day* and saw that Betty Finnin was fiction editor. My story wasn't fiction, but I addressed the envelope to her anyway.

It was gone, gone, gone for six weeks. So, unsolicited manuscripts were just thrown away?

Eventually a letter dated September 30, 1947, came which stated:

> *Dear Mrs. Mosley:*
>
> *I would like to have "The Stono Mountain, Sweet Cream Shoes" for our magazine now if our offer of $400 is acceptable to you. We would, of course, want the privilege of cutting and editing as we deem advisable.*
>
> *If this is agreeable to you, we would like to have a short biographical sketch and an informal snapshot or two, to use in the front of the book — if space permits.*

> *Meanwhile, we're holding your script until we hear*
> *from you.*
>
> *Sincerely,*
>
> *Betty Finnin*
> *Fiction Editor*

I answered by return mail. Uh, yes, I would consider $400. Betty didn't have a decimal point. I looked hard for it, thinking it might be $4.00. So I added the decimal point, just to be sure!

It was the beginning of a long and satisfying new career.

Comedian Jimmy Durante often said, after telling a joke and getting a good response, "I got a million of 'em, folks." I thought that if my little tales were what editors wanted, "I have a million of 'em."

Ben Hibbs at the *Saturday Evening Post*, Betty Finnin at *Woman's Day*, Maude Longwell at *Farm Journal*, Bill Birnie at *Reader's Digest*, Arthur Gordon at *Guideposts*, Eugene Butler at *Progressive Farmer*, and many others were very helpful to me. They seemed to detect a tiny spark and blew on it the breath of encouragement to keep it alive.

By 1953, I had had published in various magazines enough stories with the same setting and same characters (the farmstead, family, and neighbors) to make a book. I added a theme to run through it, giving it a sense of oneness, and thus *The Mockingbird Piano*, my first book, was published in March of that year by the Westminister Press. I had no agent, just sent it in "cold," as they say in the writing world. I signed the contract, and the overhead light reflected especially bright on the gold point of my pen. "Hello, God. Thank you. Use me."

The Mockingbird Piano won the Missouri Writers' Guild Award for that year. This award precipitated a journey to Columbia, Missouri, during Missouri School of Journalism's special week, the first of several such weeks I attended in succession.

A few days after returning home from this pleasant ceremony, I received a letter from the *Saturday Evening Post*. It arrived after dark by special delivery. "I think I'll sit down to read this," I told Edward, for I knew I had just recently sent them a story. I sat on the floor just in case I might fall out of a chair.

It read:

May 25, 1953

Dear Mrs. Mosley:

*I am very happy to be able to report that we are buy-
ing "Whittlin' Man." We all like it very much and feel
that it's a sweet story.*

*When we buy material from new writers, it is our
custom to ask them to have two business acquaintances
send us letters of reference for our files. We also would
like to have biographical material and a picture of your-
self, if you have one, in case our Keeping Posted editor
wants to use it in the issue in which your story appears.
When all this has been received, a check for $850 will go
out to you on the following Tuesday, our regular payment day.*

Congratulations on your first sale to the Post, *and I
hope you are as well pleased as we all are here.*

With best wishes, I am,

Sincerely,

Patricia Walsh

I read it aloud and rocked back and forth like someone doing
a modern-day aerobic exercise.

The title of this story was changed by the *Post* to "Primitive
Young Man." The two business acquaintances I picked to send letters of reference were Fred Naeter, co-owner of the *Southeast Missourian* newspaper at that time, and Homer George, a pharmacist,
owner of the Broadway Prescription Shop.

In the 1950s, I wrote seven more stories for the *Post*. When the
magazine was sold, but kept the same name, I sold one more story
to them, "Biglow Baily Day," which I consider one of my best stories.

My longest-running adventure in writing has been a newspaper column. This was started in 1955 when co-writer friend Thomza Zimmerman and I thought we might start a small syndicated

column for weekly newspapers in Southeast Missouri. It was to be an exchange of letters, she writing one week and I the next. The title of the column was "From Dawn To Dusk," a title Thomza had been using for her column in her local hometown's newspaper.

We wrote of the little things in our daily lives. Our purpose was to try to help others find joy in the simple things of life. It caught on. At one time we had ten weekly newspapers subscribing.

Thomza Zimmerman (1904 – 2004)

Dad Goes On to That Other Dimension

Not only did Dad experience the tragedy of losing his right arm, there were other accidents. Earlier, while working at a granite quarry about five miles north of our farm home, a boulder he was trying to maneuver into a loader slipped in some way so as to hit the end of the crowbar he was working with and drove it into his side, missing a kidney by only a fraction of an inch, so said the doctor.

Lou and I were hoeing corn that day in the fifteen-acre field when we saw our wagon and horses emerge from a wooden area and come slowly down alongside the field. Perplexed at the odd hour for Dad to be coming home, and wondering, "Who was that driver?" we ran toward the wagon. As we ran, we threw off our dark red, dried corn-silk wigs enclosed in hairnets we were fond of wearing to lift our lives out of the humdrums.

The driver, another quarry workman, gestured for us to stand back. "Your dad has been hurt," he said. Even now I can recall the fear with which we followed the wagon home, wanting to cry out, "How bad?" but fearing to do so, lest we learn.

Our horses pulled the wagon ever so slowly along the lanes, across the gravelly riverbed. Barefooted, we softly followed. On

131

a bank where the wagon tilted upward a little, we saw the blood and Dad's ashen face.

"Lucky," the doctor later said to the group of us huddled in the kitchen, awaiting the report. "Went right between vital organs."

There was a common sigh of relief, but I was somewhat puzzled. What were vital organs? I thought everything inside was vital.

The bruising, swelling, and, no doubt, pain were awful. It took a long time to heal. Dad never worked at the quarry again.

I soon learned what vital organs were and that the heart was at the top of the list. When it stopped, "Taps!"

In 1930, Dad had his first heart attack. From there on it was trouble. Not frequent at first but from time to time, he was hospitalized at the Bonne Terre Hospital, the nearest one in our county. No bypass surgery then. No transplants.

In 1959, he could not make it back from his last attack. He died February 9, 1959, at the Bonne Terre Hospital. Dad, who was always there for us, making plans, making big plans, was gone.

On hot, humid summer evenings as we lay on quilts in the front yard, trying to catch any stray breeze, he would often say to us, "See that hill in front of us?" It was his way of pulling us up from lethargy. Of course we could see that tree-covered hill in front of us, rising up from a creek not over a hundred yards away. "Someday we might make a sheep pasture there," he would plan. "Imagine that hill all a green pasture with five thousand white sheep grazing." Not fifty, nor five hundred, but five thousand. Why not?

Another evening he would present a mind's eye picture of it becoming a vineyard or an apple orchard or maybe a range for Arabian horses.

He had a "thing" about light, too. Literal light. He was the first in the community to bring home a Coleman lamp. He rigged up the carbide light system for the farm home. When we moved to Doe Run, which was still in the kerosene-lamp stage, he and a partner formed the Doe Run and Delassus Light and Power Company, which brought electricity to our little village.

When I was called to "Come home; Dad has died," I found Mama in the kitchen, her head on the table, encircled by her arms. I put my hand on her shoulder and said, "It's all right, Mama." I wondered if she felt as I had the many years ago when Grandpa had placed his hand on my shoulder and said, "It's all right." It surely wasn't all right for our torn hearts, but we all knew and accepted that it was the nature of things to live and then die. What made it bearable was the promise that we might live again, as had been demonstrated a long time ago by One who was called The Light of the World. This same One also told of a Heavenly Father who was always looking for his lost children — lost from the path he had cleared for us.

Wilson L. Bell (1888–1959)

After Dad's death, I thought of Dad being a reflection of that Heavenly Father looking for a lost child, only on an earthly lost-from-sight basis.

Although there were six older ones to look after me, I did escape from their sight once in a while, not intentionally, but being led away by some pretty flower in the yard and then the garden, the orchard, meadow, riverbank.

I've often been told of the panic that pervaded the premises when it was discovered that I, barely able to walk, was missing. All afternoon the six of them dropped what they were doing to search for me in every conceivable place they thought I might be, so I was later told.

Darkness was creeping over the landscape. I'm sure it meant nothing to me. They said they called and called, but I did not answer. Soon, Daddy, out of breath, running alongside the riverbank to where I had strayed, snatched me up in his arms and hurried home with me, so the old story goes.

There was another time Daddy came to find me. I remember it quite distinctly.*

---

* "Cockleburs Will Getcha If You Don't Watch Out," *Southeast Missourian*, October 13, 1991.

I, in about the fourth grade, was coming home from school. Lou had gone on ahead because I had stayed to dust the erasers or do some little chore about the school to help the teacher. The sun was getting very low. I decided to take a little-used shortcut through a fallow field that hugged the riverbank. I hadn't taken this shortcut all year.

First, there was this overloaded cocklebur bush. It stopped me momentarily, snatching at my cotton dress, my long, cotton stockings, my shoelaces, my hair. Oh, yes, my hair. Cockleburs grow tall in rich river bottomland. But what was one cocklebur bush to a country girl? I stomped it down and proceeded, unaware that perhaps thirty cockleburs were attached to me like barnacles. They reached out with their spiny hooks to embrace other nearby cockleburs like long-lost sisters and brothers.

Shadows gathered in the low places. Evening river sounds became more pronounced — bullfrogs, tree frogs, crickets. I must hurry. They'd be worried about me at home. And there were my chores. I decided to run, not give the cockleburs a chance to grab. It was a grievous mistake. Sturdy, vibrant specimens of cocklebur bushes awaited my passage, a veritable sea of them. They came at me from all sides, overhead, underneath. They stuck to new places and to the cockleburs that were already on me, two and three deep.

If I pushed one bush aside, another sprang at me. I could see the bloody scratches on my hands. No doubt they were on my face, too. I tasted blood.

I'll go back, I thought, and take the long way around. But, looking back, I saw the cocklebur bushes had closed ranks behind me. I was in a living trap.

I discarded my books and lunch box to put up a more worthy fight. But fighting a rich patch of cockleburs growing on fertile land is a lost cause. Soon I saw that I was almost literally covered with the hateful things. I had become a cocklebur-baby.

Faintly I heard someone call my name. An owl? There was an old Indian legend . . . but I answered. If it

was Daddy, I remembered he'd always told me that if I
got lost to not wander around but stay in one place; he'd
find me.

I kept answering and soon Daddy loomed before me.
I guessed it was Daddy. He was wearing cocklebur cloth-
ing but his face looked familiar. He picked me up and
carried me out of that awful place. I put my arms around
his neck, but dropped them quickly when I saw him
flinch. I cried and he laughed. He cried and I laughed.

When we got home, after dark, every living thing
who saw us laughed or barked or mooed or meowed.
Mama gave me a haircut. It started a new fashion called
the Cocklebur Tangle!

1950–1960

The World Passing Before Me

At first there was no other world for me but the farmhouse, the outbuildings, the near fields and pastures, my parents, grandparents, and sisters, Tabby Cat, Penny the dog, the foxhounds, the farm animals, and chickens. It was such a good world. I had no knowledge that there was anything beyond the scallop of hills that surrounded us, with the river and railroad running through.

Then I became aware that there were other people, who lived somewhere beyond the hills. What were called aunts, uncles, and cousins came to "invade" my world for a few days and then disappear.

There was Sunday school, even before regular school. At the white frame church at Loughboro, not far from the schoolhouse, I was presented with colorful little cards with pictures of persons wearing strange clothes. "James, John, Judas, Jesus, and others," my Sunday-school teacher identified. "They lived in a land faraway."

A land faraway? Was this Bonne Terre whence came the aunts, uncles, and cousins?

Then came S.W.'s funeral, and I was, along with the family, taken, wide-eyed, through Elvins, Riverside, Flat River, and Deslodge to Bonne Terre. I'm sure it must have seemed faraway to me. Thus the "outer world" began to pass before my eyes.

From time to time during those years, when supper was over and we were all in the kitchen doing the things we wanted to do, Dad or Grandpa would look up from some big sheets of paper I came to know as the *Farmington News*, and say something that always started out with, "I see where. . ."

I can't remember the tidbits of news they were noting aloud for the benefit of other members of the family, but reviewing history of the time, it might have been, "I see where President Wilson has made William Jennings Bryan Secretary of State." We never called him William Bryan or just Bryan but always William Jennings Bryan. They may have said, "I see where the Germans have sunk the *Lusitania*, and there were Americans on the ship," or "I see where the bank says loans to farmers are more easily made now."

Then came school, and there was that round globe that fascinated me so. Planet Earth, so they said. I learned where on that globe, James, John, Judas, and Jesus had lived. Indeed, it was faraway. "About nine thousand miles as the crow flies," the teacher estimated. I knew that we walked approximately three miles to school. Walking three-thousand times that distance was almost more than I could imagine. The globe was so little, but my concept of the world was enlarging.

Then came the Atwater Kent radio, with a lot of static, but we were getting closer and closer to world events as they happened.

In a high-school class, or maybe a supplemental session to history, there was a study of worldwide current events. None of these events seemed so immediately important to us, though, as the fact that our boys' and girls' basketball teams beat Esther High School last Friday night. But in these Current Events sessions we heard about something called television. "You get a picture of things as they happen, way far off," it was explained. Someone surely must have asked, "How?" But how to explain that when the teacher probably, along with the rest of us, didn't yet understand telephone and radio?

On and on went progression toward bringing the whole world and outerspace into focus. The Current Events description of things to come, came. In the 1950s, Edward and I bought our first television set, and since then the green couch across the room from

The old green couch

the RCA, then the Zenith, then the Magnovox became a reviewing stand for the world passing before our eyes. I've seen, first in black and white, then color, all the big world-happenings this last half of the twentieth century. The instantaneous viewing of things happening where John, James, Judas, and Jesus lived seemed to make the world shrink to the size of the old grade-school globe. Now, instead of it taking me nine years and eight months of walking three miles a day to get there (walking on water), as I once calculated, I can fly there by crow route in about twenty-four hours.

So what were some of the first big world happenings we saw from the green couch reviewing stand? War, of course. Always and always war, it seemed.

The League of Nations, an organization that had come into being when I was eight years old and which hoped to promote world peace, but didn't, was succeeded by the United Nations in 1945. This organization has a Security Council which makes rulings in war and peace and furnishes troops from members of the organization to enforce their rulings. Most of the troops, so far, have always been those of the United States. I suppose it will ever be thus.

When Communist North Korea invaded South Korea, the U.N. Council said North Korea was at fault and ordered the U.N. troops into Korea to "arrest" things. Another weary war dragged on, but was almost like a postscript to World War II, which had ended just five years previously.

Dwight Eisenhower had succeeded Harry Truman as president, and he was able to settle the Korean War by drawing a dividing line at the thirty-seventh parallel with North Koreans to stay on one side and South Koreans on the other. It has proved to be an uneasy settlement, with troops on both sides guarding the demarcation line ever since and with suspicions in the 1990s that North Korea is making a nuclear bomb.

Two other televised pictures that we witnessed and which were harbingers of things to come in the next decade were President Eisenhower holding up a "shingle" of a metal heat shield that had proved to be effective in resisting the burning of objects when they plunged at great speed from outer space into the earth's atmosphere, and the National Guard in 1957, standing at the entrance to Central High School in Little Rock, Arkansas, to ensure the safe passage of black students into the school. This was an attempt to test the 1954 ruling by the United States Supreme Court in the case of *Brown v. Board of Education* of Topeka that so-called separate but equal U.S. public schools were illegal and with all due speed should desegregate.

Goodbye to the Chickens

Had we looked more closely, I suppose we could have had a better notion of what was coming in the incredible sixties, but there was always the day-to-day living, the taking charge, the moving forward on the home front.

After being taken into the city limits, it seemed that the first "country" things to go were the chickens. I hated that, for it was still pleasant to spread the fresh, summer-smelling straw on the floor, to gather the eggs, to just sit on a bale of straw in the hideaway of the chicken house and think about sundry things while the querulous hens clucked and the roosters strutted. But chickens, pigs, horses, and cows were not welcome in the city, and the city was "swallowing" us. Along the horseshoe-shaped drive of East and West Rodney where there had been only five houses, the lots were being snatched up and homes built. There are eighty-six houses now facing these drives and more along Chrysler and Adeline Streets, which have been cut through the interior of the "horseshoe." Little private drives branching off outward from East and West Rodney afford room for other houses. A cow could not now find its way around on the old Haman Farm.

Thinking the price of real estate had peaked, we sold the south part of our lot to Keith Miller. We sold it with the provision that only one house be built there and so placed that it would not obstruct our view to the south. Such a house was built, but I'm not sure our original stipulations could hold up anymore.

The second chicken house that we had built was demolished first. The first chicken house stood for a long time thereafter. Stephen and friends, having removed the roosts and the row of nests, used it as a clubhouse. At one time, the inside walls were nearly covered with baseball cards. "If only we hadn't tacked them," Stephen lamented in later years when "good condition" baseball cards became very valuable.

The woven wire fence around the chicken yard and the south part of our lot came down, except that which ran alongside our driveway. For many more years thereafter, it served as a support for the row of luxuriant Paul's Scarlet roses that we had planted there, one hundred feet of them.

A cindered path, bordered by old-fashioned purple irises, led from the south side of the garage alongside the roses to a seat under an apple tree. When the roses and irises were in bloom at the same time, it was a pleasant little path to travel.

I never gave up my gardening, although the plot grew smaller and smaller, and the days were over when, upon hearing a team of horses pulling a wagon down the street, I could go out and hail it to ask the driver if he'd plow my garden. However, I still managed to get the soil turned up and over in the spring. Garden tillers had come into vogue for "city" gardeners, although in my opinion they were not

Jean Bell Mosley among the hollyhocks that bordered her garden

nearly so effective as the old plowshare that went much deeper and laid the soil over in shiny brown furrows.

A great joy of my life has been to put seeds into the ground and watch for their sprouting. The bean seed pushed the soil into a little, brown, cracked hummock as if some minuscule mole had come near the surface. Soon a pale green stem, still crooked, could be seen through the crack in the hummock if I got down low enough to look, which I did. The next day the crinkled green beginning of a leaf would break through. By the third day, the whole bean plant would be there, ready to begin its life cycle. I would touch the little leaves tenderly. All seeds manifested their sprouting differently. I loved them all, and the whole ambiance of the garden—the warm spring sunshine, the songs of the returning birds, the breezes in my hair, the feeling that I was doing something worthwhile. Perplexing things always became clearer to me in my garden.

"You've made a rare day today, God," I would whisper. In answer, an apple blossom drifting from a nearby tree might land in my bean row, or a robin, following along behind my hoe or trowel, would cock his head and seemingly wink at me.

I have pleasant recurring dreams, no two the same, wherein I have returned to a long-neglected garden, maybe years later, and find things still pushing up through the soil. I try to interpret these dreams. Have I neglected something? Is something I once planted, maybe in my mind or someone else's, still there? Do I need to get on with some sort of "cultivation" or loving care?

In spite of my thought that such dreams may be reminders of something I'm neglecting, they are good dreams, for at least the sprouted things are still there, green and healthy. I always awake refreshed.

Hello, Community!

With Stephen in school, Edward working steadily, and my toe in the door of saleable freelance writing, I began to take a larger part in community affairs, but not very large. The lure of home and the fascination with this newly discovered gift of writing was strong.

In the ensuing years, I joined the Rodney Vista Homemaker's Club, Parent Teacher Association, Quest Club MFWC (Missouri

Federation Women's Club), Chapter G.F. of PEO, the Cape Girardeau Writers' Guild, the Missouri State Writers' Guild, and a local bridge club.

The Rodney Vista Homemakers' Club was a part of the Missouri Extension Service to homemakers. It consisted of housewives living in the Cape Girardeau suburb west of Highway 61, or Kingshighway as it was later known. We met monthly in the afternoons, took our preschool children with us, studied ways of doing home chores better — how to clean steam irons, cook oatmeal, prepare nutritous meals from the five food groups, etc. The County Extension Agent met with us from time to time, giving us the latest tips on canning, cooking, decorating, raising children, and many other things. Some of our activities included rolling bandages from old white sheets for the local Cancer Society's cabinet, sponsoring chili suppers and talent shows, the proceeds of which were given to the Girl Scouts and Boy Scouts. Always we prepared Christmas and Thanksgiving baskets for the less fortunate, and generally had a good time just enjoying each other's company.

One lasting memento I have from those Homemakers' Club days is a hex sign that has been in the gable of my garage for years. Sometimes directions to my house are given as, "The garage has a hex sign in the gable." One of our club projects was the making of serving trays from rounds of aluminum. We crimped the sides of the rounds with pliers so that a "piecrust" would stand up. Different designs were made in the bottom of the tray by the process of glueing in a design, then pouring in acid that would "eat" the metal out around the design.

I ordered an eighteen-inch diameter round but never did make a tray of it. Later I painted the Daddy Hex sign on it in brilliant colored enamels and nailed it in the center of the white gable. About every two years I change the colors by repainting. I am not superstitious about hex signs, but I do think they make color-

Hex sign that hung on Jean Bell Mosley's garage

ful decorations. This Daddy Hex sign was a quilt pattern found on the cover of a roll of Mountain Mist quilting cotton. I enlarged it to fit my aluminum circle. The legend of the Daddy Hex sign is that it is supposed to ward off evil spirits.

When Stephen started kindergarten, I became a zealous member of PTA. Being put in charge of securing parental subscriptions to the PTA magazine, I had every set of parents subscribing.

Louise Gross, the kindergarten teacher, conceived the idea of enlarging the children's playgound by clearing a steep-sided ravine to the north of the playground, very brushy and poison-ivy infested. The area was known as the Home of the Birds because great flocks of blackbirds and starlings made this area their roosting place. We parents slaved at that task and exchanged remedies for aching backs and poison-ivy blisters. A steep rock stairway was put into place, leading down into this extended playground. All parents were uneasy about that stairway, especially those of little boys who liked to run and chase.

I promoted the idea of putting lifesize, wooden cutouts of the characters in *The Story of Little Black Sambo* down in the ravine, the little book at that time being popular with the youngsters.Internet information now, in the last decade of the twentieth century, declares that not many people under the age of forty know the story and that, because of race relations, the book has quietly disappeared from most bookshelves.

Quest Club MFWC, like the Rodney Vista Homemakers' Club, is for women, but the objects and aims are broader. There is hardly a facet of life that the Federated Women's Club does not touch, although their one main object is supporting Girls Town, a place to care for uncared-for girls.

PEO is an international sisterhood much concerned with philanthropic and educational matters. Members support Cottey College in Nevada, Missouri. Many scholarships are given to women.

The Cape Girardeau Writers' Guild, in the beginning, was composed of members who had some area of interest in writing and some who actually worked at writing. It was quite active in the 1950s and 1960s. We met in members' homes where we talked of what writing projects we had completed, what we had underway, or what aspirations we had for future projects. It was special to meet at the J.W. Gerhardt home on Apple Creek, where the lower room walls were natural rock outcropping. Gerhardt was an architect and building contractor. Sometimes his friend, James

Cape Girardeau Writers' Guild

Picture taken early 1950s at J.W. Gerhardt's home in Apple Creek, Missouri. Back row, standing from left to right: Helen Collins, Ann West, Thomza Zimmerman, Gladsia Russell, Earl Collins, Judith Crow, Odell Williams, Lura Vineyard, Clara Hoffman, Edward Mosley, Elizabeth Walther, (person unknown), Mary Z. Reed, Frances Selle.

Seated, middle row, from left to right: (person unknown), Stella Riggs, Jessie Thilenius, Jeptha Riggs, Stephen Mosley, Jean Bell Mosley, Aileen Lorberg.

Seated on floor from left to right: Beulah Riley, Vic Russell, J.W. Gerhardt, (person unknown)

Logan, nurseryman and gourmet cook, would be there to prepare wonderful meals for us.

For many years the Cape Girardeau Writers' Guild would have an annual spring banquet at which some well-known writer would be the guest speaker. The Guild faltered near the end of the century.

The Missouri State Writers' Guild was composed of members of local guilds who had had at least three published pieces. This guild's annual spring meeting coincided with Journalism Week at Missouri University School of Journalism. I went regularly for several years, quickly becoming vice-president and then president of the Guild. I gave several speeches during Journalism Week before the student body and the State Writers' Guild members.

As for bridge clubs, they are social get-togethers, not altogether unlike the pioneer women's quilting bees, except that we play the card game instead of quilting. It is a good place to share

143

Jean Bell Mosley, speaking at Journalism Week

1954

1955

1956

life experiences, form lasting friendships, and have good "woman talk." It is the great pastime for the local ladies.

I served on the board of the Cape Girardeau Public Library and the publications board at Southeast Missouri State University. I had no great input for either, just filled out the membership. Perhaps I was asked to serve because of my stated love for books and the fact that I had had some published. I did make a few speeches on behalf of a bond issue to be floated for the public library. It failed, but other financial means soon enabled the city to relocate and build a new library.

When the local Zoning Committee held hearings on whether or not an apartment building could be built at the southeast corner of Marie Louise Lane and East Rodney, I appeared before the committee to object. The permit was not issued, but a nice two-family duplex was erected that appears to be just a handsome residence.

I appeared before the City Council to object to any public restrooms that might have been contemplated in the Missouri Conservation building, and I also objected to an adjacent wading pool. The public restrooms did not materialize. The wading pool was built, but after some years was demolished because it did become a place of leaf and picnic-trash collection, as I had predicted.

Small victories.

Days of Contentment

In spite of the distant rumblings of discontent in the later part of the 1950s, my days were full of peace. I found great satisfaction in homemaking. The pleasant odors of Windex, Mr. Clean, Pledge, and other cleaning supplies added to my joy of making windows sparkle, floors shine, and furniture gleam. The so-called feminist movement which was smoldering, awaiting quick winds to fan it into flames, was outside the parameters of my thoughts. A home where there was love, peace, and joy, good food, good rest, good friends coming were the embers I wanted to fan.

To knead the yeasty-smelling bread dough, crack the lovely eggs on the rim of the blue crock, shape the fluted edge of a pie crust, create a warm spicy odor in the kitchen, or that of sturdy soup simmering, were things I enjoyed.

Lora Pitney and Jean Bell Mosley
Displaying quilt blocks for which they received honorable mention in a contest.
Hanging on the clothesline in the background are quilts made by Jean Bell Mos-
ley and her mother.

To hang my beautiful handmade quilts on the clothesline for an airing on some brisk, blue-sky spring day was a happy thread woven into the tapestry of my life. Once a Tiger Swallowtail butterfly lit in the center block of my flower-garden quilt as it hung over the clothesline. Stayed there for a long time, as if it wished me to see it. "I saw it, Lord. Thank you."

The idea of being a second-class citizen as Simone de Beauvoir had deemed women to be in her book *The Second Sex* might as well have been written in Sanskrit or hieroglyphics for all the understanding I had of it.

Later, when it was declared by some of the leaders of this feminist movement that the image of happy female domesticity pleased advertisers and kept women readers caged in a docile mood, I laughed all the way to my hammock.

My hammock was not just any old hammock but one made of wooden barrel staves put together with strong wires, just like the

146

one I had swung in in other halcyon days when visiting Grandma Casey in Fredericktown.

My hammock was fastened between two apple trees that we had earlier planted in the chicken yard. The chickens were gone by this time, and green grass grew all around, plus a myraid of daffodils, irises, and peonies I had planted where the chicken scratch yard had been. Clumps of hollyhocks still stood at places where the fence had been.

The apple trees had grown tall and sturdy and just the right distance apart to fasten a hammock. Padded with old quilts, the hammock was a comfortable place to be when the trees were in bloom, all through the summer as the little apples swelled, and into the Indian Summer days when the apples were ripe enough to fall in a slight breeze. Some of them even fell into the hammock where I lay, far away from the feminist movement, rumors of racial discontent, and distant war.

Nearly every spring, summer, and autumn afternoon, I would take a favorite book out to the hammock and read while the birds sang, crickets fiddled, and grasshoppers hopped. What books were these? Thoreau's *Walden*, Grayson's *Adventures of David Grayson*, Frost's and Riley's poems, Archibald Rutledge's *Peace in the Heart*, Gladys Taber's Stillmeadow books, and for probably the fiftieth time, *The Wind in the Willows*, to study Grahame's felicity with words.

One of the cats in my long series of cats would come to curl up beside me and purr contentedly. Blue jays, peering down at us from the canopy of green leaves, somehow seemed to understand that their vocal opposition to our presence would not be appropriate here.

Sometimes I would close my eyes and ask God to let me "see" a message from Him when I opened them again, just like I had that long-ago day of the carbide light. I was never disappointed. Once a piece of white lint, drifting from a cottonwood tree, landed in the exact center of an apple blossom, hung up on the pistil and stamens. I thought, I must pick that out so a bee can come and mix the pollen, but as I waited, a sparrow flew in, daintily picked out the lint and flew off to resume the making of her nest. "Oh, God," I chuckled, "how you do arrange circumstance, what economy of nature you have ordained, and your perfect timing for me to see." The cat would wake up, stretch, settle back down, and soon would be purring again.

It would have been on such a hammock day that I wrote "Foot of the Rainbow"*:

I once asked Aunt Marg, "What makes the dew?"

Aunt Marg lived in a magical world of her own, on the far side of some rainbow. Her answers to my questions were far more to my liking than any I found in a textbook.

"Why, honey," she explained, "at night the world washes its face and the dew is what's left over."

Her explanation is so believable, especially on a morning in June when the earth is so fresh and vibrant and, as Lowell said, "We see it (life) glisten."

To step outside at dawn, one finds that not only has the earth recently bathed but perfume has been splashed on, too. The fragrance from the clover blends with honeysuckle and mock orange to make a perfume that hasn't been bottled, unless at the far side of some rainbow.

The early-morning rabbits leave intricate dew-shaken trails in the grass. Thinking the pattern to be some new musical score, written in the night, the mockingbird in the apple tree, looking down, tries to sing it, while a woodpecker down in the park offers his drumbeat.

After inspecting the zinnia and marigold seedlings, I take an improvised seat under the arching branch of a tall-growing climbing rose to meditate awhile on the seeds. Ah, the eternal mystery of a little brown scrap of apparently nothing, springing to green life in six days! They alone contain all the visual proof we need for the shortcut to good living by faith and promise. I wonder what Aunt Marg would have said if I'd asked her what was in the seeds that made them sprout. "Little samples of God's power," seems a fitting answer.

The decibel of sound slowly rises in June. There is bee buzz and the first stridulations of the crickets. The rattle of grasshopper wings will join the symphony of jarflies and tree frogs. The children, free of school, and their dogs, glad of it, make the hand of the sound register leap wildly.

---

* *Tipoff Magazine*, June 1979.

*Like some old King Cole in his counting house, I
start to list my June riches. The nearby wren just turning himself inside out with song is so insistent, I had to
list him first and then make three mental ditto marks to
include the one in the lilac bush, the one on the fence,
and the one on the weathervane. Next are the roses. Not
just those in my yard, which are few, but my neighbors'
and all those all over town, even the pretty pink sweet-
briars blooming off on remote hillsides which I see in my
mind's eye only. But they are mine!*

*For a while my dew diamonds are exposed as the sun
searches them out in the grass. There is one glinting red
over by the birdbath. Another, blue-green, lies at the foot
of the martin house. The martins must see it, too, for you
never heard such chortling talk.*

*Underlying all these fanciful jewels and rare musical
performances is the real wealth of June – the persistence
of the fundamentals. Grass grows. Seeds sprout. Rivers
flow. Shadows are cast at the same angle as last year.
Forces and rhythms are at work that transcend man's
ideas and plans.*

*From my rosy bower I look across the street at my
mailbox and am tempted to go pull off the numbers and
write, "Foot of the Rainbow."*

Long Fuses Being Lit

Just as in my high-school days when we were more interested
in the basketball games than in current worldwide events, so in
the 1950s, the local happenings, particularly Stephen's basketball
games, claimed our immediate attention rather than the world
affairs, especially those going on half a world away in Southeast
Asia.

We knew, somewhat vaguely from skimmed-over newspaper
accounts and half-listened-to TV news, that the French who had
long controlled that area known as Vietnam had been defeated by
an uprising of the Vietnamese people. What Edward and I and a
lot of other people didn't pay much attention to at the time was
that when the French sued for peace, terms of which were known

149

as the Geneva Accords, many nations that had been involved signed the Accords. The United States did not, and therein lay a problem, but someone would take care of it, wouldn't they?

The southeast portion of our own United States was simmering, too. Ever since the Supreme Court in the 1954 *Brown v. Board of Education* case had declared segregation in schools to be unlawful and for segregation to cease, news came boiling out of the south that Rosa Parks, a black woman, had refused to give up her seat in a bus to a white man, and a Reverend Martin Luther King Jr. was organizing the Southern Christian Leadership Conference to make peaceful demonstrations demanding civil rights. Countering this were White Citizens Councils and a flurry of racial incidents. But someone would take care of this, wouldn't they?

What were these things compared to our city's building a floodwall to keep out almost-annual floods of the downtown area, Stephen shooting a goal from mid-court in the last second to beat Perryville, Edward operating more sophisticated and complex printing presses, and me in the midst of a "cyclone of writing!"

My time at the typewriter had doubled, maybe tripled. It seemed I was trying to make up for "lost time." I would have twelve to fifteen story manuscripts circulating at one time. Most of them sold, ranging in payment from $2.50 to $2,500, and a few at $3,000.

My five-drawer steel filing cabinet I bought from Arnold Roth when he purchased a new one became stuffed with copies of manuscripts, letters, and speeches.

Yes, speeches. It seems that when one's thoughts get published, it is assumed the writer

Jean Bell Mosley at her writing desk

can give speeches. So I gave speeches all over the state and in southern Illinois. It was time-consuming and took away from my writing time.

Program chairpersons were always on the lookout for program material, and I was fodder. My speeches at Writer's Conferences, Missouri Journalism Week, Associated Press meetings, service clubs, and clubs ad infinitum were mostly about writing or the telling of some story I had written.

I did not claim to know all about writing, and I prefaced many of my speeches with this bit of verse:

> *I knew a writer who would cure*
> *The state of mind we all endure,*
> *Declaring war on his neuroses,*
> *The root, he said, of his psychoses.*
> *So off he went and had him fixed,*
> *All wires straightened that were mixed.*
> *Creating thus a second plight,*
> *When sane, he found he couldn't write.*

I don't know the author of those lines, but it sounds like Ogden Nash or Richard Armour.

Embedded in many of my talks was this quotation from William Faulkner's Nobel Prize acceptance speech, "The . . . writer must leave no room in his workshop for anything but love, honor, pity, pride, compassion, and sacrifice." I would sometimes examine my manuscripts to see if I was coming anywhere close to Faulkner's standards.

In moments of reflection, I try to sort out which events in my writing career were the most thrilling. Was it the first sale? The first story sold to *Saturday Evening Post*? The first article to *Reader's Digest*? Publication of my first book? Receipt of the C.S. Lewis silver medal for *The Deep Forest Award*? They were all very satisfying moments, but I believe the most satisfactory was when A.S. Burack, editor of *The Writer*, a leading trade magazine for writers, asked me to write for his magazine. Some quotes from his letters were: "It occurs to me that anyone with your ability would have some valuable advice to pass on to writers who are just trying to get a foothold in the writing profession." "Your article, 'Triple Threat Flashback' certainly brightened our day! It is one of the best articles we have read in a long time. . . ." "The texture of the story

('One Night Together' in *Saturday Evening Post*), the feeling of purity and simplicity that you manage to get across is remarkable."

These comments were a balm to my writing ego and somewhat like receiving a diploma, a certified graduation.

I wrote other articles for *The Writer*, but writing about writing was hard for me to do. Having tumbled unexpectedly into the writing world with no formal training or experience except college Freshmen English Composition and senior college thesis, I could never shake off the feeling that my "diploma" was an honorary one.

International and national affairs have a dreary insistence of sifting down through layers of everyday living to nibble and bite at zones of comfort, and to make one question if one is just riding on the backs of those who are down in the trenches taking care of things.

The United States, which had not signed the Geneva Accords, decided to try to hold on to the southern portion of Vietnam, on which they had a tenuous claim, in order, so it was said, to stop the spread of Communism and to have a toehold in that corner of the world. Thereafter, just as strange words like Ypres, Verdun, Belleau, El Alamein, Anzio, St. Lo, Bastogne, Pingyang, Pusan, Seoul, Iwo Jima, Eniwetok had earlier crept into our vocabulary, now we heard Ho Chi Minh, Ngo Dinh Diem, Tonkin, Mekong, Cordillers. Thinking back, it seems we learned a lot of geography by warfare.

1960–1970

The Explosive Sixties

So the first half of the twentieth century came to a close. Eleven presidents had served. Three wars had been fought. The Depression had come and gone. I was forty-seven years old. Surely my life span was more than half over. But, quoting beloved poet Robert Frost, and thinking of all the things I still wanted to do, I would reassure myself, "I have miles to go before I sleep."

By the end of the 1950s, I had enough stories published, a la *The Mockingbird Piano*, to make another book. It was somewhat of a sequel to *The Mockingbird Piano* but yet stood alone on its own. Thus my second book, *Wide Meadows*, was published by Caxton Printers in 1960. It was chosen as a *Christian Herald-Farm Journal* selection and also as an American Ambassador Book selected by the English Speaking Union to interpret the lives, background, character, and ideas of the American people in other countries. Portions of this book were transposed into Braille.

Among the promos was this statement: "Glowingly alive in every page are the lovable schoolgirls, Lou and Jean. You will meet the neighbors, too, and in the last chapter, you will rejoice with Jean as she finds where God has signed his name!"

Still, I wanted to write a biblical novel, a sort of love letter to God with whom I so often talked and who talked back to me in so many different ways. But the fuses that had been lit, one sputtering away toward Southeast Asia, the other toward the Southeast United States, were about to reach their explosive destinations, and these ominous sputterings slowed my progress. Would we have racial troubles in the local school as in Little Rock? Were we going to have to fight yet another war to hold on to South Vietnam? How long would it take? Stephen was sixteen years old, two years away from draft age.

Years ago, from the safety of the barn, I had watched Dad blow up old stumps in the apple orchard. He would attach a long black fuse to a stick of dynamite which he buried under the dead stump. Then he would light the fuse and find a safe place to await the explosion. The fuse would sputter along under the Early Harvest apple tree, the Maiden Blush, the Russet, to finally ignite the stick of dynamite under the old Sheep's Nose stump. Boom! Bits of the stump, grass, and dirt would explode into the air and when everything had settled down, the landscape had changed.

The explosive devices at the end of the long "fuses" leading to the southern states and half a world away were not like a single stick of dynamite, over with and done. They were multi-multiple, one setting off another and another and another. When things settled back down (some are still ongoing), the cultural, political, psychological, military, and moral landscape of America was changed.

Some of the changes were good; we went to the moon and back. Black America rose up, spoke out, fought back, and the Civil

Rights Act came into being. Some were bad: 58,156 Americans killed in Vietnam. Martin Luther King Jr., John F. Kennedy, Robert Kennedy assassinated. Ku Klux Klan uprisings. Murders of southern blacks and some whites who went to help. The decline of the nuclear family, the basic building block of society.

From the safety of the green couch across from the TV, I saw John Glenn take off for orbiting the Earth — Earth, that old round globe at Loughboro School. Tears of pride ran down my cheeks. Tears of pride for what America could do. I saw Neil Armstrong land on the moon. *Land on the moon!* I go out now at night, look at the moon, and whisper, "We've been there." It is still almost incomprehensible. I saw and heard Martin Luther King Jr. give his "I Have a Dream" speech.

The ensuing Vietnam War seemed to have been fought ten feet away from me, in color. To see the Vietnamese man deliberately shot in the head in a vacated street in Vietnam, the bodies of the My Lai massacre lying in a ravine, a Buddhist monk burning himself to death on a Saigon street was more than I wanted to see of the world.

I acquired the ability to send my mind out to walk in old meadows, down ancient woods' roads, alongside flowing streams as surcease, but not entirely without a string of guilt attached. Someone had to face the problems of the world, attempt to right the wrongs. Why should I be out in the meadows and woods mentally, or in the hammock physically, escaping from reality? What was my role?

It seemed more than ever as I pondered the question that my role would be to use words, to hold up before readers, if I could get any, a gentler way of life, attempt to make them see, hear, and feel, even for just the moment, the little joys of life — crumbs if you will. Sometimes, when I think my words to be clumsily used, trite, or of little consequence compared to the big movers and shakers of literature, I remember the Syrophoenician woman pointing out to Jesus that even crumbs are useful. Then is when I might write such crumbs as "Little Places of Retirement"* as follows:

> *The before-dawn songs of the robins, the sudden*
> *cheerful call of an early-returning purple martin are like*
> *the siren's songs from the Lorelei, calling me outside.*

---
* *Southeast Missourian*, April 12, 1992.

But this is not a wicked siren luring me to destruction, rather to rejuvenation.

Each season has its charm and its comforts, but towards the end of that season they grow a bit stale and one wants to burst out like a butterfly from a winter cocoon.

All the books I planned to read this past winter have been read. The crocheted rag wall hanging has been crocheted but not yet hung. All the words I needed to write have been written. I'm ready to descend the five non-icy steps and frolic like a young filly around and around the yard. That's only my mental attitude. In physical reality, I'll walk slowly around like a retired mare put out to pasture.

It doesn't take a lot of alacrity to sit in the sunshine on the big stump where the wild cherry tree was, weave in and out amongst the cedars, and follow a mole's tracks, trying to mash down his trail.

The yard is awash with violets. Sometimes, instead of the stump, I sit right down in the middle of them. Can't quite manage the lotus position anymore. Don't know that I ever could. And I never needed a mantra to meditate. I just watch the bees flying from dandelion to dandelion and think about how well cared for they are. About the time they tire of the dandelion wine, there will be the Dutch clover, then the autumn olive. Autumn olive, how funny, since it blooms in spring. Its fragrance is inimitable and I suppose the nectar is too. When the little creamy white blossoms unfold, the bushes tremble with happy bee life.

There are many sticks and twigs to pick up, so with a little red wagon, I go around tossing them into its bed as frisky as a child pulling a wagonload of teddy bears. Well, no, that's not quite right either, physically speaking. But with the newly oiled wagon wheels, and on a downhill slope, it fulfills my recommended daily requirements of exercise. Not that I do it for exercise. There's a gene in Jean that in springtime says, "Clean up that little corner, and when you're through, do that one over there and there and there."

The gene manifested its authority early. Where the log smokehouse formed a right-angle corner with the picket fence on the farmstead yard, I felt compelled and pleasantly satisfied to clean it out in the spring. Hollyhocks were springing upward at the base of the logs and a rambling rosebush, beginning to leaf out, either held up the pickets or vice versa. Over winter, weeds sprang up in the corner – burdock, chickweeds, feverfew, etc. Dogs loved that corner to chew on bones and leave them there. Windblown leaves and other refuse caught in the corner.

Without any bidding from anyone, I raked, pulled weeds, chopped down the healthy burdock, and made myself a little place of retirement. Retirement in the sense that I could go there to be alone, no chores or duties weighing heavily. I could read my little storybooks or just sit in the warm sunshine watching the working of early spring.

Sometimes I asked Grandma for a few zinnia seeds she would have saved from the past season and sowed them where I had destroyed the burdock. With the sound of frogs in the meadow's low places, cackle of hens rejoicing over yet another produced egg, the odor of the good earth mingling with woodsmoke from the chimney, I did not know I was ingraining a rite that would last to the final decade of the century. I only knew how good it felt to bring a little neatness into a small corner where I could be alone with my thoughts and activities.

Now, as I pull the wagon around, noting the Johnny-jump-ups I'm running over, the chickweed that needs pulling up, a little bare place where some zinnias might be sown, I think of my old book friend, David Grayson, who said, " . . . if once a man has a taste of true and happy retirement, though it be but a short hour, or day, now and then, he has found, or is beginning to find, a sure place of refuge, of blessed renewal, toward which in the busiest hours he will find his thoughts wistfully stealing."

My constant but unseen friend, Jesus, knew the most about the benefits of being apart for a while. While I pick up real sticks and debris to toss on the burning

pile, He picked up the sticks and dregs of humanity to
offer them a new life, an eternal life!

Our daily lives did not change much during these turbulent sixties. Entries were made daily in my journal:

August 7, 1961
  The Russians have done it again. Gherman Titov is orbiting the earth right now. Round and round he goes.

August 28, 1961
  A small yellow butterfly lit on my hand today. "Hello, God. Thank you."

September 4, 1961
  Two kittens fell into the empty cistern today. Fire Chief Lewis came out to rescue them.

Not a lot, if any, of the antiwar demonstrations went on in our relatively peaceful riverside city. There were few racial conflicts. Drugs were slow to come.

It was up and off to work for Edward, up and off to school for Stephen, and up and off to my writing desk for me. That is, after making beds, washing dishes, planning supper, maybe washing, ironing, sweeping, and dusting. But I was at home working at my own speed, handling my own dear things — the blue and white dishes, the pretty quilts, the sun-dried sheets — thinking my own thoughts, talking to God, and looking for his answer always.

We had breakfast and supper together, usually at the kitchen table, for the dining-room table had become a study table for Stephen who was out of high school in the spring of 1962 and into Southeast Missouri State University that September.

This dining-room table was constantly spread with textbooks, notebooks, papers, pencils, pens, clippings, Sigma Chi mugs, all the accoutrements of a college student determined to "get an education."

Reader's Digest

My desk, too, was strewn with papers, notebooks, and reference books. During the 1970s some of my "little crumbs" of writing grew in substance and style, at least, so editors said.

On a beautiful day in May when the irises and roses were blooming, I walked leisurely to the mailbox and pulled out a letter that had a return address of: *Reader's Digest*, Pleasantville, New York. I remembered that I had sent them a manuscript way back in February, so what could this letter be?

Striving for composure, I walked slowly all the way back into the house, sat down, slit the envelope very neatly, took out the small sheet, and read:

May 2, 1963

Dear Mrs. Mosley:

What must you think of us — holding up your story, "The Day The Cows Didn't Come Home," for so long?

The delay resulted from the article being read by several of the staff in turn and I'm happy to report that the decision in favor of it was unanimous. A check for $1,500 is enclosed.

Thank you for giving us first chance at this delightful story. If you care to send us other material, we'll be glad to read it.

Sincerely yours,

(Mrs.) Helen Givins

I called Edward at his work and heard the joy in his voice as he received the good news. Then I made a most understated entry in my journal:

May, 4, 1965
Sold to Reader's Digest *today!*

The journal entry before this was:

May 3, 1963

The fine thing about man is that potentially he can do anything with himself!

Every once in a while a person gets the urge to turn over a new leaf, make a new beginning, either to accomplish an old aim or take aim at a new one. And the good thing is, there is nothing to keep him from it.

The greatest thing to be considered here is willpower. For only through willpower can some hard things be accomplished.

The journal entry after the understated *Reader's Digest* sale was:

May 5, 1963

Had a curretment today.

Dr. D.B. Elrod, the surgeon; Dr. Alyea the anesthetist.

Life! Such a mixture of things—cabbages and kings, joys and stings.

Not only had the *Reader's Digest* bought "The Day The Cows Didn't Come Home," they, later in the year, said it had been chosen as a "First Person Award" and sent an additional $1,000.

The piece started my "writing fling" with the *Reader's Digest*. During the 1960s and 1970s they bought thirteen other pieces, one was another "First Person Award" and one a "Drama In Real Life."

These writings helped me to believe that I was doing some good. Letters and telephone calls seemed to indicate that. Some of the articles were put into textbooks, gift books, and inspirational books.

In the meantime the journal entries went on. Such as:

March 1, 1964

March winds are sweeping the floor of the earth. It gives me an urge to do a little housecleaning. I, nostalgically, want to put some kerosene on the broom, as in the old days, and set the furniture outside to sun.

Edward and I went over to Horseshoe Lake this afternoon. We saw thousands of geese on the water and in the fields. At "Buddy's" eating place on the way home we bought some ham which I will fry for supper. It was a pleasant drive.

June 16, 1964
*June mornings are rare treasures. A cool breeze
ruffles the window curtains. Birds, cats, and butterflies
are abroad. Am making some patchwork pillowcases for
sofa pillows.*

June 25, 1964
*Life goes through us and we separate the cream from
the milk just like in the old DeLaval cream separator.*

July 2, 1964
*Edward to Dr. Wilson. Chest X-ray and cardiogram.
All OK.*

Sept. 12, 1964
Louis LaCoss, Editor Emeritus, St. Louis Globe-
Democrat, *said in today's paper, "If for no other reason
than curiosity, one should wish that his days will be
many more just to see how the whole mess works out."*

Sept. 21, 1964
*51st birthday! I am joyful, happy, and enthusiastic
about life and living.*

Nov. 4, 1964
Leonard Mayberry fixed my shelves above stove.

Dec. 19, 1964
*Menu for Christmas dinner: Chicken pie, mashed
potatoes, peas in a carrot ring, coconut cake, cranberry
salad, slaw, punch relishes.*

By the mid-sixties I decided that if ever I was to write the biblical novel I wanted to, this was the decade to do it.

There had been so many wonderful biblical novels already
published, how could I tackle one that would be different? I had
often thought about Zebedee, the father of the apostles James and
John. When Jesus came by, choosing his disciples, the brothers so
readily dropped their fishing nets and followed Jesus. Did Zebedee resent his sons being chosen? Taken away from the family
business? Did he, like so many would do today, not recognize

who this Jesus was? I knew of no other book that had Zebedee as a main character. Indeed, he is just sort of mentioned in passing in the Bible. So I chose him around whom to weave my fictional story. I followed the chronology of the Gospel of John.

I had entitled the book, *My Brother, My Sister*. Broadman Press, the publisher, chose the title *The Crosses at Zarin*.

I did my best writing on the novel on the banks of Wessel's Pond. After supper, with Stephen settled down to studying or off on a date, Edward and I would drive out to Wessel's Pond, about seven miles away, to fish. It was a relaxing time for Edward who loved to fish. Relaxing for me, too, although at this time I went for a different purpose.

There was a rustic picnic table on the bank. I spread my writing materials on it and wrote most of the book there during the summer sunset hours. Evening breezes rippled the waters of the pond which caught the last sunbeams of the day. In my mind's eye, the pond became the Lake of Galilee.

In the spring, blossoms from an overhead persimmon tree fell on my papers, and in the fall, sometimes a ripe persimmon would splatter on my pages. We often stayed until the whippoorwills began to call and a star or two came out in the night sky.

Sometimes other folks were there. Once a small, bright-eyed lad stopped at my table. He had two little fishes on a string he wanted to show me. "What's your name?" I asked. "Andrew," he replied. A young lad, two fishes, Andrew, Lake Galilee, a.k.a. Wessel's Pond—a shivery little feeling played around my spine.

Back home, after this pleasant interlude, Edward and I felt compelled to listen to the local and national news before going to bed.

The local news was never very disturbing. Progress on the floodwall to protect downtown from the ever-flooding Mississippi River was reported. Interstate highway I-55 was opened from nearby Scott City on the south to nearby Fruitland on the north. All that construction noise to the west I had heard for many months could now be "traveled" upon. The new Central High School was well-liked by the community, and Santa Claus came to the Town Plaza Shopping Center via helicopter!

The national news was more depressing. Despite the fact that the young, handsome John Kennedy had become our president and, with his lovely wife Jacqueline, had precipitated what were to be known as the Camelot years, acting on the advice of some of his "Knights of the Round Table," he embarrassed himself and the nation with the infamous Bay of Pigs fiasco, a failed invasion of Cuba, a Communist island with allegiance to the Soviet Union. The Soviet Union was our enemy in a cold war that had come into existence after the end of World War II.

Edward and I, sitting on the green couch, watching such news reports, decided it would be better thereafter to go to bed without listening to the national news. But then came the Cuban missile standoff. Krushchev, Soviet leader, had secretly delivered missiles to Cuba. Kennedy ordered them removed and blockaded Cuba. Soviet ships menacingly faced American ships. America collectively shivered. Thereafter, Edward and I decided to stay up for the national news lest we be "fried" in our beds by nuclear missiles. Not that the place of death made any difference; it was just that we'd have died "without boots on!"

The Crosses at Zarin

Publication date for *The Crosses at Zarin*, the book I had largely written on the banks of Wessel's Pond, was Tuesday, August 1, 1967. I began the day by sitting in the porch swing watching a Heavenly Blue morning glory uncurl and talking to my friend. It went something like this: "God, thank you for the gift of another new day where I can see where you are and where you have been. I sit here beside you with nothing but praise, thanksgiving, and rejoicing that you are here and now and ever will be, and that I can talk to you, friend to friend.

"You know that today the book I've wanted to write about your Son will be published. Thank you for the strength and ability you have given me to do this. May it unfurl like that morning glory there and come to full loveliness, attracting readers who in these bewildering days of seeming chaos need to find comfort in your promise that he whose mind is stayed on you will be kept in perfect peace.

"You know my mind is stayed on you, for I see you everywhere I look. How beautiful the feathers of the cardinal that just flitted before me, almost as red as that tomato you made peeping at me through green foliage in the garden plot. The guard hairs on the tail of that squirrel sitting up there in the nearby oak are picking up beams from the early sun. It is like splintered light from that carbide light of long ago.

"If my book, being published today, is not a great light, may it be at least a little beam as bright as one of those guard hairs. Although my book says it is dedicated to my friend, Thomza, it and everything I do is dedicated to you. I trust the Holy Spirit will dust off, straighten up, correct anything that is imperfect of mine before it is handed to you."

Broadman Publishers arranged a book-signing tour for me at Mobile, Alabama. They proposed to arrange a flight from Cape Girardeau to Atlanta and then on to Mobile. Unused to making my way through a large airport, I told Broadman I'd rather go by train, since it would be less expensive, and take my college-age son with me. They acquiesced.

Stephen and I boarded "City of New Orleans" train which left Anna, Illinois, at 1:20 PM, August 14, and arrived in New Orleans at 12:25 AM, August 15. I had hoped to see some large antebellum homes along the route, but since trains usually travel through the less scenic parts of town, we saw no great plantation or city homes. Spanish moss hanging from the more southern trees and an increase in the black population at train stations were about all the new things we noticed. We did have our evening meal on the train, which I had looked forward to, but it wasn't very good.

We took a cab from the train station to Travel Lodge and stayed all that night and the next day at New Orleans. It was raining, and the first things we had to buy were umbrellas. We were to go to the Baptist Seminary at New Orleans, where I was to autograph some books for the library. The head librarian was to take us to lunch. Somewhat to our disappointment and perplexity, the librarian said she was so harried that day due to some crisis at the library that she had no time for lunch. She stuffed a twenty-dollar bill in Stephen's pocket and told us to "go have lunch." We couldn't help feeling a little snubbed and wondered if this lunch date was just some last-minute thought of Bob Phelps, Broadman's sales representative, who had initially planned only for a trip to Mobile.

We not only went to lunch, but took a bus tour of New Orleans and saw all the famous places.

We left New Orleans at 8:30 PM on August 15, bound for Mobile. Of course we were keeping in close touch with Edward about where we were and where we were going.

The trip from New Orleans to Mobile was across Lake Pontchartrain. It so happened that a boat was passing through the lake, and the railroad tracks, as in a drawbridge, had to be raised for its passage. This took a long time, so it was well after midnight when we arrived at Mobile. Nevertheless, I called Edward, who was very upset and worried about our being so late with a call he had expected much earlier. He was always worried when Stephen or I were away from home.

We spent the 16th and 17th at Mobile. The book-signing parties were at a bookstore in a shopping mall that had just recently opened and at a local library. Neither session was very successful. Either not much publicity had preceded my visit, or folks just didn't want to buy the book. Saleswise, I would call the whole trip a flop. But then we did get to see a part of the southland we had never seen before.

Mr. Phelps ushered us around at Mobile and attempted to take us to see Bellingraph Gardens, but when we got only halfway there, he decided we would miss our train back to New Orleans if he didn't turn around right then and go back to Mobile.

We arrived back in New Orleans in time to have supper at Brennan's and walk the streets in the French Quarter, stopping every once in a while to listen to the music coming from open shops along the way.

Next morning we boarded the train for Anna, Illinois, at 7:10 AM and arrived in Anna at 5:00 PM. Edward met us and his smile was the broadest I had ever seen. I was enormously glad to be back too, for in Mobile I had my first touch of depression. More of this depression was to come later.

The Crosses at Zarin went into its second printing shortly after publication, and Broadman called it their best-seller. New York Times and other big metropolitan newspapers seldom, if ever, consider religious books for their best-seller lists.

1970 – 1980

Sometimes It Took More than Aspirins

The sixties were "bookended" with physical distress for me. My first bout with major surgery came at the beginning of the decade. While bathing, one day, I discovered a lump on one side of my throat. It was a sudden discovery and scary. How had I missed it? Heretofore, aspirins, turpentine, Vicks, Rosebud salve, and seemingly outrageous poultices had cured almost all my ailments. I was pretty sure this lump couldn't be dissolved by aspirins. It was late afternoon when the discovery was made, so I didn't get to Dr. Garland Reynolds' office until the next day. "It's got to come out," he pronounced. In less than four days it was out, along with half of my thyroid gland. "Nonmalignant," I heard the nurse say as I was beginning to wake up from the anesthesia. Sweet word that, "nonmalignant."

After initial recovery, the surgeon, Dr. Frank Hall, prescribed thyroid medication to make up for the missing half gland. It made me grind my teeth and, as the cliché goes, "climb the wall." After several experimental diminishing doses, it was decided I didn't need any such medication.

It was very painful to swallow after the surgery. It seemed my food had to go up and over a sore, arched bridge to get to my stomach. I remembered the song of my high-school days, "I'm dancing with tears in my eyes," and tried valiantly to sing, "I'm eating with tears in my eyes," if Edward or Stephen should happen in at mealtime and be alarmed at my tears.

This was my first adventure with a pain shot, too. I had just been given such a shot when a most delicious lemon-custard dessert was placed before me. I was so hungry from not eating because it hurt so bad; the custard was the first thing that went down without pain. I had taken only one bite when I became so sleepy, I could not lift the spoon for a second bite.

At the end of the decade, I went through the "funnies" of postmenopause. A ten-year postmenopause! I seemed to have sailed right through initial menopause without any of the usual symptoms, but alas, it came. Right there, down south, it came while on the book-signing tour. I thought at first it was something I'd eaten on the train, or the seeming heaviness of the southern atmosphere. What was this awful thing that closed in, held me trapped? "God?" I queried.

I don't even want to recall all the details, but the bad comes with the good.

It was the accompanying depression that was so bad. I found crocheting and embroidering to be a way to get through it. My friend, Thomza, already experienced in this unhappy time of life said, "Now, just remember, Jean, you will get over this."

In the spring I sat in the porch swing embroidering pillowcases, looking at the green leaves coming out and saying, "By the time they fall, this will be over." By the time the leaves fell, I was still embroidering pillowcases and saying, "Before the leaves turn green again, this will be over."

It did leave, backing out slowly like some old stubborn camel who had nosed his way into "my tent," uninvited. Dr. Dennis Elrod helped that "camel" out of my living space, and life went on as before. Something good ought to come out of menopause. I have yet to find it. Perhaps many pairs of embroidered pillowcases to give as gifts?

At the beginning of each new decade I always look forward, hoping that it is going to be better than the last one. But right away came a deluge of unhappy events: Kent State tragedy, Mama's death, Edward's heart attack.

On an early day in May 1970, Kent State students in Ohio, protesting the Vietnam War, were fired upon by the National Guard. Four were killed. My hands gripped the edges of the green couch as the TV announcer made the grave statement. Was the Vietnam War going to cause a civil war in the United States? Were Americans killing Americans already, over a war half a world away?

By now Nixon was president, having succeeded Lyndon Johnson who became president when John F. Kennedy was assassinated. Nixon had promised he would end the war in Vietnam and eventually he did, but not before extending it, secretly, into Cambodia. When this was revealed, the antiwar demonstrations increased. Edward and I sat watching the thousands of marchers in Washington. Marching for peace.

In June of that same year, Daniel Ellsbery turned over to the *New York Times* what were known as the Pentagon Papers. They revealed that our government had lied and misrepresented the

Vietman War to the American people, and the war began to slowly wind down. We had been defeated. A first for America.

Goodbye to Mama

After Dad died, Mama stayed for a while, alone, at their white frame house on Columbia Street in Farmington. In their late years, both Mama and Dad worked at the mental institution in Farmington, known as No. 4, and they had made their residence either on the grounds of the hospital or later at this location on Columbia Street.

Mama, all her life, had been surrounded by abundant family members, so she found it very lonesome living alone. When her elder spinster sister, Minnie Casey, who lived in Oakland, California, begged her to come stay with her for a while, Mama went, making the long train trip by herself.

Aunt Minnie lived a very Spartan life, and when Mama came back to Missouri for a visit after two years, she was very thin. I hated to see her go back to California, but she had promised Aunt Minnie to come back, and back she went.

During this second stay she had an emergency glaucoma operation. This, together with seemingly inevitable cataracts, dimmed her vision considerably. She thought it time to come home for good, and so did Lillian, Lucille, and I.

Mama paid to have the second storey of Lucille's home in Farmington made into an apartment, and there she lived for a while. Then she began dividing her time, staying at Lillian's and with me, maybe for a couple months at a time.

Myrtle Casey Bell (1886–1971)

Edward and I had already made the screened porch on the south side of the house into a downstairs room for Stephen. By this time Stephen was away teaching school, so Mama took that room.

While staying with me, she suffered her first heart attack, a rather massive one, and thereafter suffered angina pains the rest of her life.

While staying with Lillian she suffered a cerebral hemorrhage and never regained consciousness, although she was at the Farmington Community Hospital for several days before her death.

On the day of the hemorrhage, Lillian, in another room, heard Mama go to the bathroom and come back to sit in her favorite chair. When Mama failed to respond to something Lillian said, Lillian went to investigate and found Mama sitting in the chair, unconscious, her dress neatly arranged and her cane hanging over the arm of the chair. Mama was gone, she of the "two orange ice-cream sodas, please"; she who spoke the word "murmuring," like the deep strains of a cello; she who rewove a tear in a coat sleeve with some strands of her long, black hair. She was eighty-five. She is buried alongside Dad at the Farmington Memorial Gardens Cemetery.

In addition to the above-mentioned memories, and amongst the hundreds of others, there was the brown, acorn, butterfly dress.*

> When I was putting together my trousseau, Mama said, "Now you'll have to have a new housedress."
>
> Note "a" housedress, not four or five. It was the pits of the Depression. To use the word "trousseau" is almost laughable.
>
> Mama wisely knew that the majority of a 1930s housewife's days were going to be spent in housedresses — a housedress. Breakfast, dinner, and supper, your new husband was going to look across the table and very likely see you in the same dress.
>
> We consulted the Sears, Roebuck catalog.
>
> At that time, Sears sold dress fabrics and had little swatches of the cotton, voile, bastiste, etc., glued into the catalog so you wouldn't be ordering a pig in a poke.
>
> Slacks had not yet come into fashion, nor the later habit of changing dresses every day.

---

* *Southeast Missourian*, May 15, 1994.

A housedress, if of the proper color, could be worn for three days without washing, starching, ironing, and putting it on again, fresh.

We fingered all the swatches, thought of any trim we might already have in the scrap bag or any that might be salvaged from other almost worn-out clothes.

After much deliberation, I chose a brown cotton print that had little, yellowish acorns in it. At that time I could have identified acorns from the white, red, black, post, and burr oak trees. We had them all on our home place, and I knew where they were.

So perhaps that's why I chose this particular fabric.

"Now you must have pockets," Mama said, and I agreed. I have always disliked garments without pockets.

"Buttoned down the front," I suggested, remembering some yellow buttons I'd seen in the button box.

"I think pinafore ruffles at the sleeve-shoulder seams would be nice," Mama planned.

"What's that?"

Mama drew me a picture, and I liked it a lot. I thought I would look sort of butterfly-like and said so.

We talked about butterflies as we cut and shaped.

Would they look like the brown fritillary or the painted lady ones that came to flit around our summertime zinnias? Oh, it was so good to plan and work with Mama.

"I'd like yellow rickrack around the pinafore ruffles," I suggested. Mama didn't say anything, and I knew she was wondering if we ought to afford that.

"The ruffles will have to be starched and ironed," Mama warned.

"And we'll need a wide hem, so it can be let up and down as the fashion changes," she added. I knew that. The dress was to last and last. My hems had gone up and down since the sixth grade.

We worked on that dress as some mothers and daughters would work on a bridal gown. After all, a bridal gown was worn once; the everyday dress would go on and on.

It did, and every time I ironed it, the brown dye in the fabric exuded a crushed acorn odor. Serendipity!

With the passing of Mama, Edward and I were now both bereft of parents. His father, Edgar Scott Mosley, who had helped build our house, indeed did all the carpentry work and who delighted, later, to work in our big garden, died in 1953. He was a big man of few words.

Edward's mother, Ruth Parthena (Curd), often playfully called R.P., passed away in 1956. They were both gentle people, not easily disturbed by anything, perhaps because they had already put many hard years behind them before coming to Cape Girardeau to live at 501 Themis Street.

Mr. Mosley, in the late 1890s and early 1900s, had helped clear the swamps of Southeast Missouri to make it the rich farming land that it is today. Rich people reaped the rewards of the hard work, buying up the land as soon as it was cleared.

Now, late in this century, there is a movement in conservation circles and other organizations to return more wetlands to their original state. So it goes. Something that seems good at the time is found, in later years, to be something not so good, all things considered, like wildlife.

Clearing the swamps was a dirty, dangerous business. Sometimes roughnecks were employed to cut down the trees and rid the stumps, hip deep in black muck, fighting mosquitoes and snakes all the while.

Mrs. Mosley often told of the time when she almost shot her husband, Edward's father (before Edward was born), through the locked door of her home, thinking it was one of the roughnecks who had come at an odd hour when her husband was not at home.

Through it all, they raised four children to adults: Sylvester, Juel, Edward, and Bernice. Three more children died in infancy or while still very young.

While Mr. Mosley did his carpentry work, Mrs. Mosley kept room-and-boarders at the gracious white frame house with seven bedrooms. When she got a few dollars ahead, she would buy something pretty — a lace collar, a brooch, a pretty dish — which revealed the feminine longings beneath her workday world. I have some of these "whims": four milk-glass salad plates, a blue vase, a flow-blue teapot.

Heart Attack!

At about midnight, March 12, 1972, Edward experienced pain in the left of his chest. He tried to minimize it, as men do, denying it was anything to worry about. But I took him, kicking and screaming, to the doctor the next morning. He had an EKG and was sent to Lovinggood-Horn Laboratory for blood tests. Back home, at about 3:30, Dr. Charles Wilson ordered him to the hospital. He went to room 160 first and then to Intensive Care. There had been a coronary occlusion. In other words, a blockage in the flow of blood through the heart. Lying flat on his back, all "wired up," he was like a caged tiger.

"Now what, God?" I asked, while waiting in the Intensive Care waiting room. When a loved one is in Intensive Care, a five-minute visitation every three hours is allowed. I spent a lot of time in that waiting room. To try to keep myself steady, I wrote in my mind, a thing at which I was getting fairly adept:

> *Those two young girls over there. They are here every day at the hours designated for the five-minute visit. With their gayly patterned jeans and blouses and long, shining hair, they seem alien to the prescients where possible death hovers just around the corner for some loved one. They sit so close to each other, their faces ashen and immobile. So young. They say nothing, as if even to break the silence would cause some other tenuously held thing to break. I keep the silence with them.*
>
> *And that lone woman over there, unknowingly, incessantly, she drums on the chair arm with fingers that have seen too much arthritis and probably even now are aching. From time to time she swallows noisily. Her chin quivers, then she tosses her head and passes a hand over her face as if to get rid of some miasma of overwhelming anxiety and grief. She takes out a worn compact and inspects her eyes. She must not go into the ailing patient with reddened eyes, but a face full of hope and cheer. She struggles. I struggle with her.*
>
> *An old man accompanied by a daughter, I suppose, sits and toys with his cane. His hair is white, and his face lined and leathery. They speak softly from time to time of mother. He is more resigned, more at peace than*

the daughter, for he has experienced more of everything. She knows that, too, but her heart cries out, "Not yet. Not yet." My heart cries with her.

The telephone rings before the appointed hour. Everyone jumps.Someone arises to answer and turns to call out a certain name. That person leaves. The others resume their vigil.

A group of women sitting around a table are talking about inconsequential things. The casual observer and listener would think them unfeeling and out of order to be talking of so many eggs in a recipe and the minimum amount of double knit it takes to make slacks, but I know the mind veers towards miniatures of reality when vague fear threatens.

I concentrate on a miniature of reality myself. There is a hangnail on my finger. I put all my efforts into removing it.

Suddenly, with no warning, a surgeon comes into the room to talk to a family group. All is deathly quiet. One cannot help hearing the muffled talking. "It has spread. All we could do." They are strangers, but my heart aches, too.

I walk over to a window and look out where some daffodils are nodding in the spring breeze. "Mrs. Mosley?" someone at the telephone calls my name. It is my time for visitation.

"All right, God. Come, let's go see how he is."

Long bedrest was what was then prescribed for coronary patients, and Edward endured that until dismissal the first week in April and then some more time at home.

Edward shared a hospital room with Edward Blumenberg, affable Cape County Assessor. I suppose my Edward, in the long hospital hours, spoke to Edward B. of his worries of never being able to work on the printing presses again because it required heavy lifting of paper and other things, and the doctor had warned him against that. So the two Edwards "hatched up" the idea that, since it was election year, I should run for Cape County Treasurer. The idea was unsettling to me, but I tried not to show it. Back to office hours? Back to public work? Probably there would be new equipment I'd have to learn to operate. A political "upstart" may not be well received by the staunch officeholders.

172

But it seemed to alleviate Edward's worry about how we would get along financially, so I agreed to run, although I did not share his financial worry. If the worst came to the worst, there would be Social Security Disability and a tiny pension. My writing was financially rewarding but erratic.

Although a lifelong Republican and never having missed a voting opportunity, I had never taken an active part in the political structure, other than knowing who the officeholders were and supporting them.

Practically out of the politically unknown ranks, I (gulp) filed for County Treasurer. A Mr. Ludwig, the person with whom I had to file, was unfriendly, informing me that this was not a popularity contest. Thus, my toe in the world of politics got stepped on right away.

I did all the things that someone running for office did — showing up at church suppers and other public meetings all over the county. My nametag and smile firmly fixed, I visited with all the committee men and women I could find, ran a newspaper ad, put a sign in my yard, all the time secretly fearing I might win. By the way, the sign in my yard got pulled up and taken away the first night by someone from the loyal opposition, I suppose. Ah, politics.

I lost in the county primary by less than 200 votes. The thought has occurred to me since that if I had hired a horseman to gallop rapidly around schoolhouses, yelling, "Vote for Mosley," a la that rider around the Loughboro schoolhouse described earlier, it might have impressed a sufficient number of teachers to vote for me. But, alas, in 1972, there would have been legal charges of trespassing, damages to school property, disturbance of the peace, etc. We were in the super-litigious era that continues to this day.

Edward, of course, was disappointed, and I sort of pretended to be, but was secretly relieved, especially since I thought my adventure had served the purpose of consuming time while Edward regained his strength.

Folks thought I took my defeat so graciously! They commiserated with me, pointing out that few women ever held county office, which was true at that time.

On my first daily walk around the Arena racetrack thereafter, I picked some of the lowly dog fennel along the way, and it never looked so pretty nor smelled so good. Discarded soda-can tab openers reflected sunlight all along the way. "Thank you, God."

Changes

I think, in time, Edward was glad, too, that I didn't win. After his recuperation, for the next four years, we spent days and days in the Indian relic country of Southeast Missouri. Knowing many farmers in that region, we got permission to roam their fields, fencerows, and creek banks for the artifacts. We did no digging but collected quite a lot, the best of which were displayed at the local museum for many years.

An authority on such artifacts from the University of Missouri studied our collection, assigning age and rarity. Among our best specimens were a perfect banner stone, a perfect white Clovis point, and several perfect Dalton points in addition to drills, plumb bobs, beads, tomahawks, hatchets, and hundreds of arrowheads.

Edward found this activity so all-absorbing, he did not hunt or fish anymore. I not only enjoyed looking for the relics, but being out in the fields, meadows, old fencerows, by creek banks suited me just fine. Sometimes while Edward kept on roaming the fields, I might sit in the shade of a tree, take out a pen and small notebook, which were always in some pocket, and write something about the resting fields of America* such as this:

> The resting fields of America have never been promoted as attractions for tourists. What's a big expanse of corn stubble or bean leavings? Winding rivers, steep bluffs, placid lakes, mighty mountains are the things pictured on come-and-see-'em brochures and postcards. But the fields are part of America the Beautiful, even when they are not waving their amber grains. They lie so peaceful and still under the shifting sun, some flat, some artfully sloping up to the horizon. You have to see these resting fields through eyes that have seen them full cycle, over and over again, to know they are poems in terms of corn, wheat, cotton, sheen of new turned soil, coolness to bare feet, sweat to the brow, brown wombs of the spiritual as well as the material. So friendly, so good are the fields.
>
> I have known the young robust fields, newly cleared, dark, rich, bursting with turnips and potatoes, pumpkins

---

* *Kansas City Star*, September 10, 1972.

and sugarcane. They are hurried. Up from old-leaf mold,
dead grasses, burnt brush, they smell of fertility. They
are vain — young upstarts with morning glories making
work for hoes and rakes and plows and cultivators.

Mature fields, long devoid of cockleburs, bindweed,
and rotting stumps, go about their business as usual,
straightforward in straw hat and sturdy blue overalls.
Corn does not grow quite as tall, wheat quite as rank as
in the new fields. But here is steady, reliable purpose.

In quiet hours, it is to the old fields my thoughts re-
turn. Pleasant are they, full of daisies, timothy, dewberry
vines, with clumps of black-eyed Susans, Queen Anne's
lace, fleabane, all alight with the glow of yellow candle-
sticks of mullein. Here the butterflies flit from flower to
flower.

These are the resting fields, tranquil, serene. They
have seen crops and crops. Long-tailed plow horses
and big-eared mules have, in other years, tugged and
strained and pulled, making the deep virgin furrows.
But now they rest, gaining strength for some future use.

Happiness lives in such fields, though you will not,
searching, meet her head-on.

Being addicted to the work ethic as Edward was, he was very disappointed that, after a suitable period of recuperation, the Southeast Missouri Printing and Litho Company for whom he had heretofore worked all his working life did not offer him some sort of less strenuous work than the heavy lifting required at the presses. There were many things that he could have done. He even suggested being a salesman on a commission basis, but, no, not that either. I suppose the already-employed salesmen objected.

After trying all avenues and arguments, Edward subsequently went to another local newspaper, *The Bulletin Journal*, and, citing his long experience in the printing business, was awarded a salesman's position on a commission basis. Being employed again did much to rally his self-esteem.

Stephen Leaves Home

Stephen left home slowly and by degrees, which made it easier for all of us.

After graduating from college, he went to teach at the high school at New Athens, Illinois. He came home on weekends. So it seemed he was still at home. After the school year at New Athens, he decided that if he was to climb the salary ladder, he'd better go for his master's degree. He resigned at New Athens to come home and work on his further education, attending Southeast Missouri State University for the 1967–68 year.

In the spring of 1968, he was employed as a teacher in the Sikeston, Missouri, middle school. He commuted from home for a little while before moving into a local apartment, not alone, but with two cats. He had been around cats all his life, and I suppose he thought them as necessary as a chair, table, or bed. He continued teaching at Sikeston Middle School until 1972, finishing his master's degree in summer terms.

Stephen's high-school graduation was such a satisfying affair. It was in Houck Field (the football gridiron). The sun was just setting and already there was a moon in the sky. A soft breeze teased the tassels hanging from the mortarboards. His master's degree graduation, in the Houck Field House, was less pleasant. The packed house was so stifling hot, the speaker who gave about a thirty-second speech got tremendous applause.

All through high school and college, Stephen had dated many pretty girls, but when he met Peggy Matthews of Sikeston, I suppose he thought, "This is it." And it was for twelve years. They were married in front of the fireplace at Peggy's home in Sikeston, 824 N. Ranney, April 21, 1973, twenty-seven years and one day after Stephen's birth. It was Stephen's first marriage, Peggy's second. The happy event of this marriage was the birth of a beautiful granddaughter, Lauren Patricia Mosley.

However, before Lauren's arrival, there was another sadness to endure.

To Keep On Keeping On

With Mama's death, Edward's heart attack, my own period of depression, and the ongoing national unrest, it would have been easy to slip into some "Slough of Despond" or "Dismal Swamp" of inactivity.

Always, though, there seemed to be something to snatch me back to my chosen path, a reflected light somewhere which reminded me of that day I realized God talked in many ways, maybe even sadness. And there was my daily reaffirmation that there is a Divine Order in the universe, and I am somewhere in that order and have a part to play, even though it be as a little cogwheel, the workings of which Grandpa had explained to me when we studied the inside workings of his watch.

Just as William Faulkner's Nobel Prize acceptance speech had influenced me at the beginning of my writing career, here in the forlorn seventies, E.B. White, he of *Charlotte's Web*, was doing the same. He said in his 1971 National Medal for Literature acceptance speech:

> *I have always felt that the first duty of a writer was to ascend — to make flights, carrying others along if they could manage it. . . . To do this takes courage, even a certain conceit. . . . Today with so much of earth damaged and endangered, with so much of life dispiriting or joyless, a writer's courage can easily fail him. I feel this daily . . . but despair is no good — for the writer, for anyone. Only hope can carry us aloft, can keep us afloat . . . and a certain faith that the incredible structure (the earth) . . . cannot end in ruin and disaster. This faith is a writer's faith, for writing itself is an act of faith, nothing else. And it must be the writer, above all others, who keeps it alive — choked with laughter or with pain.*

So I plodded on, especially in my weekly newspaper column, hoping I could assist others to "take flight" as E.B. White had said, even if it would be only a moment or two of thoughtfulness for my reader, as in the following, "Thoughts on Things Everlasting."*

---

* *Southeast Missourian*, September 22, 1987.

My pancake turner got jammed in the cabinet drawer. The plastic handle snapped off sharply, leaving only a bobtailed stub to hold on to. My irritation at myself for so forcefully slamming the drawer and at the pancake turner's ease of breakage were out of proportion to the non-importance or economical disaster of the event. I mumbled and grumbled and spoke sharply to the person I could see in the shiny side of the coffeepot.

I like for my kitchen tools to last and last; rather pride myself on their long lives. The wooden rolling pin, the metal measuring spoons and cups, slaw cutter, potato slicer, are all the same ones I started housekeeping with.

There is in the family, somewhere, a metal can opener that is serving a fifth generation and could go on doing service for years unless some granddaughter on down the line gets sentimental about it, frames it and hangs it up for all to see.

The charm of the can opener, other than its long life, is its simplicity. There is no corkscrew attached, no bottle opener, no puncturing device. It opens tin cans. You couldn't do anything else with it. Oh, maybe throw it at someone in a fit of rage, but we aren't a throwing family. It is the personification of singleness of purpose.

Lasting things with singleness of purpose! How gently they lie on my mind. In an age when it is use and discard, tire of things and throw them away, it is good to see something going on and on and on, even if it is only a can opener.

I think cults and offbeat religions spring up because some people want to try something new, something different, throw out the old, tired basics. The Israelites' flight from Egypt, the wanderings in the wilderness, the Ark of the Covenant, the Exile, Isaiah's and Micah's prophecies, the Birth, Death, Resurrection, and provision for salvation? "They're all so hoary with age," say the impatient, impertinent ones. "Let's get at it some new way, try something different, take our stand on some other rock."

I would like to challenge these "New-wayers" to get at the laws of gravity in some new way, to make the sun rise in the west, to have Venus and Jupiter change places. These things have real long whiskers they could pull and pull on forever to try to reshape or rearrange. How about "As a man thinketh in his heart, so he isn't?" Or "Raise up a child in the way he should go and he'll depart from it every time?" These things would be new but, I'm afraid, as easily demolished as a plastic spoon in a disposal.

Sometimes I have difficulty following the melody of a song when it is played in jazz time. There are all those little musical runs and side roads, but I know the melody is there and how mistaken I'd be to follow a little trill and say, "Hey, I've found the melody."

I thought the following "Tangled Like Tar Baby in a Hedgerow,"* might not choke anyone with laughter as E.B. White suggested, but maybe make them grin:

"You got ter get outer here and see what's goin' on in de thicket," I sez to myself, sez I, reverting to my Uncle Remus dialect in order to lift the day out of wintertime Slough of Mediocrity.

Donning my fur cap and struggling into my rabbit coat (it's mock raccoon really, and getting a litle tight), I went forth to the thicket, ordinarily known to me as the hedgerow, but today was to be up and out of the ordinary.

Halfway down the thicket-hedgerow Brer Rabbit hopped out in front of me. "Good Mawin," sez I. Brer Rabbit ain't sayin' nothin'.

"But," I sez around to myself, sez I, "Brer Rabbit's got ter have a winter home in there." Then, thinking I hadn't seen a rabbit's winter home in a long time, I had an overwhelming desire to find it.

I pushed aside the thick briars of the old fencerow multiflora roses and leaned in. Stooped down. Didn't see anything. Pressed aside some stickery barberry that was once a fence hedge, clean and trimmed, but now grown wild along with the thousand other things. Went forward a few stooped-down steps. I felt something closing behind me. It was the thorny rose canes. They clung tenaciously to my rabbit-raccoon coat.

---

* *Southeast Missourian*, February 19, 1993.

I parted a few more vines and inched forward. These vines didn't have thorns. I got the sinking feeling they were poison oak I saw growing along there last summer. Too late now, if they so be. I went along, half sitting down, like a Russian folk dancer. In fact, I couldn't stand upright now, for the roses and barberry and wild grape vines and possibly poison oak had closed like a Venus's-flytrap above me.

Ever try to turn around, half sitting like a Russian folk dancer, in a fur coat, in a bramble of barberry stickers and thorny roses, with knees past the felicitous manner of rising? And, look, here was something else. Spanish needles. They were aching to be transferred to another location to help populate the Spanish needle world.

My furry cap was far above me now, resting in the embrace of the multiflora rosebushes. Multiflora rosebushes? Hadn't I read they were bull-proof?

"You done got yoself 'tached to a Tar Baby," I sez, sez I. I tried to think of how Brer Rabbit had pried himself loose from the Tar Baby, but my recollection powers were as tangled as my arms, legs, torso, hair, and emotions. I smelled blood, too. I forgot all about Brer Rabbit's winter home. The idea was to get out of there.

"Now what I'll have to do is get down low and practically crawl out of here," I said, in my sane, no-nonsense Midwestern voice.

Back home, straggled and draggled and bloody, too, I hastened to find the Uncle Remus book and reread how Brer Rabbit had loosened himself from the Tar Baby. He didn't. Uncle Remus left him there, stuck-up, offering only that there was a rumor, "Some say Jedge B'ar came 'long en loosed im — some say he didn't."

There is some sort of little moral to my adventure, just as Uncle Remus' stories sometimes have a moral. I had no more business disturbing Brer Rabbit's winter home than he did mine.

But it wasn't a mundane day. I got out by myself without any Brer Passerby coming to loosen me, or Brer Policeman coming to read me my rights.

The sad seventies seemed relentless. My beloved pet cat, Black Silk, died. She was soft, cuddly, and loving. She could speak to me in "sign" language. Whenever I started down the sidewalk, keys in hand to go to town, she would reach a paw out in front of my ankles to indicate she didn't want me to go away. When curled up in my lap, lying beside me on the couch, or snoozing on my typewriter table while I typed, if I spoke loudly to someone in another room, she would instantly reach up a soft paw and place it over my mouth as if to say, "Hush."

I wrapped her in one of those many embroidered pillowcases I had made, choosing a pretty one, and buried her under a cedar tree in the backyard. It was a graveyard for all our dead pets.

Worse than that, my sister Lou's husband, Earl, died. Edward was in the hospital at the time with phlebitis. Stephen stayed with Edward, while only Peggy and I went to the funeral. At the time, Lucille had a broken arm and was in much pain. Everything seemed askew.

Then came a chilling series of entries in my journal:

February 2, 1974
Edward had bloody stool. Called Dr. Wilson. Entered hospital at 11:00. No hemorrhoids. No growth in rectum. Possibly diverticulitis.

February 8, 1974
Edward's trouble diagnosed as diverticulitis.

May 16, 1974
Edward in hospital for sigmoidoscopy. Spastic colon in Dr. Wilson's opinion.

May 20, 1974
Edward still in hospital. Stomach x-ray, and "air blown" x-ray to follow.

May 20, 1974
Dr. Shoss, after the "air blown" x-ray, said there was a possible thickening of tissue where small intestine enters large intestine.
Dr. Wilson prescribed a stronger tranquilizer. No exploratory surgery was recommended. We did not suggest one.

August 14, 1974
   Edward to hospital again for follow-up on x-ray to see if any change had occurred.

February 18, 1975
   Took Edward to hospital about noon.

February 20, 1975
   Entered hospital to visit with Edward. His chin was quivering. I asked what the trouble was. Not being able to answer, Mrs. Adams, the nurse, trying to make it easy said, "Oh, they found a little spot on his liver."

   When Dr. Wilson arrived, he spoke to me in the hallway of the hospital, confirming a cancer in the intestine had traveled to the liver. An office visit to Dr. Wilson, later that day, determined that surgery was advised.

February 26, 1975
   Edward will have surgery today at 1:00 PM. Operation was over by 2:15.
   Dr. Charles McGinty (surgeon) spoke to me at end of hall near ICU. He said the right colon was cancerous and that the liver was affected. Now we will think in terms of chemotherapy.

   Before healing from the original surgery, another operation had to be made since the first stitches had burst open. The second operation was performed by Drs. Melvin Kasten and Bob Hunt, Dr. McGinty being away during the emergency.
   There was a long period before the incision healed. I took Edward to Dr. McGinty's office for the dressings until he thought I could manage. He gave me the necessary surgical scissors, dressings, tape, etc.

May 7, 1975
   Edward got his first treatment of floura-urasil this AM, an injection in the arm. The plan is to give a series of treatments, once a week at Doctor Wilson's office, preceded by a blood check at Lovinggood's laboratory the day before. Then skip a week or two. From then on it will

be weekly visits to the lab to check on Edward's red and white blood cells. If the count is suitable, it will be off to the doctor's office for another injection.

At one time, it looked as if the treatments might work, at least for a long time. Dr. McGinty once said, "Ed, I see no reason why you can't live as long as you want to put up with these treatments."

It was a great statement to lift our spirits, at least for a little while. The treatments, thankfully, did not make Edward sick, but at length he could tell he was getting weaker and weaker.

On a bitter, deep-snow and icy day, Jan. 29, 1977, he died at Southeast Missouri Hospital. Stephen and I were both present. He is buried at Memorial Park Cemetery, Cape Girardeau, Missouri.

The Deep Forest Award

The decade moved on toward its close. It wasn't the best of the century. But there were some bright spots. In 1974, the American Association of University Women, Missouri division, sponsored a Festival for Missouri women in the arts. My region's center was nearby Jackson, Missouri. There were various awards to be given for the visual and performing arts, including writing. I entered a short-story contest.

Still being affected by my love for *The Wind in the Willows*, I wrote a story with anthropomorphized animals as the characters, with no other names than Rabbit, Beaver, Chuck, Squirrel, Mr. and Mrs. Raccoon, Head Frog and the Lesser Frogs, Little Mocker (a mockingbird), and the Keeper of All Creatures (God). There were many meadow mice to whom I did give names, usually those of whom I knew and loved—Lauren, Margaret, Gladys, Thurman, Stephen, etc.

Since acronyms were in such vogue, I entitled the story, "The DFRBGM Award." It won first prize regionally, was sent on for state competition where it again won first place. Hummm, I thought, it must be fairly good. So off it went to *Cricket* magazine. The editors there liked, bought, and published it. The sensible editors changed the title to "The Deep Forest Award," DFRBGM being so unpronounceable. Humm, I thought again. Maybe I could extend this story to book length. So during the dreary days of the late seventies, I mentally immersed myself in the pleasant setting of a deep forest bordered by a grassy meadow through which ran a rustling brook. Hence, DFGMRB.

The lovable characters of this community were always looking out for each other and very conscious of The Keeper Of All Creatures.

During the days of Edward's chemotherapy and endless lab trips, I could mentally enter the deep forest or grassy meadow for a few hours of escape from what I knew was coming. I could, for a few precious moments, identify with Mrs. Raccoon, one of the main characters, as I placed her high up in the white oak tree, looking out of her little round doorway and seeing:

> *The lowering sun was making golden threads of long floating spiderwebs. Mrs. Raccoon watched them lodge on the tree branches, wild asters, stumps, brambles, and briars. They seemed to be weaving an intricate protective golden web around them all. And inside the web was a roseate glow from end-of-day sunshine, livened by shouts of merriment from those beginning to mix the scrabbledobies, those arranging the pawpaws in attractive little stacks, and those just talking over the happenings of the day. She looked in the direction of the now abandoned and uncovered Little Toy Computer. Rays from the setting sun caught and hung on a brass corner. One corner seemed to send a special red-gold beam right up to where she was sitting. No matter which way she turned her head it was there, almost as if it had her trapped. She knew, of course, that she could go back farther into the room, or even down the tree and get out of it, but she rather liked the warmth and glow and the airy, graceful feeling of being held up by a sunbeam that had no substance.*
>
> *Such a feeling reminded Mrs. Raccoon of the time she had tried so hard to explain the Keeper of All Creatures to little Mocker; how He did not keep anyone harshly chained, but that His chain, if anything, was more like warm sunbeams linking His creatures together.*
>
> *At that moment the sunbeam from the computer almost blinded her. Then, suddenly it went away. No matter how she turned, twisted, or stretched, she could*

not get it back. She looked at the computer in a thought-
ful, puzzled sort of way. Of course, she could see that
shadows were gathering down below, but it was almost
as if the computer had given her a big parting wink.

From somewhere down deep inside, a thought began
to take shape. She remembered she had also told Little
Mocker that although no one ever saw the Keeper, she
sometimes felt as if she had seen where He had just been.

Mrs. Raccoon trembled with mingled awe and
reverence. She looked again at the computer. Her heart
swelled. Her eyes gleamed. "Surely I've seen where the
Keeper has just been and He left a message!" she whis-
pered.*

With this passage, I was trying to recreate a feeling in the
reader somewhat like I had experienced that long-ago afternoon
when the carbide light reflector shone in my eyes and the feeling I
had that I was in God's presence.

The resulting book was *The Deep Forest Award*, published by
Crossway Books in America and as *Little Mocker's Great Adventure*
in the United Kingdom. It was also put on tape by the Christian
Blind Mission International for the reading-impaired, and subsequently was a C.S. Lewis silver medal winner.

Home Improvements

During the years of Edward's sickness, things around our
premises began to look shabby. A sort of gray pall seemed to
descend and cling to everything. It was not our first priority to
remove it.

A few months after Edward's death, I knew that if I didn't do
some needful things, I might not have the nerve later. So, from
time to time, there came a new stove, a new refrigerator, washer
and dryer, new kitchen linoleum, new green carpet all over the
downstairs rooms, a new car, a new trellised privacy fence at the
rear of our lot, and many other little things. One spring thereafter,
I went to visit some friends, the Harold Aldrich family. They occu-

---

* *The Deep Forest Award*, Crossway Books, 1985.

pied, at that time, the old Stacy farm, the farm that adjoined ours way back in the early part of the century. The visit was unplanned. My sisters and I were just driving by, crossing and recrossing old familiar roads. When we came to the Aldrich home, it was like stepping into a fairyland. There was the same old house, the same old bell mounted on a pole that called countless workers from the fields, but now the place, unknown to us, had become a show spot of the National Iris Society. At the time of this visit there were great beds and rows of the most beautiful blooming irises, and overhead soared a myriad of purple martins, making their most happy chuckling sounds. I could hardly wait to get home to establish my own "fairyland of irises and purple martins."

Two seasons later, I had a great curving bed of colorful irises, all secured and planted by myself. At the end of the row was a birdbath, and overhead soared purple martins.

When the martin house was put up, I wondered if any of the lovable birds would come. The first spring after its erection, I walked out the back walk one day and there on the lower porch of the house were two little dark-colored birds huddled together. It was still cold, last of March. I knew that if I could just see their forked tails, I'd know they were martins, but I didn't want to scare them away for fear they wouldn't come back. I stood there for a long time in the cold. When they did fly away, I saw their forked tails. I've had flocks of the cheerful martins ever since.

Curving bed of irises
at the home of Jean Bell Mosley

Thereafter I took a consuming interest in my backyard. Forsythia, mock orange, calacanthus, bush honeysuckle, old-fashioned roses, tiger lilies, phlox, daylilies, peonies, clematis, rudbeckia, sundrops, columbine, daisies, hollyhocks took their places. With annuals sown here and there, the premises became a mecca for honeybees, bumblebees, butterflies, hummingbirds, and all manner of beetles and bugs that liked flowers too. I could spend hours sitting way back, almost hidden in the blooming mock orange, inhaling the fragrance and listening to the bumblebees, some of whose wings would brush my cheeks. I never feared them, nor they me. Many times a cardinal would be nesting in the same bush, and we were all just co-existing like, shall I say, "a peaceable kingdom"?

I encouraged the rabbits and squirrels, the tortoises, any manner of wildlife, to take up residence. Didn't even mind a little garter snake and her offpsring, in spite of my early acquaintance with snakes. Once in a while a possum or 'coon would waddle through the backyard.

The birds came, all of them native to our region, and a few which were not. The big swallowtails — tiger, zebra, etc., came. It was all almost enough to make me withdraw from society and live in my own little world, but not quite.

Days that saw a rabbit sitting on my porch, a butterfly alighting on a sleeping kitten, a squirrel looping downward from a high wire, yet holding on to let another squirrel pass, made for big bold entries in my journals.

Off to California

Since Lou and I had both lost our husbands during the 1970s, our Aunt Nellie who lived in Walnut Creek, California, thought it would be good for us to come west for a visit.

Aunt Nellie had married our mother's brother, Thurman Casey. Uncle Thurman had migrated to California some time in the late 1920s. He had purchased a large English walnut ranch, made other wise investments, and became wealthy, although by the time of our visit, Uncle Thurman was dead.

Lou and I departed on June 5, 1977, from the St. Louis airport on a TWA Jet.

I noticed that on our rapid incline, Lou was leaning back with eyes closed. I didn't know if she was having a "scene" of going to the moon or praying for a safe journey.

This was my first airplane ride, and I enjoyed it very much since I had a window seat and could see the fields, canyons, and mountains I was flying over.

A cousin by marriage, Paul O'Bannon, met us at the San Francisco airport and took us eastward to Aunt Nellie's home. California was in the middle of a drought, and I was not impressed at all by the countryside.

By the time of our visit, the ranch home had been remodeled and a lot next door had been donated to what became the location of the beautiful Thurman Casey Memorial Library. It was a relatively new building at the time of our visit. Prominently displayed in a glass case were my books, *The Mockingbird Piano*, *Wide Meadows*, and *The Crosses at Zarin*, with the notation that they had been written by Thurman Casey's niece. I was treated royally.

One day during our two-week visit, Cousin Paul came to take us to see the sights of San Francisco. We ate at Fisherman's Wharf, went down the crooked Lombardo Street, toured China Town, saw but didn't ride the trolley cars. I walked almost halfway across the Golden Gate Bridge. Would have gone farther, but it was a chilly, misty day. At the Japanese Gardens, we, surprisingly, saw my friends from Cape Girardeau, Dr. and Mrs. Raymond Ritter.

We returned to Walnut Creek by a different route, because Paul wanted to show us as much of the country as he could. I saw houses built on what looked like little shelves high up on steep mountains and wondered why anyone would want to live up there. I wondered more some years later when the horrible California fires came, the terrible mudslides, and the inevitable earthquakes. I supposed Californians wondered why we Missourians would want to live in Tornado Alley, as the Mississippi Valley is known.

Aunt Nellie had orange trees in her yard, and each morning I could go out and pick myself a fresh orange for breakfast. She also had a beautiful long-haired dog named Red. She loved and doted on that dog. In her letters to us, she was always writing about Red and sending pictures of him. While visiting, she would let me take him on early morning walks around a couple of blocks. Once, oh trembling heart, he somehow slipped his leash and was headed for a busy highway. I cringed, prayed, grew faint, called softly, walked slowly, but he managed to keep two steps ahead of me. After excruciating eons it seemed, he stopped long enough to sniff at some likely looking molehills. I lunged forward and got a good strong bodyhold on that dog. I never took Red for another walk, complaining of one thing or another—heat, headache, whatever I could think of.

There was a huge live oak tree just outside Aunt Nellie's kitchen door. One afternoon, sitting beneath it, the hot winds (must have been Santa Ana winds) in my face, I thought for a moment I was re-experiencing that touch of despression I had had in Mobile. What was it, I wondered? Some provincial Missourian who couldn't stand other atmospheres?

Aunt Nellie had been good to us, but I was so glad to get on that TWA jet and head for St. Louis.

We had to fly above the clouds coming back home and circle up through Iowa and down. Stephen met us at the airport. He wanted to know if I wanted to stay in St. Louis overnight. "No, let's go home," I said without hesitation.

Lauren's Arrival

Some of my journal entries in 1978 speak for themselves.

January 16, 1978
Fourteen inches of snow and still snowing.

January 25, 1978
Snowing again, serious business-like snow, as if it meant to reach the eaves by twilight.

February 9, 1978
Made sourdough bread today.

February 25, 1978
Stephen called and said, "Hello, Grandma," which was his way of telling me he and Peggy were going to have a baby!

March 1, 1978
Stephen and Peggy up today for celebration dinner of the coming event in September.

April 15, 1978
Foeste's planted Bradford pear tree, north side of triple windows, and pin oak in north front yard.

April 18, 1978
Church Circle at my house.

April 19, 1978
   The park workers are cutting down the dead maple overhanging my mailbox.

May 3, 1978
   Won first prize in State GFWC contest for crocheted white afghan.

May 14, 1978
   Doctoring for poison ivy.

June 26, 1978
   Working on baby jacket and cap.

July 19, 1978
   Arthur Gordon, editor of Guideposts *called from New York. Invited me to the annual* Guideposts *workshop at Rye, N.Y., on Long Island Sound for last week in September. Said Marjorie Holmes, Catherine Marshall, Elizabeth and John Sherrill, and Norman Vincent Peale and his wife Ruth would be there. I told him I had not entered the contest, but he said he'd put my recently purchased "Thanksgiving Prayers" in the hopper for it and that it was a foregone conclusion it would be a winner. Said he wanted me to come to "add class" to the 14 other writers who would be there! (Such flattery.) I told him my first grandchild's expected arrival would be about that week and I didn't want to be away for that event, but that I'd get in touch with him later.*

August 1, 1978
   First day of bagged trash collected at the curb by the city.

August 21, 1978
   Called Mr. Gordon at Guideposts *and told him I would come. I thought it would be good for my career, but worried still that I'd be gone when the baby arrived.*

September 9, 1978
   Dan Cotner and I received Dingledein Award for outstanding accomplishments in music and writing.

September 18, 1978
  Plane tickets to New York arrived today. Still jittery about missing baby's arrival.

September 22, 1978
  Lauren Patricia Mosley arrived at 3:36 PM. Steve called to say Peggy had gone to hospital. I dropped everything and left for Sikeston immediately. She was already in this world when I arrived. Cute, cute, cute! Little toes, turned-up nose, little red, wrinkled bit of humanity, destined to become Miss America, no doubt.

So Lauren cooperated right from the beginning, arriving before I was to depart for New York two days later.

Guideposts magazine says of itself, "[It is] a practical guide to successful living, is a monthly inspirational, interfaith, nonprofit publication written by people from all walks of life. Its articles present tested methods for developing courage, strength, and positive attitudes through faith in God."

All walks of life. That includes me, I thought. I walk a path too, one that has led me to stop at moments and mentally shout, "Oh, God, how great is life. Thank you for letting me find joy along the way."

The week at the *Guideposts* workshop was a major joy along the way. Although I had been to "The Big Easy" and "The City by the Bay," I had had someone along. This trip to "The Big Apple," alone, seemed a big undertaking. *Guideposts* had said they would meet me at LaGuardia airport, just tell them what I would be wearing. What I would be wearing! A hundred other people may be wearing the dark red James Kenrob knit suit that I would be wearing. But there, right at the end of the plane's stairway, was a representative holding up a big placard on a long pole that said, "Guideposts."

The trip had been pleasant. Again I had a window seat, and as the "Big Apple's" skyscrapers loomed ahead, at one point I looked down and there right below me was my old friend, the Statue of Liberty. Same old statue I had seen in my Loughboro history books, had written stories about, had drawn pictures of, had memorized Emma Lazarus' inscription on it. My feelings at that moment must have been of some kin to those coming through Ellis Island in the early years.

The workshop, or retreat as some choose to call it, was held in what is known as the Wainwright Mansion on Long Island. Surrounded by a wooded area, the rear and spacious lawn slopes down to the sound.

At the far southern part of the Sound, which is visible from this spacious rear lawn, sailboats anchor for the night. At sunset, the sails turn pinkish-red, and if any of us happened to be on the lawn or walking along the shore, we'd almost spontaneously do a harmonious rendition of "Red Sails in the Sunset" or even a solo if alone.

Aside from the lectures and work sessions, we had free time to use as we wanted, walking about the estate, sitting in little groups discussing our life situations, praying together either aloud or silently. There was a lot of love floating around. By the middle of the week, one really felt close to others.

Of the fifteen admitted to the workshop that year, thirteen of them were women. In addition to these fifteen, four or five various editors from *Guideposts* were there all the time. Because of the beauty and serenity of the place, I felt it more of a retreat than a workshop.

Jean Bell Mosley at the Guideposts *workshop, Rye, New York, watching "Red Sails in the Sunset," Long Island Sound*

The mansion is a large three-storey affair. I don't know how many rooms it has. There is the main section, with a wide hallway leading through from front to back with a wing on each side. Each wing, among other things, has a garden room which looks out on the Sound. It was built by General Jonathan M. Wainwright. This is not the Wainwright of Pacific fame, but Jonathan Mayhew Wainwright, a first cousin of Jonathan B. Wainwright. He was billeted in France in World War I and admired his residence there so much that he vowed if he ever got back home he would build another mansion just like it. He did. And I think that he could not have found a lovelier spot.

We had to choose our flight time so that we would arrive at either LaGuardia or Kennedy Airports in time to get to Rye for the 7:00 dinner, which would be our first session.

If arrivals were anywhere close together, a station wagon waited until it was filled, and then another would take its place. Frank Elam from Arkansas and I were the last ones in to fill one station wagon, so I didn't have to wait at the airport for anyone else, like some had to.

There were seven of us in the station wagon, plus all our luggage, so we were cozy. Before we'd gone ten miles, we were all on a first-name basis.

Rye is only about twenty miles from LaGuardia, so it wasn't long before we were turning in through some big stone gates that led to the mansion.

Mrs. Wainwright outlived her husband, and after his death she donated the house and grounds to be used as a Center for Human Development.

All meals were served buffet style, with the food set up on long tables in the wide hallway. We formed a circle and held hands for the blessing. Each time a different person gave the blessing.

After dinner and about a fifteen-minute break, we went to the lounge for an official welcome and workshop instructions. Sometime as we were assembling, Dr. Peale and his wife Ruth came in, as did Arthur Gordon and his wife. Arthur Gordon was, at that time, editorial director of the *Guideposts* magazine.

Dr. Peale and his wife went around to each one, shook hands, and talked briefly.

Van Varner, Senior Staff Editor, introduced himself and said that he was to be our "Den Mother." He was one of the most affable and quick-witted persons I have ever met. He asked each

of us to introduce ourselves and give just a few personal facts—
where we were from, our family, and something about our writing
careers. Then he officially introduced Ruth and Norman Vincent
Peale. Both spoke to us, giving the history and aims of *Guideposts*.

Dr. Peale said that writing in the *Guideposts* style was not easy,
which puffed all of us up a little, for we wouldn't have been there
unless we had written for *Guideposts*.

The general format of each day was this: A big brass gong at
the foot of a long, winding staircase was sounded about an hour
before breakfast. Breakfast was at 8:30. At 9:30 we gathered in the
lounge for a general workshop assembly. At 11:15 we gathered for
smaller workshop sessions wherein we criticized manuscripts. At
1:00 we had lunch and then free time until 4:00. I spent most of
this free time walking the grounds or just sitting down by the water. Sometimes someone would join me. Lots of others spent their
time reading and studying the manuscripts to be discussed the
next day. I found that I did this better in the early morning hours
before anyone else was up. I'd creep out of bed, get to the bathroom, dress, and go to the music room for my study. I don't know
how many I awakened at what they must have considered the
middle of the night. But then I had to put up with inconveniences,

Authors Catherine Marshall and Jean Bell Mosley

194

too. We lived dormitory style. I shared one huge bedroom with four other ladies, and the one in the bed next to mine was from Hawaii and was a chain smoker.

At 4:00 PM some editor from *Guideposts* would speak to us on some facet of writing. The first 4:00 PM general meeting was conducted by Arthur Gordon, the second by Catherine Marshall. We knew that she would be there, so we ladies decided to dress in our long dresses for the occasion, only to find Catherine was dressed in a street-length, shirtwaist pink crepe de chine. Each one of us got to chat briefly with Catherine and have our picture taken with her.

One evening as I entered the dining room, Marjorie Holmes arose from her seat and came, almost running, to hug me. "Oh, Jean Bell Mosley, I've wanted to meet you for so long."It was exactly what I was going to say to her. She said that she had once written me a fan letter and that I had so graciously replied. My, I was glad I'd answered that letter! To be so greeted and hugged by Marjorie in front of all the others set me up a little in the eyes of others. (Never in the "scenes" Lou and I had, did I ever have one like this.)

As always, in such glittering moments, I thought of the little girl who went after dark to close the henhouse door, or at 4:00 PM summertime, riding Old Nell the mare up some Ozark mountainside to find the cows and bring them home, and, most especially, walking home from school when I felt such a sweet nearness to God.

It was a wonderful week, and when I got back home, there was little, one-week-old Lauren, lying in her yellow crib, ready to be loved by Grandma.

Jean Bell Mosley and granddaughter Lauren Patricia Mosley

1980–1990

Lauren's Early Years

Perhaps Lauren's earliest memories of me will be entwined with small scraps of silk, calico, lace, and little houses.

Being a saver of leftovers from just about everything that comes into my house, there is always a generous supply of snippets and shells and silvery bells.

Our favorite pastime on Saturdays when she would come to visit with me would be the making of little sachets. We would pull out the whole contents of the scrap-filled cedar chest, and she would pick and choose the little pieces she liked best. At first we would cut out single little circles of lace, net, calico, or silk, put a certain amount of dried potpourri in the center, gather up the edges of the fabric, tie a ribbon around it, thus making a squat little sack of fragrance. We delighted in setting them all in a row on some window sill.

As she grew older, we progressed to "little pillows," as she called them. We would cut out two sides of circles, squares, or heart-shaped pieces of fabric, sew them together, leaving an opening, of course, and stuff them with dacron or cotton dabbed with a generous amount of floral scented oils. Our favorite was violet.

Later came lace-edged ones, embroidered ones, and trimmings of whatever we could think of.

In my early years, Mama and Grandma spent hours with me making doll dresses out of such saved scraps. By Lauren's time, the beginning of the Cabbage Patch dolls era, dolls came already dressed in such fancy and beautiful dresses, one didn't think of making them wardrobes of leftover scraps. It was also the era of the preprinted fabric for making stuffed dolls, animals, etc. Lauren did like these, especially a stuffed doll named Strawberry Shortcake. In a tussel with a playmate, the head of Strawberry Shortcake was pulled off. Stephen, drying Lauren's tears, said something like, "Don't cry. Grandma will fix it." So I did, wondering if, for Lauren, I had been catapulted into the region of being the one who could fix everything.

One Christmas we decided to start a little village, the buildings to be made of cardboard houses such as milk cartons or even smaller boxes. We would cover these with calico and cut gables, and would glue on a roof, usually of cardboard-backed red felt. Around the edges of the roofs we would "freeze" on "icicles" of white edgings with a hot-glue gun.

We made several houses, a school, log cabin, store, and a church. When we came to the church I said, "Now, Lauren, pick out the cloth we'll use for the church." I was interested to see what she would choose.

The scraps were searched through and through, over and over, and finally she said, "This." It was a small length of pale satin, the most elegant scrap in the whole bunch. It was as if she had some reason to believe that a church should be of the finest material. It pleased me.

We made stained-glass windows for the church with colored sequins, a bell tower with a tiny bell suspended in it, and a cross of toothpicks was dipped in gold paint and glued to the roof of the bell tower.

Some of our later houses at other Christmases grew more sophisticated. They had porches, wings, ells, balconies, and even dormer windows. We added little figures of humans, purchased from Woolworth's, to scatter around the holiday village.

The village came into everyday prominence during the holidays. At other times the houses rested on a long shelf in what I call my "overrun" room.

In suitable weather we took nature walks in the park, always carrying a basket to fill with whatever we found to be interesting—bird feathers, oak balls, hedge apples, seed pods, hickory nuts, persimmons, acorns, a pretty leaf. In springtime we might sit down in a patch of clover and make clover bracelets or necklaces.

Lots of times we walked alongside the creek looking for the muskrat. Sometimes I'd ask her to tell me a story and *The Velveteen Rabbit* would take up our whole walk.

When Stephen was little, he would sit for long stretches at a time while I read to him all the old childrens' classics. But Lauren had little patience for this. She was an "on-the-move" child.

When Lauren was a little older she often brought along a little girlfriend to visit. They delighted in going upstairs, which we often referred to as the attic, and dressing up in old garments to come down and let us guess who they were trying to be. It was apparent that Lauren had a talent for putting things together with a flair and modeling them in a professional, different-poses manner.

I tried to make some little dresses for Lauren, remembering how much I loved the dresses Mama made for me, but was never very successful, her not being around every day for me to fit. However, I did make her an "official" Little Orphan Annie red dress with white collars and cuffs, which was quite a success. I bought a curly red wig, and she made a cute little Annie.

Lauren loved to come to Grandma's, I think, primarily, to eat some of my wheat germ, yeast-raised bread. She would eat great buttered slices of it, except the crusts. She was here for every birthday, at which she would light a candle her father had received from his kindergarten teacher one year — yes, the one who had called him Edward. The candle is of pink wax with "Happy Birthday" on it in silver. We light it for everyone's birthday, and I think that it still has half a century to go.

In 1985 my book *The Deep Forest Award* was published. Jane Stacy, Southeast Missouri State University University Alumni Director, hosted an autographing party for me at the University President's home. Since the book was dedicated to Lauren, some of my friends wanted her to autograph it, too, under her name, so she dutifully sat at the table with me, dressed in a little velvet dress and printed LAUREN under her name, until she had had enough and went in the direction of cookies and punch.

I often wondered if Lauren, now a young lady,

Lauren Patricia Mosley
(Junior year at Drury College in
Springfield, Missouri)

198

ever remembered those early years at Grandma's. A story she wrote for a creative-writing experience in an English class set my mind at rest. Presented to me at Christmas 1995, it reads:

Homemade Love

"Hello, come in, how is everybody? Oh, there's my favorite granddaughter!" I then get a big hug from Grandma Mosley. Grandma Mosley's house is such a neat place to visit. This house holds old memories, and new memories are made every time I visit.

Grandma Mosley's house is red brick with white shutters and has window boxes full of bright flowers. This is the house where my dad grew up, and the big oak trees in the yard give hints of its age. The sidewalk to the back door is lined on both sides with daylilies, hollyhocks, and petunias. These flowers bloom every spring, and occasionally new ones will pop up.

On the back porch is a swing hanging from the ceiling. Grandma Mosley starts each day by drinking her coffee and watching the purple martins and wrens from this squeaky seat.

There are three cowbells hanging on the outside door. These are the doorbells. I give them a push and they send out their loud "clangs." Before waiting for an answer, I walk into the kitchen. The kitchen smells like homemade bread. There is always something baking in the oven. I look through the clear oven window and see a green-bean casserole today. On the counter is a small glass bowl of black olives – my favorite.

The kitchen leads directly to the dining room which is always dressed for the occasion. On the four-place, rectangular-shaped table is a homemade tablecloth and white and blue dishes. These dishes must be very old because I usually get warned to "Be careful with those," when I clear the table.

Entering the living room is like entering a tiny world of Christmas. Around that time of year, Grandma Mosley sets out our Christmas Village. These are houses, stores, and buildings made out of milk cartons and other boxes covered with fabric. We worked long and hard collecting boxes and gluing and cutting one year to make this original display. We gathered milk cartons and cut off their tops to glue on Kleenex boxes for roofs, and no one could ever guess that under that bright red material were such insignificant things.

Besides these numerous adornments, the living room also holds a couch, a TV (which is usually tuned to a basketball game), and three comfortable chairs. On the far shelf are her books. The Mockingbird Piano, The Deep Forest Award, Seeds on the Wind *are just a few that she wrote herself. Small knicknacks are placed throughout the house. Most of them represent characters in her books. Crystal mice, raccoons, frogs, and owls each carry their own story, and Grandma Mosley can tell about each one.*

The back room probably holds the most memories for me. This is Grandma Mosley's writing room. It is a simple place: a small table with a typewriter and dictionary, a larger table with all sorts of papers and notes.

There is a sewing machine, a shelf of books, and a file cabinet. On the wall are plaques representing many of my grandmother's achievements and also some original illustrations from her stories and books.

When I was younger, every time I visited, Grandma would help me make a "craft." Sometimes we sewed a fancy pillow. Sometimes we cut out pictures and made a book, and sometimes we made dolls. "Not too much glue, Lauren; it will never dry." Grandma sewed and I threaded the needle. We were a team. Neither of us had ever seen anything prettier than what we made! There is one place in the house that Grandma frowns upon when I enter. "Oh, don't go up there and look at my mess!" But I always do. In the doorway are pencil marks keeping track of my growth. They get closer together as I get older, and I still have trouble believing I was so short.

The steps to the attic are lined with magazines. "One of these days you're going to break your legs trying to get up those steps." Nah, plenty of room. The attic is full of Dad's old toys, baseball uniforms, furniture, and everything else that is not fitting for downstairs. It

*has a certain smell of old clothes and holiday decorations
not used anymore. In the summer it is an oven, in the
winter, a freezer. I never spend much time in the attic,
but I can always discover tokens of times past such as a
funny old shirt or a musty book.*

*Back down the stairs in the dining room, the musty
smell is gone and again the scent of bread fills the air.
The cuckoo pops out of its clock house and gives its
hourly call. The wall from which it hangs is pale green.*

*Every time I go to Grandma's house, I hear a new
story, find an unusual treasure, and gobble up lots of
delicious food. This house tells a continuous story of my
grandmother and her countless accomplishments.*

"Come back and see me soon, OK?"

"You promise to make bread?" I ask with a grin.

"Well, I guess I could do that," she replies.

*She watches me as I disappear down her flower-
bordered sidewalk. I'll be back in no time.*

Last Visit to the Old Farmhouse

Nearly every year my sisters and I, after we had established
our own homes, would set aside a day to drive down the crooked,
woodsy road to the farmhouse where we were reared.

A last visit was in 1980. Tuesday, October 14, to be exact. It
says so in my daily journal.

The house, occupied by several families after we left, had, by
that October visit, been vacant for some time and seemed lonesome, but the river, fields, mountains, and meadows were still
there, unchanged.

October was at its best that year. Had we known it was to be
our last time to open the familiar door, climb the stairs, and enter
our old bedroom, we wouldn't have been so happy as we were.

The last tenant had secured carpet samples from some store,
and the floor of our bedroom, never carpeted while we were there,
was completely covered with blocks of colorful, deep-piled carpet
samples, tacked together so that it looked like wall to wall carpet-
ing.

Simms Mountain

The only piece of furniture was a rocking chair someone had left. Curtis, Lillian's husband, was with us, as well as his dog, Cape, so named because he had been secured in Cape Girardeau.

We let Curtis occupy the chair. Cape lay at his feet. Lillian, Lou, and I sat on the colorful floor where we could look out the window that provided a view of the barn, the meadow, the sugar-maple grove. Through a fringe of bordering trees we had glimpses of the river. Beyond the river and another field, the sides of Simms Mountain rose up like a carnival of gypsies in all their fall finery. The two, sky-pointing sour gum trees that marked a legal corner of the farm, and which would have been brilliant crimson at this time, were gone, but we could see more little scarlet gum trees taking their place at the edge of the mountain. High-flying Monarch butterflies fluttered southward in the fantastically brilliant blue sky. There were cows in the meadow which some current neighbor had rented for pasture.

We had brought a basket lunch and decided to eat it right there where the view was better than that from the kitchen. Before we laid a cloth on the carpet, we took turns saying prayers. I can't remember the words of our prayers, but they had to do with thankfulness for the time we had lived there, the guidance we were given, and the goodness and mercy that had followed us. I wanted to vocally end my prayer with, "Thank you, God, for letting me see that carbide light and the 'light' that followed," but only God and I would have known what I meant, so I whispered it inwardly.

"The dresser was there," Lillian said, pointing to the south wall of the room.

"For a while," Lou responded. "Before that, it was over there." She pointed to another wall. "I remember well, because that is where I put the boxed valentine that Leemon gave me one year." Big boxed valentines were the height of expressed sentiment then. They cost a mighty fifty cents.

"And I remember that spot so well," I told them, pointing to a place on the ceiling above the door to our room.

"Why?" came concerted, puzzled questions. Even Cape seemed to raise a lazy eyebrow.

It did seem an unlikely spot to be remembered. I tried to explain.

The lamplight from Mama's and Dad's room, across the upstairs hallway, by some mysterious architectural happenstance, threw a funnel-shaped pattern there on our ceiling, after our lamplight had been blown out. I went to sleep looking at that funnel-shaped light because it brought such a safe and comfortable feeling that all was well. Mama and Dad were just across the hall, "funneling" their love to us.

Reflected light has played such a big part in my life. I once read a devotional about reflected light. The writer told about a discarded copper skillet that hung from a nail near a basement window. When the sun's rays struck a certain spot on the skillet, it reflected a light into a dark corner where lay some old, shriveling potatoes. This meager light caused the potatoes to sprout, the lesson being that if we can only reflect a little light we may bring new life to something.

As we munched away at our sandwiches, we recalled the straw ticks and feather beds and handmade quilts, unbleached muslin-sheets that had a seam down the middle. If two slept together, as Lou and I did, one had better stay on her side of the seam, unless it was a cold winter night. Lillian had a bed to herself. "Right over there," she said, pointing to the exact site of her bed that never changed. Sometimes Lou and I moved our bed to a different spot just to make something new that didn't cost anything.

"Remember our scenes?" I asked Lou.

Lou gave me a frowning glance as if I had stumbled into some secret area. "Or Grandma's passage-of-time quilt?" she hurried to respond, slamming the door on what she must have still thought was our own private territory.

At the time of our "scenes," we didn't know fancier and more precise words and phrases such as "fantasizing" or "conjuring up" of mental visions. Perhaps we were precursors of Thurber's Walter Mitty.

Where we came up with the word "scenes," who knows?

After we had said our nightly prayer and before falling asleep, we would imagine ourselves to be something we weren't, always doing something gloriously satisfying and stunning. One of my favorite "scenes" was being at a huge church-meeting somewhere, always someplace strange to me. The pianist had failed to appear and the minister had asked if there was anyone in the congregation who could play the piano. I would modestly arise, walk to the piano and play it so beautifully the congregation would be in tears. In reality I could barely manage "The Old Rugged Cross" and the aforementioned "The Trail of the Lonesome Pine." There was a variation on this theme. Sometimes the soloist would be absent and I would substitute. I've always been told that I can't sound the true notes, but do well in the cracks between the notes.

Lou's favorite would be to drive a hitch of ten horses around the courthouse square at Farmington while onlookers applauded, especially Leemon.

We often shared with each other what our "scenes" had been, and there was always mutual admiration of our mental inventions.

We never accomplished any of the grand things we imagined, but we did learn the efficacy of imagination. Lou became somewhat of an interior decorator, imagining what an empty room would look like if a chair was placed there, a sofa here, a credenza against yon wall, burgandy drapes, a plant, a lamp, etc., and then bringing it to life in either her home or someone else's.

I became somewhat of a writer, imagining what would happen if a soldier, returning late from a war, had found his house in Fish Town Row dismantled and the parts used by others.*

When we left that October day, there were no backward glances. I think we felt the buildings would be there, at least as long as we were here.

Pictures of the farmhouse were taken later at the request of Mereta Williams, for the place had been put forward as a Missouri Literary Landmark.

---

* "Biglow Bailey Day," *Saturday Evening Post*, June 1975.

Thank goodness the pictures were taken, for a rich man subsequently bought the farm, burned all the buildings, filled up the cellar and well, and proceeded to make a nature habitat of the whole place. The Belmont Branch Railroad had already been abandoned, the rails and ties removed.

The next time we went to visit, all was level, raw ground. The only thing we found was one square nail, the kind used in the last century in erecting the front part of the dear old house.

The new owner built a log house. Who knows, maybe things are starting all over again.

Arabian Nightmare

I'm not sure Lou or I ever had any "scenes" wherein we were a Scheherazade or any other Persian princess. It was too foreign to our way of life. We knew where Persia was. The old Loughboro school globe had it located, in purple. And I remember reading, at an early age, something in the *Book of Knowledge* about the Garden of Persia where daisies, lilies, and irises grew so tall one could easily get lost in them. A description like that would stick in my mind. Our irises were only a little over knee-high. Sinbad, Aladdin, Ali Baba were stuck there too, strange fellows in a strange land.

Somewhere in the post- "scenes" years when I was occupied with aforementioned things, Persia became Iran and Iraq. In the late 1970s, news began to trickle into my consciousness about shahs, the Peacock throne, revolutions, and wars where old purple Persia had been.

A white-bearded, turbaned fellow called Ayatollah Khomeini was on the TV screen almost nightly, having replaced Shah Pahlavi as the Iranian ruler. I never followed the affairs closely. Tehran and Baghdad—so far away. But suddenly, at least it seemed suddenly to me, there it was passing before me like some more ugly stitches on the unrolling tapestry of time. Because we didn't want our Cold War enemy, Russia, to get control of Iran and to keep the oil flowing (we are dependent on Mideast oil), we got mixed up in wars between Iran and Iraq, way over there where irises grew so tall and where, once upon a time, men tried to build a tower to reach heaven.

Late in 1979, the chilling news came over the airwaves that Iranian militants had climbed over the tall gates of our embassy in Tehran and within ninety minutes had taken possession of it, holding fifty-two Americans as hostages in protest of our letting the deposed Shah Pahlavi enter the United States.

Nothing like this to jerk you fast forward through the decades from purple Persia to present-day Iran and Iraq. I sat slumped on the old green couch, watching, by myself now, and wondering if we were going to have another war. I was running out of fingers on one hand to count the wars I had been through.

Jimmy Carter was now our president and America became obsessed with how to get the hostages freed. Every night when CBS anchorman Walter Cronkite and later, Dan Rather, came on with the evening news, there in the upper left-hand corner of the TV screen was the number of days the hostages had been held. At the beginning, I thought it would be sixty days or somewhere near that. But as the days marched on, days full of political intrigues and machinations, botched attempts and failures to rescue, the thoughts of Scheherazade's 1001 nights began to nibble at my estimation.

There was a lot of maneuvering of the political insiders, both Iranian and American, to make sure the hostages weren't released during Carter's administration. So, for 440 days they were held.

Five minutes after Ronald Reagan, who succeeded Carter as president, was inaugurated came the news of the release of the hostages.

Many books have subsequently been written and congressional inquires made about the tangled affairs and covert operations of this era.

My reaction to the release of the hostages and simultaneous inauguration of Reagan was entered in my daily journal in this manner:

January 20, 1981
Up early to watch the inauguration and the near-return of the hostages. The inauguration was absolutely superb. Nancy Reagan wore a red coat and a little braided circlet of the same material for a hat.

All during the scenes of the President-elect going from the White House to the capital, escorted by Carter, the taking of the oath, the parade, interruptions of the broadcast were being made to trace the progress of the hostages out of Iran.

When the last unit in the parade, the Mormon Tabernacle Choir, stopped before the reviewing stand and sang "Battle Hymn of the Republic," I suspect there were few dry eyes of those watching all over America, including mine. There was a great feeling of unity across the land.

When the planes carrying the hostages landed at Algiers and took off again, there was an indescribable feeling of happiness and good will.

Reagan's day was so good and unmarred, he said it was like a dream from which he didn't want to awaken. He said, "It's a great New Beginning for the American people."

Reagan's statement, "It's a new beginning," became somewhat of a theme of his administration. Although his administration was bogged down by congressional inquiries of secret deals to supply Iran with arms in exchange for the hostages, such inquiries known as the Iran-Contra Affair, his eight years in the president's office picked America up from "Dismal Swamp" and gave her renewed energy to go onward.

New Beginnings

New beginnings is a phrase dear to my heart, and I was glad to hear Reagan speak of it to the nation. I experienced the exhilarating sensation afforded by a new beginning when first I learned that if I made too many mistakes and smudgy erasures on a sheet of tablet paper, I could tear it off and begin anew. Although I was trained to make my tablet paper last (a tablet cost 5¢), if on a page I had added 8 plus 8 to be 14, or the alphabet to read abecd, etc., I could tear the page off and begin again on a fresh, unmarred page.

Finding the exact words to describe the sensation afforded by a new beginning is difficult. Maybe exciting, energizing, sense of cleanness will come close. One feels a curious airiness, as if having dropped wearisome, heavy baggage in order to skip lightly along the path of new ideas, new inspirations, new goals.

Long ago I began making little booklets, all of which were entitled "New Beginnings." I folded typing paper crosswise, sewing machine-stitched along the fold. These were always designed for a forty-day period. Why? Perhaps because forty days is a biblical number. Maybe I felt that I could sustain anything for forty days. Many times I didn't.

Typical "new beginning" goals, often repeated, were:

1. Consider each new day a big, fat dazzling gift from God.
2. Quit presenting to the world a facade that is not really me.
3. Be more patient with people whose dreams are not my dreams.
4. Write a cheerful note to someone every day.
5. Always remember the day God answered.
6. Read more in the Great Guidebook that says: "Behold, I make all things new." "Get yourselves a new heart and a new spirit." "Be ye renewed by the renewing of your mind." "I have set before you an open door."

These little booklets can still be found stuck in between books on the shelf or maybe in the books. They testify to the fact that I did not always stay with my forty-day effort. I suspect, though, that if I could find a suitable number of them and calculate where I quit before the forty-day period, I would find more "kept" days than "unkept." And maybe three days after I had "strayed away" I began a new one! I believed so thoroughly in Thoreau's statement, "If one advances confidently in the direction of his dreams and endeavors to live the life which he has imagined, he will meet with a success unexpected in common hours."

Now, in the 1980s, nearly all my little forty-day New Beginning booklets have an entry saying: *Write something every day for your autobiography.* Thus, this book has taken shape.

Home

By the time the 1980s arrived, I was so lovingly rooted to my little brick home that I felt it to be a part of me, somewhat like a turtle and his shell. Not that I couldn't get away from it, but oh the sweet knowledge that it was there to come back to after having been out relating to the world's many facets of living—discussing, agreeing, objecting, purposing, explaining, helping, hindering, forgiving, and generally responding to a thousand stimuli. How comforting to feel the old familiar doorknob in my hand, to give it a twist and once again be home.

Home is a place that has never been definitively described, for it means so many different things to different people. Home is where the heart is, say some. Home is the place you hang your hat. Home is where, if you go there, they have to take you in. So go the many attempts at describing a home. One of my dictionaries gives eleven definitions. The fourth one suits me, "An environment or haven of shelter, of happiness and love."

In the farm days, we once had a horse, Russell, who was willing to pull the buggy alone for long distances away from home, or the big farm wagon with a teammate, but the minute, on the return journey at day's end, when he entered a certain area where he sensed familiarity, he began to trot faster and faster, to throw his head back and shake his mane, his nostrils flaring as if to inhale every wisp of some well-remembered odor. By the time we got to the last long hill leading up to his home, the barn, there was no checking his haste, no matter how much we pulled back on the reins or how much his more lackadaisical teammate objected. We always left the barnyard gate open when out with Russell, for fear he'd jump the fence gate, buggy or wagon and all, in his eagerness to get back to his "home of shelter and happiness."

Unhitched, he would quiver with seeming delight beneath the curry comb and turn to look at us often with his great, liquid, brown eyes as we rubbed him down. Entering his stall where corn and hay awaited, he would make soft velvety whinnies that spoke of utter comfort and peace. There would be answering whinnies down the row of stalls. He had been out in the sharp-edged world and had returned home to smell the combined odors of cracked corn, hay, leather harness, cow stalls on the other side of the partition, and the pungent manure pile itself, to hear the soft moos and neighs and the clucking of a few laggard hens as they hurried for the twilight henhouse.

I think of Russell often as I pull away from the complexities of the modern highway near eventide, round a curve fairly fast, go past familiar houses, yards, trees, and shrubs even faster, a la Russell, to squeak the car's brakes and turn into my own driveway.

Whatever neighbor's dog or cat may be there to greet me as I go up the walk, I stop to greet it too, a rub here, a pat there. If the neighborhood children are still out playing in their yards and see me, they shout a greeting. Streetlights are coming on as if to lengthen the day.

Inside the house, some sort of tenseness drops away from me as if I'm shedding an old, heavy, ill-fitting coat. My out-in-the-sharp-edged-world clothing is replaced by my in-home, softly lined garments. My feet wriggle comfortably as they feel the change from tight leather to fuzzy lined slippers, and my body quivers deliciously with comfort as did Russell's hairy hide. I might even whinny or make some suitable purring sounds with home-sweet-home contentment.

Once, in the midst of a holiday family-reunion meal, when there was a lull in the conversation, Lillian, with no lead-into conversations, looked around and said, "I wish everyone had a home." We continued eating in silence, each one no doubt thinking of those who might not be so lucky. Mentally I reviewed the dictionary definitions of home. Does "environment or haven of shelter" cover an out-of-the-wind doorway? Or lying on a sidewalk grate for warmth in the wintertime? Some of the homeless may say, yes, they are familiar places, a hub which one can return to and look out on the spokes of his world. Still, I'm sure Lillian's wish and mine, too, is for everyone to have a home with walls and a roof, warmth in cold, shelter from the rain, and especially an at-home feeling in the universe wherever he or she may be at gentle twilight time.

Oops!

My journal entries for 1981, 1982, and 1983 were full of notations about Church Circle, Quest Club, Writers' Guild meetings, giving a program here, there, everywhere, Lauren and Stephen's visits with me, my visits with Lillian and Lucille, and all the little blessings and wonders of just seeing and noticing things that seem like spoken sentences from God. Then early in 1984 came this entry:

Feb 8, 1984
Gave Arts report at Aileen Wheking's for Quest
Club. Felt bad physically afterwards, so left the meeting
and came home. Blood pressure was high (by my kit)
but soon dropped. Knowing my blood-pressure problem,
such things scare me a bit.

Feb 9, 1984
Life seems so good and pleasant after a little scare. It
is pleasant not to be pressured, rushed, or have anything
to do at a set time.

And life was good, but later that day, about 4:00 PM, I had a
recurrence of the "bad feeling." I called my friend, Ruth May, who
came to take me to Dr. Ronald Robinson's office. He did an EKG
and gave me a nitroglycerine pill and sent me directly to Southeast Missouri Hospital. On the sheet of paper Dr. Robinson had
given me to take to the hospital were the words, "Coronary infarc-
tion." I had seen those words before on Edward's hospital papers.

Oxygen, heparin lock, nitro-patches, heart monitor followed in
quick succession. Medication, headaches, blood thinner, and plans
for an arteriogram followed.

Dr. Allen Spitler was called in as my cardiologist. Seven days
later, the arteriogram was performed at about 2:30 PM.

I was given some kind of tranquilizer before going down to
what seemed like some sort of shabby tunnel to an x-ray department. The hospital was under renovation at this particular time.
The nurses and interns rolling me along on the gurney laughingly assured me they weren't taking me to any trash pile. When
we arrived at the proper place, I was rolled onto a sort of canvas
semi-hammock. I learned later, it was called a cradle. I sent my
mind back to the hammock that had hung between the apple trees
where I had spent so many pleasant hours, Black Silk purring
beside me.

An x-ray square was positioned above me. I was covered
with a plastic sheet, just as they did for operations. I pretended
it was one of the old quilts I had padded the hammock with. The
lab men and Dr. Spitler kept up a running conversation between
themselves and with me. I wonder if I said something like,
"There's going to be a lot of apples this year."

I was given a shot of something I believe they called valium. Then a little sting was felt in the groin where and when the catheter was inserted. I felt no movement of the catheter at all as it went up through the artery. Then, several times the doctors asked me to breathe deeply and cough.

I had a hiatal-hernia attack of hot saliva welling up in my throat and told the doctors so. They gave me Mylanta which I sipped through some kind of narrow opening. Sipping it while lying down, I took the hiccoughs and thought I'd maybe have to do the procedure all over again, but I guess the hiccoughs made no difference.

I was turned from side to side, all the time hearing the nurse reading, aloud, my blood pressure, which fell, as I suppose is normal. Then there was a warm sensation when the dye was released into the heart chamber, just as had been predicted, and of which I read about in the brochures that had been given to me beforehand.

When it was over, which didn't last long—about ten or fifteen minutes—and the catheter was removed, there was a warm, liquid sensation as if I were wetting something, but wasn't, just as the literature had said. Then, back to my room.

Dr. Spitler was up almost immediately to give me a report and a picture of what had happened. It seemed an artery was about 60 percent clogged. But the doctor and everyone else concerned were happy about the results. It would be treated with medication.

Stephen and Viney Ralph Woods Marry

Sometimes, in my daily journals, when there had been lengthy notations and descriptions of what had transpired that day, I would write short notations in the margins, indicating what I thought to be the special thing. A sampling of such marginal notations are: Purple martins arrived today. Bill R. came to paint woodwork of house. New blacktop driveway today. Nominated Wendy Rust for Missouri Mother of the Year (she won).

On August 8, 1988, I wrote in the margin "8-8-88." Some years later I read the entries for that day to see why I had thought the marginal notation of "8-8-88" was of importance. The entries read:

August 8, 1988

Before daylight while it was still dark, I sat on the
front porch to look at the crescent moon and the big star
nearby. A hoot owl, in brown velvet hoots, sounded from
Bob's maple tree.

Gladys H. called to say this was a sad week for her.
They are selling her old home place in Jonesboro, Arkan-
sas, and moving her mother into an apartment.

Theresa Hale called, asking me to give a program to
her Garden Club, April 14. I accepted.

Got out "The Rustling Brook"and started writing
on it again.

Donna Mosley called to say Russell's leg cancer can
be controlled without amputation.

Rejoice!

I reread the passage to see what it was that had prompted me
to make such a marginal notation. Of course I was glad that my
nephew's leg cancer could be controlled. I was not too happy about
giving yet another program. I mentally sympathized with Gladys
about the sale of her old home and my thoughts went back to the
sale of our old farm home. But that "8-8-88"marginal notation? After some moments of reflection, I realized that never again would
those "8's" stack up like that for me. They seldom do for anyone.

Then on April 21, 1989, there was this marginal notation,
"Wedding!" And the entry:

April 21, 1989

Beautiful day! Francine, from Francine's Flower
Shop, brought the triple window-ledge decorations —
three white geometrically carved containers holding
peachy-red colotcheas and lots of long trailing ferns.

I had the three-tiered plant stand placed at the left
side of the archway between the living and dining rooms.
Flower pots, covered with pink net, with a ruffle at the
top, were filled with all colors of impatiens. Two big
palms, the pots also covered with pink net, stood on the
floor at the sides of the triple window ledge. The wedding
took place at that end of the room.

Stephen and Jimmy Woods (Viney's son) and
Lauren arrived first, Stephen and Jimmy in tuxedos and

Lauren in a long pink and green, lace-trimmed dress. Then came the photographer. After that, Viney and Ellie (Viney's daughter) arrived. Viney had a long-sleeved, creamy white dress, with a low, pleated flounce and appliqués of white and creamy satin leaves. The back had an insert of net flowers and leaves. Ellie had a pink and blue silk print. I wore a dusty rose silk dress, pleated skirt, and pleated top with low waistband.

Judge Bill Rader, who performed the ceremony, wore a double-breasted light gray flannel suit. Lauren carried the rings on the little rose-crocheted cushion I made of Mama's four Irish crocheted squares. It was centered with a small silk rose corsage which Lauren later wore after the ceremony.

Wedding of Steve Mosley and Viney Woods
Back row: Steve and Viney
Middle Row: Ellen Woods, Jean Bell Mosley, and
Jimmy Woods
Bottom Row: Lauren Mosley

> Rader's ceremony included passages from First
> Corinthians and Elizabeth Barrett Browning's "How do
> I love thee? Let me count the ways."
>
> We had a champagne toast and I burned my sesame-
> seed toast squares in the oven while looking for the bride
> and groom, who were still having pictures taken outside
> in the yard.
>
> In less than fifteen minutes I had a new daugh-
> ter-in-law, a handsome step-grandson, and a beautiful
> step-granddaughter.
>
> Afterwards Viney and Stephen opened wedding
> gifts. I gave them a crystal pitcher with two one-hun-
> dred-dollar bills inside. Then we went to the N'Orleans
> for a dinner.

Viney held an important position with the American Cancer Society. Stephen, still teaching at Sikeston High School, had been living alone (no, with a cat!) at his eight-unit apartment building on Davis Street in Sikeston since 1985. After marriage, they moved into Viney's home on Salcedo Road in Sikeston. Later they moved to a lovely home at 813 Park Street in Sikeston. Lauren was with them often.

1990

Rivers

By 1990, I was beginning to feel like a Cape Girardeau Old Timer. An English teacher in the city school system asked me to write three model paragraphs about Cape Girardeau for a student workbook. There were a great many who had lived here longer than I, but I was pleased to be asked.

I knew immediately that one paragraph would be about the river upon whose banks my city of Cape Girardeau was built, the Mississippi.

I love flowing waters. They speak to me of renewal and re-freshment. I have lived by rivers all my life. First there was the St.

*Looking south on St. Francis River from the Loughboro traffic bridge.
Picture taken in autumn.*

Francis, not over a quarter mile from our doorstep. It was a pussy-cat compared to the great tawny lion of the Mississippi. But in it I learned to swim, to fish, and on it, to skate. Its waters were fresh, clean, and cool. At least fresh, clear, and clean then. We thought nothing at all about cupping up a handful of its water to drink, or even, if a place was handy, to lie on our stomach and sip the cool water.

It flowed into, and lingered in, deep pools underneath over-hanging bluffs. Then, as if tired of that, flowed onto shallow, pebble-bottomed beds studded with big rocks that made the waters splash and gurgle like water fairies at play. Moving ever onward, it would flow over smoothly surfaced boulders that made it murmur mysteriously and soothingly.

It was the St. Francis that *murmured* over the rocks nearby on that day when I shut my eyes and said that simple little prayer and my life changed.

I crossed that river thousands of times by swinging bridge, by horseback, in buggies and wagons, by stepping stones when it ran shallow, or barefoot when the hot days came.

Lou and I fished for perch from a place we simply called the Flat Rock. It was a large rock shelf that jutted slightly over the

216

water. Paper ash, maples, oaks, willows, elms, and sycamores cast a dappled shade all up and down the banks on both sides.

Sometimes when we wearied of keeping an eye on the fishing corks, we would lie back and look up through the green canopy and try to spot the birds that were singing, or count the "plops" resident frogs made.

The river was as much a part of my growing up as the house, the barn, the cows, horses, hogs, chickens, and cats. It was *ours* where it passed through our fields. Like Stevenson's "Lamplighter," we felt very lucky to have it before our door, and the waters brought peace to us as it did to many more.

At one place where it passed by the meadow, it made a second channel and formed the Little Island, as we always called it. Here we raised the biggest turnips ever seen, and on its sandy bars, we picked up snail and mussel shells to admire the structure and the pearl-like inner shell.

The river had a quick temper after a sudden rain, flowing through a valley with semisteep mountains on both sides where the watershed was swift. Within a few hours our wide meadow would be a lake. If this happened in spring and fall migrating time, we could look out the kitchen window and see wild geese and ducks there, where horses and cows usually roamed. Most of the time, though, it was a playful, happy river and I loved it.

But now I was going to write a paragraph about the Mississippi River. A paragraph! Such stricture!

I wrote the paragraph. It was about the buoys that guided the traffic up and down the river.

When I came to live by the Mississippi, I felt that, river-wise, I had matriculated water-wise upward about one thousand grades. The floodwall wasn't up then, and I could go down cobblestoned Broadway, cross the railroad tracks, and watch the river coming down out of the north, sometimes peaceful, sometimes furious, sometimes stilled by great chunks of ice.

I found that before dawn is the best time to go river-visiting. I get up early to see if the day is going to be suitable. If Orion's star-studded belt is still visible and Cassiopeia's "M," or "W" is hanging up there almost overhead, I know it will be just right to watch the dawn's early light on the waters. Timing is important. I want to arrive at the water's edge while there is still a pearly-pink on the eastern horizon.

I must go through the gate in the floodwall now. If the day is calm, coming out of the misty grayness upriver, the flowing water appears to be a huge length of pink satin rolling by my feet for inspection. Just in case I might not like that hue, the pink gradually turns to apricot, and then rippled gold-liquid, colors you couldn't see in any other spectrum. Save for the gentle lap-lap at the water's edge, there is silence. Always a flock of birds fly overhead making a pretty, black, changing pattern against the sky. They fly westward as if to escape some coming fire in the east. They, too, are silent, as if in awe of what is happening on the eastern horizon.

In the hush of the hour, I feel the strength of the place. The old familiar cobblestones, nestling close to each other as if for some last-ditch stand, the newer concrete, the great metal rings at the top of boat docking posts, the thick cables strung between protecting metal posts, all speak of intense power. Even the river, although it may look like pink satin at the moment, could it speak, might say, "Power? You want power? I light up the whole Mississippi Valley from Lake Itaska to New Orleans with the electricity I furnish. When I'm rollin' good, I put 2.3 cubic feet of water into the Gulf every second."

I eye-pick a place amongst the river trees on the opposite bank where I think Phoebus "'gin rise to roll his chariot across the skies," and keep adjusting my guesses.

No matter how many sunrises a person sees, when that first little portion of the sun appears, it is still a thrill. It is so many times brighter than the concentrated bright glow all around that I'm eternally surprised that anything could still show up and stand out in that super brightness. But there it is, a little arch at first, then a half circle, a three-quarters circle. By the time the full roundness is up, I can no longer look at it head-on. I close my eyes and whisper, "God, you made a beautiful sunrise this morning."

A long train goes by on the other side of the floodwall, whistling and chugging, "Commerce, commerce! America's commerce!" Far downriver one can usually see the tugboats coming, flags flying. More silent than the trains, they echo, in watery tones, "More commerce, more commerce!" Their passing sends waves up to my feet.

If I stand where the sun makes a bridge across the river (and wherever you stand, it does this), it appears to be melted gold being offered up at my feet. I feel as rich as Croesus with all the morning freshness and beauty all around and the gift of another new day, all free.

I see, in my mind's eye, Huckleberry Finn, way over there close by those river trees. That's old Jim with him, poling along. And here, closer to midstream, are Marquette and Joliet paddling by, full of purpose. The smoke downriver? It's from the *Natchez* and the *Mississippi Queen*, or maybe even the *Cotton Blossom*. I hear, in my mind's ear, the calliope, and someone softly singing, "Old Man River, you just keep on rollin' along."

Rivers have such a singleness of purpose, which is to flow somehow, someway, to the sea, aloof from what man throws in it, floats on it, or takes from it. Locks and dams and piers and bridges, floating houseboats and other man-made things here and there can make it hesitate for a while as if momentarily perplexed, but nothing stops it for long.

Contemplating the strength of a river's determination to make its own right-of-way, in spite of what man puts in its way, makes one examine his own life. One may ask, has any obstacle been erected to divert me from my goals, my values, the things I hold dear, the end result I wish to achieve? Take a hint from the river, wash it out of your way, go around it, flow over it, keep to the course you have chosen, and as the river pilot would say, "Steady as you go."

Oops! II

By 1990, little bits and pieces of my body were beginning to feel like Old Timers too, particularly my heart, which had been pumping so faithfully since that September morning in 1913 when "all the church bells rang as I was born!"

On June 1, 1990, late in the afternoon, almost 5:00 PM, while walking up the back walkway, I was so weary of being short of breath, coupled, this day, with a vague chest discomfort, I decided to call Dr. Robinson.

Knowing my health history, the nurse said for me to come to the office "right now."

I drove to the office, No. 60, Doctor's Park. There followed an electrocardiogram, mounting chest pain, liquid Procardia, nitropills, pain shots, and a call for an ambulance and quick ride to Southeast Missouri Hospital.

As the ambulance crew wheeled me into Intensive Care Unit, I heard loud voices shouting, "Patient arriving," and I knew they meant me.

That's a hard way to become the center of attention, but for a brief time, I was. Never did those long ago "scenes" Lou and I indulged in include such as this.

Into my nose went the oxygen tubes. Into my arm went the needle, making an entrance for whatever they had in mind. On went the heart monitor and up went the pain.

Nurses and doctors hovered around and when I could converse with them, I was asked, "On a scale of one to ten, with ten being the top, how would you rate this pain?"

Being somewhat of a perfectionist with the outcome of numbers, particularly balancing my checkbook and adding accounts, I hesitated for a long time so as to get it exactly right and then said, "Minus 7." I meant 7-minus. I saw the doctors looking quizzically at each other. But it was a new little numbers game for me. I think once I replied, "6.8 squared."

Little robots took their place beside my bed. Some seemed to make a noise like coffee slowly percolating. Another, more vocal, did small screams and brought someone immediately through the doorway to hush it and make adjustments in the wires, tubes, and floating bags.

Meanwhile the heart monitor was making its little peaked ocean waves.

I did, in early years, semi-master "Ocean Waves" on the piano and, at times, having nothing else better to do, tried to make my fingers move on the bedsheet to the timing of the "ocean waves heart monitor," until some strange looks from a suddenly appearing nurse were cast my way.

These strange looks made me turn my attention to the plastic and rubber tubing. That might not have been the name of the materials that get stuck in here and there, but it looked like it. However, at that particular time I didn't want to start questioning the nurse about the real or synthetic qualities of these appurtenances. Combined with playing "Ocean Waves" on the sheets in time to the zigzag of the little green monster, er, monitor, might have been enough for the nurse to shake her head, sadly. And I didn't want to be transferred somewhere else where long sleeves go all the way around and tie in the back.

When the pain just would not stop, a conference of doctors surrounded my bed and I was told that I needed the balloon surgery, or angioplasty as it is more technically called. "Who would you like to do it?" they asked. Since Dr. Spitler had done the earlier angiogram back in 1984, I mentioned his name. Upon being told he was out for a few days, I said, "Well, let's just wait and see what develops and maybe he'll be back." Saturday and Sunday went by with no improvement. By Monday morning, Stephen said he thought I shouldn't wait any longer, and I was ready for any doctor to do anything.

By this time the reconstruction of that part of the hospital was complete, and I was wheeled down shiny hallways. Dr. William LaFoe, a young doctor, did the angioplasty. Stephen and Viney watched the procedure on a TV monitor in the nearby waiting room. At one point I heard three voices (doctors) exclaim at the same time, "There's the trouble!" It was comforting to hear such a consensus. So they went to work inflating the balloon and pushing the obstruction back into the artery wall.

Immediately the pain ceased. The catheter had to be left in for twenty-four hours. So, on Tuesday it was removed, and bad luck struck! A false anuerysm occurred at the incision place of the catheter entrance. The rarity of this was explained. Another conference of doctors confronted me with the news that it must be removed. Dr. Ramsey (unknown to me) did this, and I chose to be put to sleep for the procedure.

Upon coming out from the anesthesia, it seemed I was being hit by big boards from all sides. Soon, though, I realized where I was and the board-banging stopped.

On Monday, June 11, I was dismissed. Procardia, Tenormin, and an aspirin a day has been the medication since. Aspirins again!

What! Another War?

WWI, WWII, Korean, Vietnam, Grenada, Panama, and now Iraq? Old purple Persia where the irises grew so tall? I was weary of wars.

In the days following my "heart affair," I found it pleasant to go and sit on a bench at the top of the many stairs leading up to our old courthouse and watch the Father of Waters roll on to the sea. Towboats rode quietly on its surface. Traffic moved lazily on Spanish, Main, and Water Streets below me, continuing the slant of the land to the river. Pedestrians walked even slower along sidewalks, stopping at midblock or on corners to talk to each other. It was a kaleidoscope of a community at peace.

Sometimes someone would have left a newspaper on the bench, and just merely giving it a glance, there would be a headline about Saddam Hussein; Saddam Hussein of Iraq, hinting to Arab Nations that America was tired after the Vietnam War, the Iran-Contra affair, the terror bombing of the marine barracks in Beirut, and that the time was ripe for someone (read Saddam Hussein of Iraq) to unify the Arab nations and remove what many of them saw as the thorn of Israel; Saddam Hussein ordering his much-acclaimed army to the borders of Kuwait; Saddam Hussein, invading Kuwait as the first step in unification of the Arab nations.

The newspaper headlines were like upturned tacks left on the bench to bring one to stark reality.

Kuwait? Where in the world was Kuwait? I don't remember it being on the old Loughboro-school globe. But I soon found out. There were pictures of Kuwait and smoking, exploding bombs coming right out of the Zenith across from the old green couch.

My January 15, 1991, daily journal entry reads thus:

> *January 15, 1991*
> *No movement in Saudi Arabia war zone.*
> *Virginia Goodwin will be over this morning with some PEO material.*
> *Make orange slice cookies.*
> *At 5:50 PM United Nations (mostly U.S.) opened war against Iraq as they had warned they would. Tuned to CNN, I heard and saw the first bombs dropped on Baghdad. Bernie Shaw, John Holliman, and Peter Arnett, stationed at the Al-Rashid Hotel in Baghdad, started the broadcast for CNN. I listened and watched all night. Maybe napped after 3:00 AM but not much.*

Such stark contrast—making cookies in the morning, watching America at high-tech war by eventide.

Indeed it was high-tech. The night sky over Baghdad was lit up by exploding smart bombs, so-called "smart" because they could, more than ever before, precisely hit their targets. Anti-aircraft fire, with what seamstresses would call a running stitch of light, tried to sew the exploding night skies together, but it was a futile effort. If ever air superiority was on display, it was that night.

The three broadcasters took turns at describing the events. At one point Bernie Shaw described what to him was to be an unforgettable experience. In a momentary lull in the sounds of war, he heard a rooster crowing. Bernie's account was to be unforgettable for me, too. It prompted me to write:

A Rooster Crowed in Sinbad's Old Baghdad*

When Bernie Shaw of CNN was broadcasting from Baghdad the Wednesday night (our time) the Desert Storm started, during a lull in the busting bombs and anticraft racket, he picked out the sound of a rooster crowing. He said it was a sound he would never forget. Hearing that rooster myself, vicariously of course, I think it is a sound I'll never forget either. The sounds of war in that distant country, coming to me clearly via TV, were deafening, speaking of bloody death and fiery destructions. I shuddered. My eyes were misty, but when Bernie described the sound of that rooster crowing in the midst of devastating war, I'm sure I smiled and blinked away any tears.

The juxtaposition of that so-innocent call from that rooster was like, well, to get poetic, was like balm on a searing wound, hand on a fevered brow, rain on a parched desert.

The sound was reassuring that life goes on. Roosters crow when it gets light, even light from bursting bombs although in black night.

It was humorous in a way. What was a rooster doing in the metropolis of Baghdad? And amongst all the noise? I imagine that all the barking dogs, meowing cats, braying donkeys, and whining camels roundabout were silent.

I mentally pictured a big Rhode Island Red sitting on a roost in some little henhouse in a back alley. The artifical light reached his sleepy head and, to anthropo-

---

* *Southeast Missourian,* January 27, 1991.

morphize him, he said to himself, "Hey. Short night."
He shakes his head, red comb flapping, and looks around
at his harem. "Well, another day. Get up, hens." The
light from bursting bombs glistens on his burnished tail
feathers. He rears back proudly and proclaims a new day,
a sound heard 'round the world via Shaw's dramatic and
touching description.

I thought, too, of the rooster St. Peter heard three
times before the Crucifixion. Those roosters in the
Middle East! They're bright red punctuation marks in
the midst of world-shaking events. . . .

While mulling over Shaw's rooster, I tried to bring
up in my mind, like coaxing a genie out of a lamp, the
exact location of Baghdad. I knew, vaguely, that it was
on the Tigris River. It couldn't have been historic Baby-
lon could it, where a lot of other trouble started?

I went to my big wall map. Yep, there it was, strad-
dling the Tigris River, but about sixty miles upriver
from old biblical Tower of Babel. Straddling the Tigris!
So, that put it practically in Genesis' Garden of Eden
where once all was well.

Alas, if we could only go back. But it wasn't in
THE PLAN. So, we have battle sounds echoing through
ancient Eden, but a rooster crowing there, too, to keep us
from sinking into despair.

A memorable sight, caught instantaneously by the TV camera during the air war, was a cruise missile flying over Baghdad in daylight. Some people on the ground were pointing at it as if to call others' attention. It reminded me of those old days when, if anyone saw an airplane going over, he would rush outside and yell, "Airplane, airplane!" to alert others to the highly unusual sight.

The ground war in the desert started shortly after the first air bombardment of Baghdad. Under the direction of the Chairman of the Joint Chiefs of Staff, General Colin Powell and General Norman Schwarzkopf, the war to liberate Kuwait was quickly won. Cease-fire, duly noted in my journal, took effect on February 28, 1991.

While things were building up to the war and during the war, the ladies of my church circle undertook the making of a quilt which we called "Desert Storm." Members were given blocks to be cross-stitched in two shades of pale yellow to represent the desert sand.

So here I was again, embroidering to get over a bad time. I made each stitch meticulously, as if each one would help some soldier far away from home. Although unspoken, the circle members silently understood that while we were making our stitches we would pray for peace. The quilt would be sold at our bazaar, and most of the proceeds would go for missions promoting world peace.

World peace? "Someday, God? Someday?" I silently queried one day when I used a quilt block to wipe away a tear.

I looked outside and saw, through misty eyes, the dull colors of late winter. But there! Around the bird feeder! A flock of bright yellow goldfinches was feeding. The bright yellow ones seldom came in winter. They gave me the relayed answer. "Yes, someday. In the meantime there is that other kind of peace."

"I know about that, God. Thank you."

Lillian and Lucille

With Mama's death, that generation on both paternal and maternal sides was gone, folded into history, their pictures completed on the tapestry of time.

By this time, my sisters and I had children, hence a fourth generation from the farmstead days was underway. Indeed, a fifth, for Lillian had a grandchild, Beth Ann.

From high-school graduation on, Lillian taught school for forty-three years, first in some small, rural, one-room schools in Madison and St. Francois Counties — Miller's Chapel, Hildebrecht, Burch, and then the third grade at Doe Run for many of those years.

It was possible then to take a Teacher's Examination upon high-school graduation and, if passed, teach school. Through spring and summer months at Flat River Junior College, Southeast Missouri State University, and a semester at Missouri University, Lillian at length got her B.S. in Education degree. She was the first of us girls to be employed and was very generous with her money, saving some for college tuition and giving gifts to the rest of the family. A box-type Brownie Camera was one of her first gifts to me. It is now a highly prized collectible.

As explained earlier, on account of schooling, Lillian was a year late in coming to the farm, and three of her high-school years were spent in Fredericktown with Grandma Casey, it being so difficult to get to our local district high school five miles away. No school buses then.

The family's favorite story about Lillian was that she was always ready to face the world and its vicissitudes in whatever manner it took. An early example of this was that she always carried a rock in pocket or hand should darkness overtake her as she walked home from school or any other place. Emblematic though it may have been, she was ready to do battle with anything or anyone who meant her harm, including the rumored, dreaded black panther.

Pretty, black-haired, big-blue-eyed Lillian had some of the rough country edges filed away as she stayed with Grandma Casey and attended an "uptown" school, although she missed many of the farm experiences Lou and I had.

"Now you're the oldest. You must be a leader, set an example," Mama had cautioned her. Therefore, Lou and I never invited Lillian along if, on a hot summer day, we felt we would expire if we didn't cool off with a quart of peaches, filched from the cellar and taken to the river to eat, our feet dangling in the water.

"Thou shalt not steal," Lillian would have blazed. Nor did we tell her about our "scenes." "Daydreaming! Fantasizing!" she would have deplored.

Lillian Bell Wichman (1908–1994)

But we loved her and stood a little in awe of her uprightness, determination, and unselfishness.

After retirement from teaching, Lillian took up oil painting and, at this late date in her teaching career, became very good at it.

After a series of heart attacks, broken hip, a cracked vertebra, installation of a pacemaker, and ultimately heart failure, Lillian died in her sleep on February 8, 1994.

Lillian was a collector of many things and a keeper of many things. Her home was a treasure trove. She was good at organizing programs and delighting us all with games she would plan for holidays. She wanted to keep all her loved ones close around her and would have made a good matriarch of a clan. Indeed, she was that.

Lucille Bell Kassabaum (1910–1995)

So, for a short while there were two of us left until Lucille died, November 3, 1995, "And Then There Was One."*

There are some advantages to being the baby in a family of seven. . . . I, being the baby, was supervised and cared for by the six others. That was an asset, I suppose, but somewhat confining. I couldn't wander very far away on my own, exploring the pretty wildflowers, slopes, and hollows, although I did manage to get lost twice and had to be hunted for by the six others.

A major advantage of being the youngest is that you can learn from all the others. I watched and learned from

---

* *Southeast Missourian*, November 12, 1995.

Dad and Grandpa how to harness a horse and hitch it to the buggy and amazed them one day when I said, "Let me do that," and did.

I watched the order in which Grandma made her famous hickory-nut cake and soon was able to do it all by myself. I watched Mama cut out cloth and make a garment. I did that, too. I watched Lillian file her fingernails and copied that, although it seemed tiresome to me, especially since I could cut them with the scissors, at least on one hand.

But most of all, I learned from Lou. "Shoot, we can do that," was, more or less, her motto. When the waters of the St. Francis River were beginning to overflow the floorboards of our swinging bridge during a spring flood, I balked.

"Shoot, we can beat that water," she said and began to limp across where the floorboards were supposed to be. Limped, because she was crippled from polio since infancy.

When we wanted some high heels and Mama said we weren't old enough, shoot, we made 'em. Tied empty thread spools, in a most creative manner, to our Red Goose shoes and walked around as sophisticated as our minister's wife.

Perhaps Lou's biggest coup was the little wagon. We wanted one.

"It'll be easier for us to get around and haul our sassafras roots," I said, kicking at one of the wagon hubs Dad had brought to the farm from his Elvins Blacksmith Shop and Livery Stable.

We watched the hub roll down a slight incline.

"Shoot, let's make one," Lou said. And we did, with the aid of broomstick axles stuck through four hubs and a wooden box for a wagon bed. When finished, we sat in it, gave it a boost, and rolled all the way down through the orchard, across the slanting meadow and into the river. It didn't steer easily and we didn't want to abandon our masterpiece.

Ability to get around, cover space, that was the thing, so after many braces, crutches, and operations, in her mid-80s, she bought an electric scooter, her pride and joy.

One by one, they went. Grandma first, then Grandpa, Dad, Mama, Lillian, until there was only Lou and me.

"Shoot," Lou said to me the last time we talked, "I'm not goin' to be here much longer either, but I know where I'm goin'," Then, to lighten the moment, she added,"You turn out the lights and shut the door." It was a variation of our old farm days' caution to "Blow out the lamps and shut the door" should we all be leaving the house after dark.

"Go slowly, so I can catch up,"I started to say, but looking at her smaller and shorter leg which always slowed her gait, it didn't seem the right thing to say, so I, stumblingly, changed it to, "I imagine they have special gates for scooters."

And that was our last talk about that subject.

So, now she has gone and it is down to one, me. Being the baby isn't always an advantage. Sometimes you have to go through all the passings, one by one. But, shoot, I know, by this time, how to "turn out the lights and shut the door."

Sweeping Up the Sunshine

"You missed a spot here, Jean," Mama said one day as I was vacuuming the carpet. I was across the room from where she sat, working on a patchwork quilt. Looking back I saw the little spot she was referring to and thought it was just a little yellow scrap of fabric or ravelings she must have dropped.

I went back to sweep it up, looking at Mama's handiwork instead of at the floor where I was moving the cleaner back and forth, then moved on, assuming I had swept up the scrap.

"It's still there," Mama said. I could see that it was, so I went back, ran the sweeper first one way, then the other. "Oh, Mama, that's sunshine." She laughed, having already attempted to pick it up herself and then deciding to tease me.

The sunshine had struck a little brass squirrel I had on a window shelf, and through some quirk of adjustment in the window shade, the little "scrap" of reflected sunshine from the squirrel had come in and lay there on the green carpet as if it had a purpose. Perhaps it did. If nothing more than to provide a laugh at trying to sweep it up. And, more seriously, to think that you can, metaphorically, sweep up such sunshine and keep it in your mind and heart, as I have done with that incident.

Haven't I done so with the sunshine as it reflected on the carbide light? The post oak leaf? The horse's harness?

Such swept up and stored away "sunshine" has enlightened my "vision." It reminds me of the time when Stephen was just a little fellow and wanted to trap the sunshine.*

> *The midsummer day had been long and hot, filled with bean canning and hoptoads, pieces of string, bean canning, lost balls, jelly sandwiches, and bean canning.*
>
> *"Mommy, what makes a toad hop? Mommy! Come, lookie, here's a worm with a fur coat on. Is the sun a balloon? Who holds the string?"*
>
> *At long last he lay still in his little yellow bed, his eyelids drooping steadily. I tiptoed to lower the shades, for the man with the string hadn't yet pulled the sun below the western horizon.*
>
> *"Mommy?"*
>
> *"Yes, dear?" I sighed wearily.*
>
> *"Why don't you close all the windows and pull the shades and keep the sunshine in here all night?"*
>
> *"Well, son . . ." But he was asleep.*
>
> *Who wanted to trap the sunshine? I thought. It was so beastly hot, canning beans.*
>
> *The red-gold of the western sky had turned to pale amethyst. A farmer's wagon creaked down the road. A lone mockingbird began his evening concert in the hedge. All these things I saw and heard and felt, yet the peace that usually came with the close of day did not come. There seemed a nagging, nebulous half-question nibbling at my brain. I kept thinking, Trap the sunshine. What did the sunshine mean to him that he would want it all night?*
>
> *A brown thrush flew quietly to her nest in the lilac bush. The mist was gathering in the low places. The*

---

* *Faith Today,* October 1949.

*stars came out timidly and the fireflies matched their
radiance. Ah, I thought, these are the lasting things, the
grain separated from life's chaff, the things I want to
remember forever.*

*Suddenly I understood! Trap the golden hours!
Why, that's what he was saying. Sunshine to him was
synonymous with all the wonderful things in the world.
The soft tickly feeling of the grass to his bare feet, the
fuzzy white dandelion tops that needed to be picked
and blown, the black and yellow butterflies that needed
chasing, and the feel of Queenie's wet muzzle against his
cheek. These are the things he wanted to keep.*

*The mockingbird began his second show down in the
park. The moon rested momentarily on the top branch of
the old sycamore. It shed a silver light over everything. I
began to plan for tomorrow.*

*We would take our lunch down by the creek in the
meadow. I would show him how to catch a minnow.
Maybe we would build a dam. We'd gather great hand-
fuls of violets. The beans would get canned sometime.*

*I tiptoed back into Stephen's room. "Good-night,
sonny," I whispered. "My traps are set. Tomorrow we
will harvest the golden hours, print them indelibly on
our minds, take them down into our hearts, and close
the windows so they can't fly away. When the gloomy
days and the darkness come, we will get light from our
treasure chest of golden hours. And if you ask, in days
to come, 'Mommy, what did we do the summer I was 4?'
shall I say, 'Oh, I canned beans'? No, that was the summer we made a tent from feed sacks and camped under
the apple tree. You were an Indian chief and the world
was ours for free!"*

The century wanes. It has been an incredible span of time. I
don't know what adjective will eventually be attached to it. Explosive? Revolutionary? Quantum Leap?

For myself, I will call it the Light Century. Not enlightened as
pertains to the vast dissemination of knowledge via the Information Super Highway. Not light in that nothing much happened.
But reflected light that opened my running conversation with
God, light that makes me *look* and *see* lest I miss a single word.

Light like the kind you can sweep up and hold in your heart and mind so you can "see" your way through wars, depressions, sickness, and loss of loved ones, and be able to say with joy in your heart along the way:

"You made a good day, God."

"That butterfly! You did a good job on it."

"You tickle me with that giraffe, God, and those stripes on the zebra, and the exactly three red feathers atop the flicker's head."

"God, you know I don't academically understand it all—theology and the oligies of the 'other sheep in the pasture,' but I thank you for talking back to me in the way I can hear."

Rejoice!

Epilogue

Mom completed her autobiography in 1996. She lived a number of years beyond, most of those with sudden onset rheumatoid arthritis and attempting to recuperate from two broken hips. Though her moods naturally varied, she, of course, never wavered in her lifelong religious and spiritual foundation.

Mom vicariously shared through the media many of the monumental and lesser events of the early twenty-first century. Two that come to mind are the contested presidential election of 2000 and, perhaps the defining moment of the twenty-first century, 9/11. On a personal level, there were frequent visits from her loving granddaughter Lauren and the birth of Victoria, a beautiful great-granddaughter.

Many might have the wrong impression that Mom was almost exclusively otherworldly in her mindset and little interested in the reported day-to-day occurrences at the local, state, national, and international levels. Not true. Reading the newspaper and watching the evening news and *Larry King Live* were musts. She was also an avid sports fan, particularly passionate about the Michael Jordan-led Chicago Bulls and Tiger Woods.

Still, though unseen, it was obvious that she had a spiritual persona, a core center of her being, which gave her a "This too shall pass" perspective and ultimately provided her and, hopefully, others with a sense of the certainty of the eternal. Writing, of course, was her passion.

There came a time when her vision was virtually gone, along with any ability to type or even hold a pencil. I had been anticipating that day with a feeling of abject dread.

What would my wife Viney and I do to comfort her? How would we be able to pull her out of certain-to-come depression? Who would save the situation? Well, of course, Mom.

Lying in bed, she expressed to me a desire to write her weekly column for a local newspaper, the *Southeast Missourian*. She, along with Thomza Zimmermann of Advance, Missouri, had collaborated on a newspaper column for almost 30 years. Mom had continued for another 20 or so after Thomza retired. ("We never missed a deadline for column!" ninety-eight-year-old Thomza told me at

Mom's visitation.) Mom had missed quite a number due to the ravages of rheumatoid arthritis (Rheumy Toad being the metaphor she used for an article about it published in *Guideposts*) and two broken-hip operations. But she was determined to complete this one.

She told me to grab a legal pad and pencil on the table near her bed. I hurriedly did so, but by the time I sat down, she had closed her eyes.

I sat there quietly for a couple of minutes, assuming she had gone to sleep. Then, just as I got up and started to leave to get a soda, the words started flowing from her mouth. I wrote as fast and furiously as I could, not wanting to upset her train of thought as she dictated an entire column to me, eyes remaining closed.

When repeating this process for a couple of more weeks, I became more amazed at her ability to do this, particularly since she was somehow able to put aside the pain and the side effects of powerful prescription drugs she was experiencing.

Below is one of those columns. It deals with her unqualified love of books, along with a concern that traditional, handheld books may give way to virtually exclusive reading via the Internet.

The Magical Power of Books*

My books! My precious books. I would like to hug every one of them and once again thank all the authors and publishers for the life-enhancing qualities of books and the ability they have given me, through character identification, to live life on multiple levels.

I have books in every shelf of my erstwhile room—cookbooks in the kitchen; short articles in the bathroom; inspirational, romance, historical, and poetic in all the others.

The basement has escaped. But hundreds of old magazines are located there. I usually remember what magazine and month of the issue I'm looking for to refresh my memory of some notable article, story, or poem.

---

* *Southeast Missourian*, May 18, 2003.

There is one brief brochure that is missing. It's entitled "Five Acres and Independence." According to it, one had to have a goat for milk, about 10 laying hens, some blackberry and raspberry vines, and a generous garden plot. An apple tree and rhubarb were also necessities. Oh, it was good reading. Maybe I put it in the safety deposit box.

I was raised on a 180-acre farm. Did that make us super rich? I don't remember.

One good thing about my memory is that, though it is getting holes, I know where each book is located unless someone else has taken it out and not put it back in its appointed place. I once thought of having my library of books Dewey decimalized, but since I know where to find any particular book, I don't need Dewey.

There are two long bookshelves in two little rooms at the top of the stairs. In fact, the stairway divides them. One step up to the right, one step up to the left. On the lower shelf to the right are old daily journals. Then comes Steve's first books: the Thornton Burgess books about Ricky Raccoon, Sammy Jay, Old Granny Fox, and many more. After that, there are a series of the Bobsey Twins. I once came near to making a big mistake about these. A niece saw them and asked for them. I agreed. I thought they might help some other children love to read. The niece had to go to town for some shopping. I called Steve, by now a high-school teacher, to tell him what I had done. Mercy, I had to hold tightly to the phone to keep it off the floor.

"No, not my books!" he said. As a result, I had to renege on the gift to my niece. She understood. Maybe it was in Steve's genes, or maybe he had caught some book germ from me.

After the Bobsey Twins, the books merge into poetry, geography, history, and so on. At the end of that long row is a big box of old phonograph records, a gift from Chuck Hudson—an entertainer who played the organ and the piano at the same time, all by ear. Once he heard a song, he could duplicate it exactly. Thus, he bought all the records he could so as to stamp the music in his mind.

Across the staircase, at the opposite row of books, in order to have a sense of balance, I placed a Braille copy of my first book, *The Mockingbird Piano*. Have I mentioned we never threw away a book?

When I first got the braille copy I thought, *Aha; I'll see what the first words of* Mockingbird Piano *are in braille.* There was only a single raised dot. Was this a word or a phrase or what? I quickly gave up my study of Braille. The heavy volume stays in place to balance the phonograph records. I have a weird sense of balance.

On the bottom shelf across from the first little room is a strange collection of books—*Pilot Knob, The Lindbergh Kidnapping Case, The Calling of Dan Matthews,* and two little hardback books about 6 by 4 inches, *Evangeline* and *Hiawatha.* It's as though the publishers were struck by the two settings—"This is the forest primeval, the murmuring pines and the hemlock," and "By the shores of Gitche Gumme, by the shining Big Sea waters."

There is *Man on Fire* (St. Paul), *Steamboat 'Round the Bend,* bird books, stone books, and tree books.

Was there no "bummer" in the whole library? Yes, Solzhenitsyn's, *Gulag Archipelago, Volume I.* When this book was published, it got rave reviews and tremendous publicity. Several years later I bought a copy of it at a book sale. I did my best to try to read it, but it was very difficult reading for me. Words that have a lot of consonants without any relief from the vowels are hard for me to read and digest. And, there were a lot of such words.

For me, the big, thick book, by a Nobel Prize winning author, became a coffee-table book. I laid it in there with a tasseled bookmark hanging out of it. I moved the bookmark several times. Visitors thought I was reading it. Such hypocrisy.

I get a little panicky when I think books might someday be no more. With the ease of picking virtually anything you want to read off the Internet, I think my fears are not unfounded. Just turn on a button somewhere and you can have a book read to you. But, oh, the joy of seeing the word, taking eye measurement of it, and listening to the sound of it, if you wish to read it aloud.

Please don't take my books away from me. Thoreau, Grayson, Grahame, Hemingway, Steinbeck, Frost, Tabor—their names fall off my tongue like a jeweled rosary.

Rejoice!

Column Selections

Bits of News from the Leadbelt*

A niece and nephew, Ann and Charles Wichman, who live in Doe Run, Missouri, send me copies of the newspaper, *The Farmington Press*. Doe Run was my last home before I departed for college, school teaching, marriage, and Cape Girardeau. Doe Run was once a thriving little town, headquarters for the St. Joe Lead Company. There was a shaft leading down to some mining activities. Two large chat piles were part of the town's topography. They were not as tall and majestic as the chat dumps in Elvins, Flat River, and Desloge, which are rapidly disappearing, the chat being used for numerous purposes. There was a notable museum housing the first crystal chandelier I ever saw. I was awestruck by its beauty, seemingly hundreds of dangling prism pendants. I never saw it lit. Electricity came late to Doe Run.

Suspended from upper balcony rails were carpets—Brussels and, for all I knew, Persians. St. Joe was rich, and this was their museum. There was a row of fine, big houses across the road from the museum. In retrospect, I imagine they were company houses for St. Joe's officials. In our time, these were known as the Waltman, Manwaring, and Powell houses, names of the tenants.

When St. Joe moved its headquarters to Bonne Terre, the museum began to lose its stature and, over a number of years, came to house a flea market. However, I found some things there which were just as precious to me as a Persian rug. For instance, I found some of the old "bluebird dishes" like the ones we ate from on the farm. They were white, ironstone I believe, with bluebirds on the rims of the plates, saucers, and bowls. The cups were adorned with bluebirds as well. I was very careful not to get crumbs or gravy on the bluebirds.

So, with these memories in mind, plus thousands more, I like to keep up with what is going on in Farmington and Doe Run. In a recent edition of *The Farmington Press*, I read this little tidbit of information in the 50 years Ago column:

> *According to the Conservation Commission, the price for fur pelts were: opossums, 25¢; striped skunk, 96¢; muskrat, $1; raccoon, $1; mink, $15; weasel, 65¢; gray fox, 25¢; red fox, 35¢; bobcat, 50¢.*

---

* *Southeast Missourian*, April 6, 2003.

238

Notice how that mink pelt stands out! This stirred another memory of mine—the time Mama caught a mink. For several mornings, Mama reported that something had killed another of her precious White Leghorn hens in the night. White Leghorns were the best layers, and selling eggs was one of our cash incomes. When her outrage reached a critical mass, she vowed she would catch the thief, even if she had to sleep in the henhouse.

My sister Lou and I jumped on the prospect. We loved to sleep anywhere except in our own beds—in the hayloft, the smokehouse, the surrey, or just on a quilt spread on the ground where we could see the moon and stars.

We begged to sleep on the strawed floor of the henhouse where there might be some excitement going on.

Mama quickly nixed this idea. "It may be the black panther," she told us. Enough said. There were three things that made our toes curl with fear—the Black Panther, Britt's bull, and Sam Hildebrand. Sam had been long dead, but we didn't know that and heard only of his meanness. In due time, we learned there was no black panther. Britt's bull seemed to go on forever, but we knew he could never get in the henhouse.

Mama donned a pair of old overalls, checked the windows and door of the henhouse for faults. She then got down on her hands and knees and started crawling around the base of the walls, even under the roosts. Lou and I watched every move. Maybe we could do the same thing someday.

Back in a far corner where we kept extra hoppers and watering containers, we heard Mama exclaim, "Here it is!" She was referring to a hole in the wall and had found the entry. Methodically, she set a steel trap. There was no People for the Ethical Treatment of Animals (PETA) then to protest. Next morning, there was a mink. First one we'd ever seen.

Dad quickly put the glossy brown animal out of its misery. He took the whole animal to where they paid for such and came home with SIX DOLLARS!

Income taxes would have required that we report $6 as income, a loss of three White Leghorns, and the eggs they would have laid over time at $8.50.

Rejoice!

Newcomer Likes One-Two Dance Step*

Victoria Marie Collom made her way into our war-weary world on May 3, 2002, daughter of Ellie and Glenn Collom and granddaughter of Viney Mosley, that dedicated destroyer of darkdom. I think there is no such word as "darkdom," but it sounds dreary, doesn't it? And Viney is just the one to make it disappear. Those gathered in tight little nervous circles may have heard an occasional little musical lullaby, the hospital's way of letting us know that a new little person had come to live among us.

In another venue, I was waiting, watching, praying. The telephone rang. In the stillness, it was like John Philip Sousa slicing a musical note in the air.

In less than 15 minutes, I was at the hospital, holding a bundle of joy, feeling the good life throbbing through.

In the next few weeks, Victoria became a crawler and a two-step dancer. She would crawl across the space of her blanket on the floor, throwing toys out of the way as she moved along. Her little striped or polka-dotted bloomers would wriggle and dimple in all the proper places for a little girl.

When she reached the edge of her crawl blanket, she would turn around and come back, choosing a vocal toy which "sang," once picked up, "Jesus loves me, this I know, for the Bible tells me so." The words didn't mean anything to Victoria, but it had a good one-two beat. Thus, she would look around with those wide, joyous, bright eyes, studying the faces of those who were looking at her, seemingly communicating without speaking, "Do you want to dance?"

I was always thrilled when she chose me. There is a secret circuit between the oldest and the youngest in any room. Victoria would climb up my leg and position herself between the vise of my knees. Then, with hands in mine, we were off to a "Jesus Loves Me" variation of a John Philip Sousa "Stars and Stripes Forever" march. Nothing mattered but the one-two, one-two, and the heavily lashed blue-green-eyed contact she would make with me, holding it while showing her bubbling happiness.

Once I thought I felt a tremor in one of her legs and was ready to stop. But not Victoria. I now think it was a little different dance

---

* *Southeast Missourian*, Sunday, June 22, 2003.

step she at first started to try, but discarded quickly for the familiar one-two, one-two step.

Once I moved her arms in a waltz count. She gave me a strange look, dismissing that idea out of hand.

With her white teeth flashing and a plethora of dimples properly depressed, she will dance her sun-washed way through life with singleness of purpose, the only way to go.

Time moves on. Victoria is walking. She moves with her hands in front of her as if she doesn't want to wrongly push something nor be pushed herself during this serious undertaking. All the little wiggles and twists are still in place.

Victoria Marie's name is reminiscent of two earlier historical queens, Victoria of the United Kingdom and Marie Antoinette of France. So, what do we have coming up here? Not official royalty, I guess, since it's prohibited by the U.S. Constitution.

We'll keep watching — step one, step two.

Rejoice!

The Scholar and the Sage with a Biscuit*

Every family or extended family has its scholar. This is not by election or appointment. It is by conscientious appraisal and acceptance by all others.

Next to her dad, granddaughter Lauren is that person in our family. Ever since her rendition, explanation, and insight into the story *The Velveteen Rabbit*, she has held this exalted position.

Her narration of *The Velveteen Rabbit* lasted all the way around the former Arena Park racetrack up to where the Osage orange tree spilled its odd but pretty fruit across the park to a rest bench. It was told with much youthful exuberance. Near the end, I obnoxiously interrupted.

"Do you know what 'velveteen' is?" I asked.

"It is what the rabbit is covered with."

"Yes," I agreed, but still being grossly interruptive, I asked if she knew about velveteen and, before she could answer, launched into a lengthy explanation of how it differed from velvet because of the pile.

"Do you know what a 'pile' is?" I then queried.

"Yes, Grandma, it's a stack of stuff that needs to be hauled off."

Right then was when I knew she was destined to be the family scholar.

I wondered if I was in that pile of stuff that needed to be hauled off. I sat quietly, and let Lauren and the Velveteen Rabbit live in peace.

Fast forward about 10 years. Now, Lauren could tell me about her undergraduate work, honors presentation, enrollment in graduate school, and chosen career path of speech pathology, all while walking around the racetrack many more times than when she was a child.

I have no idea what-all speech pathology entails, but I do know my granddaughter. Here is something that is pure Lauren. Without using hyperbole and medical jargon, let me just say I recently lost my appetite and became skinnier each day. Lauren heard about the situation, drove to Cape, showed up in my room one morning, and said, "I brought you a biscuit."

A biscuit. What on earth would I do with a biscuit?

She thrust a warm, wrapped package into my hand.

---

* *Southeast Missourian*, Sunday, June 29, 2003.

"Kind of heavy for a biscuit," I remarked.

"That's because it has little slices of sausage in it."

"How did you do that?"

"It comes that way."

She broke off a small piece and put it in my mouth.

I tasted the biscuit dough, seasoned by the sausage. Suddenly, I was again interested in food.

The next bite contained a sausage seasoned by sage. I was alive again, remembering the long rows of sage we had in the long ago garden and the big dried hanks of it hanging around the kitchen.

I doubt that Lauren's wisdom in this instance came from any speech-pathology text or training. But now, I eat everything near at hand.

The scholar and the sage came at a crucial time and rescued me.

Rejoice!

Vivacious, Versatile, Victorious Viney*

I called her the Bag Lady at first. Affectionately, of course, for she is my dear Viney.

When it became too difficult for me to carry the weekly groceries up the back walk, up the five steps, across the porch, into the kitchen, she volunteered. She is a prime example of one who sees a need and fills it.

Diminutive Viney, bulging at both sides with arm-held, over-stuffed plastic bags, did it with good cheer, even indicating that, if need be, she could balance a basket of eggs atop her head. Balanced and poised, that's Viney, in more ways than one.

Then I called her the Sock and Paper Lady. This was when I became a "broken hippy" who didn't care whether I wore any socks at all, ever.

Somewhere in the collection of doctors, nurses, therapists, and manufacturers of aggravating but supposedly helpful leg apparel, someone suggested I wear elastic stockings. Not support hose that come in different colors and are manageable, but thigh-high elastic, as in rubber, and only in chalk white.

Remember the old, red inner tubes that fit into the small gauge tires of long ago? It was like trying to get your leg through one of those. By hook and crook, tug and pull, strain, and toughness of determination, I managed to get one on my good leg only to discover there was a hole in the toe of this brand new, expensive, ultra-white stocking through which four bare toes could be seen. I quickly examined the other stocking to see if it had the same defect. It did.

I couldn't begin to get the other stocking on. This is where Viney got her new title. Early in the morning on her way to work as a manager of a bank, she stopped to pick up my daily paper and came in to see if I'd taken my medicine, eaten something, and was settled in comfortably for the day. We sat in abject amazement looking at the toe holes until we noticed that they were neatly bound as one would super-strengthen a big buttonhole. So, we struggled the other stocking on, Viney changing her tug-and-pull position quite often to achieve maximum leverage.

As time passed and we made inquiry, we learned the reason

---

* *Southeast Missourian*, September 9, 2001.

for the toe holes. A nurse said, "They're so we can see if your toes are turning blue." I countered with, "And what if they are?" "You take the stockings off," she instructed. There was a short silence followed by further instructions. "And after a while you put them back on again."

Now when I hear the Bag Lady, the Sock and Paper Lady coming up the back steps, I say to myself, "Here come de Find-it-all Lady," for this daughter-in-love has an uncanny knack of knowing where things are — things that must come out in the nocturnal hours to play their version of musical chairs.

Viney finds and replaces burnt-out fuses, climbs on ladders to replace bulbs, unsticks drawers that are stuck, sticks back together again things that have become broken. She cooks, too — good stuff to tempt a jaded appetite.

Madam Improviser, I could call her when she sees a pocketed thing to wrap around my walker is needed. A thing in which to carry a bottle of water, the traveling telephone, nail file, comb, pens and pencils, cookies, tissues, pet rock, and other necessary things.

I could call her Lady Ball of Fire, but that is too common. I need something to fit the Internet space age.

I've got it!
Vmballo'joy@capetown.

Rejoice!

A Possible Change in Career[*]

I done gone and faw down and went Boom! Splattered my kneecap, I did, and put one of Rodman's fanciest tattoos on my cheek. There is no discernible, artistic pattern to the tattoo unless it be a spin-off of the Splat Realist/Blue, Black, Purple, and Glazed with Red School of Tattooistry.

There I was, just going along, happy as the little flock of finches singing nearby, when my right foot, authorized by me, decided to wander off the beaten track and try balancing on the edge of the concrete walk. It didn't balance. Down I went, a living, moving hypotenuse, opposite a perfect 90-degree angle, my chin and left kneecap trying out the density of the sidewalk. Naturally, the rest of my body was connected to the chin and knee, and went along, not having been allowed a choice, nor even a clump of cattails to break my fall or a cat's tail.

"Shucks," I said, instead of "**$%1."

It occurred to me that I should get near a telephone, so I started scooting backwards towards the nearest one I knew of — scooting, since I found out quickly that I couldn't stand up. There were five feet of uphill, concrete-walk scoots, five scoots up the back step (whew!), six scoots across the back porch, ten scoots across the kindly linoleum kitchen floor, ten more scoots across the dining room carpet (unfriendly for scooting), to where I could reach up and pull down a phone.

Unless I'm still addled, that is 36 scoots. Now, with each scoot backwards on your derrière, one's slacks and undies tend to move in the opposite direction. I'm not all that tall, and by the time I got to the phone . . . oh,well.

I flipped, tugged, and scratched the telephone book down to the floor. Where were my glasses? Out there by the sidewalk, no doubt, broken into 16 pieces. Have I memorized any of my neighbors' telephone numbers? Of course not. That's for well-organized people. I could have found "O" for operator, or 911, but I did know a clear-across-town friend's number and managed to fumble it in the proper order.

She came, as she always does when out-of-the-ordinary things happen.

---

[*] *Southeast Missourian*, October 13, 1996.

Steve and Viney were notified, too, one county south. After protracted hours of indecision when everything seemed all right, it was decided that I should go to the Emergency Room. I got quick attention there on account of the unusual facial tattoo. "But it's my knee," I kept insisting.

Bulky leg brace, crutches, pain and pain killers, instructions, have-a-good-day, etc., etc.

There is a little oozy place behind an ear, too. Do you suppose my brains are leaking out?

My writing brains? Oh well, I've always sort of leaned toward becoming a cartoonist. Whatdaya think?

Rejoice?

Vicarious Trip To Mars*

After our astronauts' trips to the moon and back, our nation's space program was pushed to the back burners of the general public's mind. It took us a long time to get over the awesomeness of the moon trip. But NASA (North American Space Administration) was diligently placing satellites in orbit whereby we could send and receive TV pictures around the curvature of the world and keep an eye on what other countries were doing. Then there slowly began to creep toward the front pages of the newspapers, periodicals, and TV broadcasts bits of news of NASA's proposal to send an unmanned spacecraft to Mars.

I began to go outside on a star studded night to see if I could locate Mars, according to where my star book said it would be. Finding, through my binoculars, what I thought to be it, I would shake my head in wonder and skepticism. The moon? Yes, it was right up there, big and close, only about 237,000 miles away. We've been there, done that! But Mars?

Soon, news of the adventure began to dominate the media. Animated pictures of just how *Pathfinder* (the spacecraft) and *Sojourner* (the little toy-like, spiked-wheeled vehicle inside the spacecraft) were to work came to us in bright colors via TV. It was almost like a fairy tale. *Sojourner* and *Pathfinder* were to be enclosed in huge airbags that would inflate when they landed on Mars. Braking rockets would slow the spacecraft when it was about seven miles above Mars. Then, about one mile above the planet, the airbags would be inflated so that the whole package would bounce softly on Mars' surface, at least softly enough so as not to damage things inside.

I examined the cushions on the old green couch, my reviewing stand for many years, to see just how much more wear they could withstand. Although the couch had been re-upholstered, nearly 45 years of sitting there, excitedly watching the world's big and little events on the TV, was wearing the cushion covers thin and the springs beneath a little weaker. Perhaps if I could stay rather still they might last through the Mars event, even the celebrations on New Year's Eve, 1999.

I watched and listened carefully as John Holliman explained just how we were to achieve this amazing adventure, the same

---

* *Southeast Missourian*, October 25, 1998.

John Holliman I had listened to when Desert Storm began over Baghdad.

I thought TV was bringing me the animated pictures in miniature and that the real spacecraft would be much larger. *Sojourner*, in the animation, resembled a windup toy Stephen had once had. In reality it was about the size of the toy, being only two feet long and one foot high.

Of course we couldn't see the actual landing since there were no photographers on Mars awaiting our coming. The spacecraft had to land, deflate the airbags, and erect its own camera before we got actual pictures of what was going on. But it was exciting to watch the scientists as they hovered in a room awaiting a signal that *Pathfinder* had landed. When they erupted in cheers, I knew something "out of this world" had really happened. There was a six-hour waiting period before pictures began coming back. It had landed in the dark hours on Mars, so they said, and had to wait for daylight there for things to start happening since both the spacecraft and *Sojourner* were powered mainly by solar energy. This up and down and squirming around on my reviewing stand was hard on the covers. I decided to place a quilt atop the cushions. It seemed fitting that I chose my Big Star quilt, the same quilt the good church ladies at Doe Run had made for my hope chest.

Just as tears had misted my vision when Alan Shepard and John Glenn had made their suborbital and orbital flight and Neil Armstrong stepped on the moon's surface, so, too, they misted my vision as I saw that little toy-like *Sojourner* roll off the spacecraft onto the surface of Mars and move about, one-half inch per second, on its spiked wheels, leaving our tracks on Mars. Oh my! Where next?

Sojourner was guided and maneuvered by signals from the scientists in Pasadena, California, toward a rock dubbed Barnacle Bill and began to send back to earth information of the chemical makeup of the rock. New terms, alpha X-ray spectometer, and subatomic particles, began to creep into my vocabulary. Other rocks as well as the soil were examined.

The 1,575 pictures that *Pathfinder* sent back to Earth seemed to support the theory that the landing region had been flooded three billion years ago. That's three followed by nine zeros.

The many rocks all leaned in one direction as if having been positioned that way by flowing water, just as the smaller rocks in the St. Francis River that flowed by my early home had been positioned over and over again by floods.

One picture that was sent back was called the Twin Peaks. They appeared to be small hills far away from where *Pathfinder* had landed. However, if kept in the same perspective of the general size of things shown, they may not be any bigger than a couple of robust hornets nests in the Ozark hills.

Although exciting as the venture had been, there was a sadness in the bleak scene. The thought of all water disappearing from Earth and nothing left but rocks made my eyes mist again. "Don't let it happen, God."

Rejoice!

Signposts Along the Trail of Joy*

Let me walk softly on this earth, leaving no scars, erecting no false signposts, yet leaving a trail of little notices by way of remembered words that urge travelers to stop here and see this. Listen and hear that. Touch, taste, and smell these things.

Let me stop by a live stream and see the waters flow around, over and above objects to make its inevitable way to the sea and think how much like life that is. One keeps rolling along, around strictures of hard places — loss of home, court cases, distancing of friends; around sharp, unexpected curves — sickness, accidents, disappointments; having to go along with nature's changes of course, sometimes running backwards for a while before one finds the true course again; bearing burdens of unwanted baggage — unfriendly people, the awful knowledge of what people do to others; yet always, like the flowing waters, make your way to your sea.

Let me take the time to see and admire a flock of blood red cardinals alight, if only momentarily, in a winter white sycamore, watch morning mists arise from a meadow to reveal a whole field of daisies, see white cloud sheep lying on a blue blanket far above the cacophony of the world, a child hurrying home to show the valentine he has made for mama.

I want to hear the music of the sphere, knowing I can't yet, but sensing, along with old Pythagoras, that it is there. He suggested that the sound waves between the planets and stars surely produce music. According to legend, when the great star Vega first shone upon the Harp of Orpheus in the constellation now known as Lyra, the result was that Orpheus' music was so enchanting that the trees bent to listen, savage beasts were soothed, and even rivers ceased their flow, lest they miss a single note.

I want to hear the hum of a furnace or crackling of logs in a fireplace, purr of a kitten, lonesomeness of the tree frog, some powerful music, and some light — "Moonlight Sonata" and "Moon River." Surely the mixture of sounds must meld somewhere in space and meet the sound of the planets and stars if it is only the sound of their movement in the universe.

I want to touch a baby's hands, feel its little fingers curl

---

* *Southeast Missourian*, September 29, 1996, written the week prior to her 80th birthday. Jean had written "My Creed" on the clipping of this article which she kept next to her chair in a treasure box.

251

around one of mine, feel the first tiny pressure of a returned hug. Let me touch the silkiness of milkweed floss on my cheek, stroke the velvet around a horse's mouth, sink my hands into the deep wool of a sheep's back. The fingers of wind in my hair and the rays of the sun on my shoulders make me feel more deeply that I'm a child of the universe. The red and purple satin of tomato and eggplant will give me eminent domain ownership when I stroke their sides, making me rich as the old sea merchants of precious silks.

Let me smell the newly turned earth in spring, the fragrance of a June morning, yeast bread baking, the load of hay fresh from the summer meadow, the peppermint that grows by the spring water.

David Grayson maintains that the sense of smell and taste have been shabbily treated in the rivalry of the senses, but one of my little work notices is, if you don't have to make a choice, enjoy them all to the deepest level, although walking softly so as to leave no scar for fellow travelers to skirt.

I have often thought of making a chronicle of the things I love to smell and taste, so I can read it over from time to time and not forget. Just this early summer, I came across a ripe Mayapple and ate it on the spot, having forgotten how good the taste. But, oh, the list would be so loooooooong.*

Rejoice!

---

* Marjorie Holmes, an award-winning Christian author, wrote: "'Signposts Along the Trail of Joy' is a masterpiece! Exactly the way I feel about life, and so beautiful it almost made me cry."

The Woolly Bullies

Son Stephen sat beside my hospital bed as waves of pain radiated out from my chest, down my arms, and into all other avenues connected with a heart attack. He occasionally pressed my hand ever so lightly. I knew he was hurting too, and between the spasms of pain, I tried to think of something that would lighten the moment. I almost had it, I thought, when the gurney was brought to wheel me away.

Awaking from surgery, my mind seemed to still be traveling in the same groove as before, searching for some light and reassuring remarks. Didn't I almost have something when they took me away? What was it? Yes! The Woolly Bullies! I was about to tell Stephen to notify the Woolly Bullies. I thought he might have known what I meant, and the worried look on his face would be replaced by his usual smile.

The Woolly Bullies, made up from our fertile imaginations, were a group of miniature human-like creatures who knew how to deal quickly and efficiently with the assorted vicissitudes of life. They weren't bullies in the sense that the dictionary might describe them as habitual ruffians. We just liked the sound of the rhyming names, prompting many giggles as the words rolled off our tongues.

In Stephen's preschool days, he was a great and interested listener to oral storytelling and reading, entering into the tales with complete character identification. We went, voraciously, through the Little Golden Books, the Thornton Burgess books, the fairy tales, the childhood series of books. Sometimes we just simply were caught without anything to read. That's when the Woolly Bullies were born. I started to tell made-up stories of their escapades which were always tenuously connected to our own daily affairs.

If the Woolly Bullies, in their ramblings through fields and forests, came to a stream of water too deep and swift to wade across, they forthwith rolled huge rocks into the water for stepping stones. The placement of these rocks were strikingly similar to the rocks Stephen and I used to cross a nearby creek.

"How many Woolly Bullies are there?" Stephen asked near the beginning of the wandering tales.

"Well, let us count them. See the one with red trousers and a green and white-striped shirt? You can see them better if you close your eyes."

"He needs a hair cut," Stephen supplied, delighting me with his ready entry into our very own imaginary world.

"And there's one in blue overalls and orange-checked shirt," I added.

Stephen continued with descriptions, pointing out one he saw that was wearing a cowboy outfit and boots just like his.

From time to time we named the Woolly Bullies—Shorty, Lefty, Flumpty, Butch, etc.

We counted a dozen or more, all very squat, not over twelve inches tall, round and sturdy with lots of dark, curly hair. One of them, of all things, had wings. I had added that.

"How come?" Stephen wanted to know, wings being alien to him except for birds, June bugs, and pictured angels.

"I suppose he is their guardian angel," I replied.

"'But Miss Dorothy (Stephen's Sunday School teacher) says you can't see a guardian angel," Stephen asserted.

"Maybe the Woolly Bullies can," I countered.

Stephen thought about that for a while, then said, "Let's call him Guardy." Thereafter Guardy had a prominent role in many of the tales. He could see snakes in the paths long before any of the others and warn them. He ordered the others to get out from under a tree when there was lightning and never get near the three-leaved poison ivy.

Once Butch Woolly Bully lost his Mickey Mouse watch. This was very relevant to Stephen's situation. This turned out to be a long story, lasting for two sessions, one before nap time and one afterward. The troop had to cross the deep creek, scan their Little League baseball diamond, and hunt alongside a field and around an old stump before they found it.

Absorbed in the story, Stephen interrupted, "I bet it was the same stump where we found my Mickey Mouse watch."

The continuing stories went on for several years. Sometimes Stephen told them. There were no basic forms to follow, just freewheeling imagination that might change the story line several times during the narration. Nearly always, though, the Woolly Bullies came upon some crisis situation and, led by Guardy, quickly did things to correct the situation and get back to their enjoyable wanderings, swinging from grapevines or skating on the frozen creek.

As Stephen climbed the reading ladder, the Woolly Bullies began to recede farther and farther into the background. But not altogether. When he read Scheherazade's unending Arabian tales, he remarked, "Reminded me, Mom, of the Woolly Bully stories."

Much later when a popular singing group came out with a song called, "Woolly Bully," we both were astonished, declaring to each other that we thought we had some sort of copyright.

Still, as Voltaire, Shakespeare, Tolstoy, etc. took over the reading material and made-up storytelling. I occasionally had sentimental pangs of sorrow for what seemed like the passing of the Woolly Bullies but kept it to myself for fear of being accused of living in the past. I wondered if, in his midlife maturity, Stephen had retained any vestiges of our funny little fictional gang or the subtle lessons I had tried to teach in the tales. I took comfort, though, that he was now writing and publishing stories of his own as well as humorous/serious commentaries on current events.

Now, as I was wheeled back from surgery and was beginning to focus on the real world, there was Stephen, again sitting at my bedside, pressing my hand ever so tenderly. "I'm all right," I managed to say through dry lips.

"I know," Stephen replied. "I notified Guardy."

Rejoice!

Jean Bell Mosley (1913–2003)

Educational Background

- Graduated from Doe Run, Missouri, High School in 1931, Valedictorian
- Graduated from Flat River Junior College (now Mineral Area Community College) in 1933 with an Associate in Education degree, Valedictorian
- Graduated from Southeast Missouri State University in 1937 with a Bachelor of Science degree in Education

Career Highlights

- Taught school at Graniteville, Missouri, Grade School 1935–1936
- Secretary/bookkeeper for an insurance agency 1938–1945; managed this agency during the WWII years
- Sold first story to *Woman's Day* magazine in 1947

Awards

- Missouri Writers Guild Award, 1953
- Cape Girardeau Writers Guild Award, Imagination in Flight
- Alumni Merit Award from Southeast Missouri State University for outstanding literary accomplishments, 1977
- Alumni Merit Award from Mineral Area Community College for outstanding literary accomplishments, 1983
- Dingeldein Award for outstanding accomplishments in the arts, 1979
- St. Francis Hospital's Woman of the Year, 1995
- "Jean Bell Mosley Day" proclaimed by Mayor of Cape Girardeau, 1979
- Girl Scout Woman of Distinction, 1992
- Women's Impact Award of the Girl Scouts of Otahki Council, Inc., March 24, 2001

Club and Society Memberships

- Chapter GF, P.E.O.
- Phi Theta Kappa, national scholarship society
- Kappa Delta Pi, international honor society in education
- Sigma Tau Delta, international English honor society, recognizes the accomplishments of professional writers who have contributed to the fields of language and literature
- Beta Sigma Phi, social society

- Quest Club, General Federation of Women's Clubs
- Missouri Writers' Guild
- Cape Girardeau Writers' Guild
- Sorosis (now Alpha Chi Omega), college sorority
- Delta Kappa Gamma Society International, honorary society of women educators

Church Affiliation
- Centenary United Methodist

The old home place where Jean Bell grew up has been designated as a national literary landmark by the National Council of Teachers of English.

Books
The Mockingbird Piano
- Published by The Westminister Press; Philadelphia, Pennsylvania: 1953
- Library of Congress Catalog Card No. 52-11541
- Won the Missouri Writers' Guild Top Award for 1953
- Available in Braille

Wide Meadows
- Published by Caxton Printers, Ltd.; Caldwell, Idaho: 1960
- Library of Congress Catalog Card No. 60-5623
- A Family Bookshelf selection (*Christian Herald* and *Farm Journal*)
- An American Ambassador Book chosen by the English Speaking Union to interpret the lives, background, character, and ideas of the American people in other countries
- Many chapters from this book have been chosen by national oral storytellers for presentations

The Crosses At Zarin
- Published by Broadman Press; Nashville, Tennessee: 1967
- Library of Congress Catalog Card No. 67-22030
- A Family Bookshelf selection
- Went into its second printing within a month after publication (sold 40,000 copies before publication)

Las Cruces De Zarin
- Published by Casa Bautista De Publicaciones; El Paso, Texas: 1970
- Paperback edition in Spanish of *The Crosses At Zarin*.

The Deep Forest Award
- Published by Crossway Books; Westchester, Illinois: 1985
- Library of Congress Catalog Card No. 84-72003
- Won the C.S. Lewis Silver Medal for the best children's religious book
- Published in England and distributed in the United Kingdom— Australia, New Zealand, etc.
- Recorded on cassette tape by The Sparrow's Nest and by The Christian Blind Mission International of Victoria, Australia, and broadcast for people with reading disabilities

Little Mocker's Great Adventure
- Published by Lion Publishing plc; Icknield Way, England: 1986
- British edition of *The Deep Forest Award*

Seeds on the Wind
- Printed by Concord Printing Services, Cape Girardeau, Missouri, 1994
- Library of Congress Card No. 94-76937

Magazines (Partial List of Publications)

Alfred Hitchcock Mystery Magazine
- "Sweet Sense of Gladness," short story (Dec. 1963)

American Farm Youth
- "Stella," short story (May 1953)

American Home
- Captioned pictures of home stairway and washstand painted by Jean Bell Mosley with Pennsylvania Dutch designs (July 1948)

American Legion Magazine
- "What is America's Sound?" article (May 1974)

Angels on Earth
- *The Glow Across the Field* by Carmen Robertson (Nov./Dec. 1998) (Work made for hire by Jean Bell Mosley)
- "Places of Enchantment" (July/Aug. 1999)
- "Green Grape Pie" (Sept. / Oct. 2002)

Anglers of Missouri
- "Give Me a Woods to Walk In," article, reprint (date unknown)

Australian Magazine
- "Primitive Young Man," short story, reprint (date unknown)
- "Wagon Tracks," short story, reprint (date unknown)
- "The Dog Stealer," short story, reprint (date unknown)

Ave Maria Magazine
- "Guide for Posterity," short story (Sept. 23, 1961)

Better English (Scholastic Magazine)
- "Stand Still to Fight," short story (1960)

Better Farming (formerly *Country Gentleman*)
- "The Barn Painter," short story (May 1955)

Board of Christian Education (Publishers of several magazines)
- "Snipe Hunt," short story, reprint (date unknown)
- "Nature of a Seed," short story, reprint (date unknown)

Bulletin of National Secretaries Association (Louisville Chapter)
- "Give Me a Woods to Walk In," article, reprint (Oct. 1970)

Bulletin-Journal (monthly magazine)
- "Easter Memories," story (1977)
- "Goin' This Way," story (1977)
- "Maybaskets," story (1977)
- "Waving Back," story (1977)
- "The Way and Woof of Our Day," story (1977)
- "Now!," story (1977)
- "The Fields of America," story (1977)
- "Summer Storm," story (1977)
- "Berry Lady," story (1977)

Centenary Circuit Rider
- Reprint from *The Crosses of Zarin*, "James, the Night After the Crucifixion" (Apr. 9, 1965)

Christian Advocate
- "Chapel in the Clearing," article (July 12, 1951)

Christian Herald
- "Joe Pye," short story (June 1958)
- "Living Off the Interest," article (Dec. 1967)

Christian Life
- "The Lord'll Pervide," short story (Apr. 1950)
- "Strange Valedictory," short story (Apr. 1951)

Christian Record Braille Foundation, Inc.
- Portions of *Wide Meadows* taped (date unknown)

Converse & Co.
- "The Republican Fox," short story, reprint (date unknown)
- "Spring Auction," short story, reprint (date unknown)
- "Lock, Stock, and Cook," short story, reprint (date unknown)
- "Snipe Hunt," short story, reprint (date unknown)
- "Stray Pup," short story, reprint (date unknown)

Covenant Press (Youth Today)
- "A String of Beads," short article (date unknown, sold in 1957)
- "The Nature of a Seed," short story, Apr. 22, 1962
- "Christmas Miracle," short story, reprint (date unknown)
- "The Tomato Patch," short story, reprint (Mar. 30, 1958)

Daily Word
- "And God Talked Back" (1985)

Evangel (Light and Life Press)
- "Aunt Myra and the Seeds," short story (Sept. 14, 1952)
- "For Graduation," short story (June 2, 1957)
- "Going Up?" short story (July 21, 1963)
- "Levee Home," short story (date unknown, sold in 1951)
- "Ninth Summer," short story (July 17, 1955)
- "A Weaver of Bethlehem," short story (date unknown)
- "Who Shall We Be Today?" short story (date unknown)

Evangelical Press
- "Point of Decision," short story, reprint (date unknown)
- "Thanksgiving Bells," a short article, reprint (date unknown)

Extension
- "Fisherman's Luck," short story (Aug. 1956)
- "Little Leaguer," short story (May 1958)
- "Barbed Wire Geese," short story (Aug. 1958)
- "New Dress for Tamby," short story (Jan. 1960)
- "The Rich Young Beggar," short story (Nov. 1962)
- "The Incredible Day of the Bee," short story (Jan. 1963)

- "A Towering Vision," short story (Apr. 1963)
- "Lonesome," short story (Apr. 1966)

Faith Today
- "How God Signs His Name," short story (Sept./Oct. 1954)
- "Tony's Christmas Gift," short story (Dec. 1955)

Family Herald and Weekly Star
- "Mrs. Wallingford's Christmas," short story (Dec. 1952)
- "The Blue Checked Linoleum," short story (date unknown)
- "Christmas in a Country Kitchen," article (Dec. 22, 1955)
- "Storm Cellar," article (date unknown)
- "The Bells of Eden Valley," novella, published:
    Chapter 1 (Mar. 6, 1958)
    Chapter 2 (Mar. 13, 1958)
    Chapter 3 (Mar. 20, 1958)
    Chapter 4 (Mar. 27, 1958)
- "Islands of Safety," article (Sept. 8, 1958)
- "A Share of Beauty," article (July 9, 1959)
- "This World's Goods," article (Jan. 14, 1960)
- "Blaze a Trail Home," article (Mar. 24, 1960)
- "Our Best Investment," short story (Mar. 12, 1959)
- "No Time Like the Present," article (May 16, 1962)
- "Why The Grace Notes," article (Apr. 15, 1965)

Farm Journal
- "The H.D.A. and Grandma's Bonnet," short story (May 1949)
- "Hills of Home, a Letter from Farm Woman" (Feb. 1950)
- "Slick Trick" (1950)
- "The Dewberry Mule," short story (July 1950)
- "Never Let Her Know," short story (Sept. 1950)
- "The Mockingbird Piano," short story (Nov. 1952)
- "The Treasured Wealth," short story (July 1954)
- "Goin' a Ways with Someone," article (Jan. 1958)
- "We Learned by the Silver Spoon," article (Sept. 1956)
- "We Learned About Eternity," article (Oct. 1958)
- "The Christmas Everyone Cried," short story (Dec. 1957)
- "Dad's Thanksgiving Surprise," short story (Nov. 1958)
- "You'll Get Something Back," article (Nov. 1959)
- "Reflective Nuggets," opinion paragraph (Dec. 1962)
- "I Wish You a Merry Christmas," article (Dec. 1967)

Farm Quarterly
- "Go Fetch the Cows," article (Summer 1952)

Forward
- "Point of Decision," short story (Nov. 11, 1951)
- "Levee Home," short story (Apr. 6, 1952)
- "The Republican Fox," short story (Nov. 1953)
- "Thanksgiving Bells," article reprint (Nov. 22, 1953)
- "Spring Auction," short story (Mar. 28, 1954)
- "Lock, Stock and Cook," short story (July 18, 1954)
- "Snipe Hunt," short story (Jan. 9, 1955)
- "Gold in the Hills," short story (date unknown)
- "Wet Weather Spring," article (Apr. 17, 1955)
- "The Magic Cabinet," article (May 1, 1955)
- "Stray Pup," short story (July 1, 1956)

Gospel Trumpet Company
- "Levee Home," short story, reprint (date unknown)

Grazia (A magazine published in Milan, Italy)
- "One Night Together," short story reprint (Feb. 26, 1956)
- "A Touch of Villainy," short story reprint (date unknown)

Guideposts
- "The Day We Looked for Perspective," short story (Mar. 1978)
- "Thanksgiving Prayers," short story (Nov. 1978)
- "Shield and Buckle," short story (Apr. 1979)
- "'The Chain' by Luther Hahs with Jean Bell Mosley," short story (Mar. 1980)
- "Bridges," short story (June 1980)
- "Ever Witness a Miracle?" short story (May 1981)
- "The Beautiful Sound of a Cracked Bell," short story (Nov. 1983)
- "The Not-Forgotten," short story (May 1988)
- "More than I Bargained For," short story (May 1998)
- "The Little Things," short story (Jan. 1999)
- "Rheumy Toad," short story (Mar. 2000)

Hjemmet (a magazine published in Copenhagen, Denmark)
- "Headin' for Trouble," short story, reprint (Nov. 1956)
- "The Way of Love," "A Gift for the Bride," "One Night Together," all short stories sold to Scandinavian Magazine, most possibly *Hjemmet*, (dates unknown)

Ideal Woodland
- "Give Me a Woods to Walk In," article, reprint (1977)

Illuminator (Braille)
- "The Tomato Patch," short story from *Woman's Day* (date unknown)

Journal of Living
- "He Wanted to Trap the Sunshine," article (Oct. 1949)

Ladies' Home Journal
- "A Gift for the Bride," short story (May 1959)
- "A Touch of Villainy," short story (June 1961)

Lutheran Digest
- "How Rich Can You Be?" article, reprint (Fall 1972)

Magnificat
- "Sit Alone with Your Thoughts," short story (Feb. 1953)

Missouri Conservationist
- "Bluffs," poem (June 1965)
- "Give Me a Woods to Walk In," article, reprint (Dec. 1971)

Missouri Life
- "Houn' Dog Woman," short story (Sept./Oct. 1973)
- "Oct. College," article (Sept./Oct. 1973)

Missouri News Magazine
- "Robins, Tea Time, Valentines, Part of MO Living Scene," article (Feb. 1956)

Mother's Home Life
- "Corn Silk," short story (Apr. 1951)
- "Indirect Attack," short story (Sept. 1956)
- "Mama Entertains," short story (Oct. 1950)
- "My Cherry Tree," a short article (Aug. 8, 1953)
- "The Announcement," short story (date unknown)

My Home (A magazine published in London, England)
- "A Gift for the Bride," short story, reprint (June 1962)

New
- "My Dad's Magnificent Vision," article (Jan. 1970)

Nelson Doubleday Publishing Company
- Booklets for the Know Your Bible Program, copyrighted 1959–1960
  Animals of the Bible
  Boys and Girls of the New Testament
  Boys and Girls of the Old Testament
  Famous Women of the New Testament
  Famous Women of the Old Testament
  Noah's Ark
  Queen Esther
  The Mother of Jesus

New Hampshire Profiles
- "Cornstalk Fiddle," short story (Dec. 1969) (Sold first to *Reader's Digest* and placed by them in *New Hampshire Profiles*)

New York Horticultural Society
- "Give Me a Woods to Walk In," article, reprint (date unknown)

Newsletter, *The Golden Age Circle of Wayne*, New Jersey
- "Give Me a Woods to Walk In," article, reprint (Oct. 11, 1967)

Our Four Footed Friends
- "Go Fetch the Cows," short story, reprint (Sept. 1952)

Ohio Woodlands
- "Give Me a Woods to Walk In," article, reprint (date unknown)

Parents Magazine
- "Honey Jam Ban Is Gone," article (July 1951)

Prinses (A magazine published in the Netherlands)
- "A Gift for the Bride," reprint (Aug. 1964)

Progressive Farmer
- "Bells of Eden Valley," short story (Mar. 1959)
- "Let Us then Be Up and Doing," short story (Sept. 1969)
- "Perspective," short story (Mar. 1971)
- "River Crossing," short story (Mar. 1958)
- "Something to Be Proud Of," short story (Jan. 1962)
- "Starshiners," short story (Mar. 1972)
- "The Journal of Laurie Sullivan," short story (Apr. 1963)
- "The Summer Between," short story (June 1958)
- "Through Smoke Clearly Seen," short story (June 1966)
- "Uncle Joe and the Pulley," short story (June 1952)

- "Wagon Tracks," short story (June 1955)
- "Winter Visitor," short story (Dec. 1959)
- "Winter Watch," short story (Feb. 1973)

Rayburn's Ozark Guide
- "'Possum Holler," article (Autumn 1948)

Reader's Digest
- "A Bucket of Clear Cool Spring Water," article (Apr. 1971)
- "A Question of Insight," a first-person award article (June 1967)
- "Are You Present?" article (Aug. 1967)
- "Ever Hear a Bluebell?" article (Jan. 1970)
- "How Rich Can You Be?" article (Apr. 1968)
- "Joy Along the Way," (Aug. 1978)
- "Living Off the Interest," article (Dec. 1967)
- "The Day the Copperhead Bit Me," article, Drama in Everyday Life series (Mar. 1973)
- "The Day the Cows Didn't Come Home," a first-person award article (Jan. 1964)
- "The Greatest Artists of All," article (Nov. 1973)
- "The Summer I Learned to See" (Aug. 1977)
- "Listen to the Sound of America," article (June 1974)
- Quotation in "Toward More Picturesque Speech," (Feb. 1964)
- Articles sold to *Reader's Digest* but not published:
  "Is a Rose Just a Rose?"
  "Can You See?"

Southeast Missouri State University
- A kindergarten brochure, "Home of the Birds" (date unknown)

Standard Nazarene Publishing House
- "Levee Home," short story, reprint (date unknown)
- "Point of Decision," short story (June 8, 1952)
- "Thanksgiving Bells," a short article, reprint (Nov. 21, 1954)

Scholastic Magazines
- *Scholastic Teacher* (Practical English)
  "Musical Mixup," short story (Oct. 11, 1961)
- *Senior Scholastic*
  "Stono Mountain Sweet Cream Shoes," short story, reprint (Nov. 28, 1951)
- *Junior Scholastic*
  "The Turkey Caller," short story, reprint (Oct. 17, 1955)

Saturday Evening Post (The "old" *Saturday Evening Post*)
- "A Lesson for Teacher," short story (Nov. 13, 1954)
- "Biglow Bailey," short story (June 1975)
- "Dance with Me," short story (Sept. 3, 1955)
- "One Night Together," short story (Nov. 5, 1955)
- "Primitive Young Man," short story (Nov. 28, 1953)
- "The Dog Stealer," short story (May 22, 1954)
- "The Way of Love," short story (Dec. 1, 1956)
- "Waiting for the Wedding," short story (June 12, 1954)
- "Woman Hater," short story (Jan. 23, 1954)

St. Louis Missouri Anglers, Inc.
- "Give Me a Woods to Walk In," article, reprint (date unknown)

Story Art
- "The Treasured Wealth," short story, reprint (July 8, 1960)
- "Something to Be Proud Of," short story, reprint (Sept. 10, 1963)
- "A New Hat for Grandma," short story, reprint (May 6, 1955)
- "We Learned by the Silver Spoon," a short article, reprint (July 8, 1957)
- "A Gift for Molly," short story, reprint (date unknown)

Swiss Magazine, published in Switzerland
- "Goin' a Piece with Someone," a short article, reprint (date un-known)

The Red Ranger
- "Never Let Her Know," short story, reprint (Mar. 1951)

The Wanderer
- "Give Me a Woods to Walk In," article, reprint (date unknown)

Together (Methodist Church magazine)
- "How God Signs His Name," short story, reprint (Aug. 1961)

Toronto Star Weekly
- "The Dewberry and the Mule," short story, reprint (Feb. 24, 1951)
- "Wagon Tracks," short story, reprint (June 11, 1955)

Town Journal
- "The Silver Spoon," a short article (Sept. 1956)

Troop Camp Hints (Monthly paper of Girl Scout Council of Greater N.Y.)
- "Give Me a Woods to Walk In," article, reprint (date unknown)

Utah P.T.A. Bulletin
- "I Wish You a Merry Christmas," article, reprint (Dec. 1, 1969 and 1970)

Wee Wisdom
- "How Bluebell Knew the Way Home" (Aug./Sept. 1986)

Weekly Unity
- "A Lamp Is to Shine," article, reprint (date unknown)

Weldon's Ladies' Journal (magazine published in London, England)
- "If You Hold Them Too Tightly," short story, reprint (Sept. 1952)

Wisconsin High School Forensic Society
- "The Tomato Patch," chosen for contest entry

Woman's Day
- "The Stono Mountain Sweet Cream Shoes," short story (Apr. 1951) (First Sale!)
- "The Tomato Patch," short story (Oct. 1951)
- "If You Hold Them Too Tightly," short story (Jan. 1952)
- "The Turkey Caller," short story (Nov. 1952)
- "Box 208, R.F.D. 2," short story (Feb. 1953)
- "A Portrait for Molly," short story (Nov. 1953)
- "End of a Dream," short story (Aug. 1954)
- "Her Man Calloway," short story (June 1956)
- "Headin' for Trouble," short story (Mar. 1959)
- "The Lamp Is to Shine," article (Dec. 1964)
- "Open the Door and Walk Out," article (Mar. 1965)
- "Give Me a Woods to Walk In," article (Nov. 1966)

Writer
- "Writing by Ear," article (Jan. 1955)
- "Triple Threat Flashback," article (Aug. 1956)
- "The Setting of Your Story," article (Nov. 1960)

Newspapers

Newspapers variously subscribing to column *From Dawn To Dusk*. Column started in 1955 and ended in 1976.

- *Advance Advocate* (later *Advance News*)
- *Bonne Terre Register*
- *Cape County Post* and *Cashbook*
- *Cape Girardeau Bulletin*
- *Charleston Enterprise-Courier*
- *Democrat News* (Fredericktown)
- *Fair Play* (Ste. Genevieve)
- *Farmington News*
- *Flat River Daily Journal*
- *Malden Newspaper*
- *Perry County Republican* (Perryville)

Other publications:

Farmington News
- "Thanksgiving Bells," article, reprint (Nov. 28, 1952)
- "The Lost Christmas Gift," short story (Dec. 25, 1953)
- "Christmas Cooking," article (Dec. 24, 1954; Dec. 19, 1963)
- "Christmas Miracle," short story (Dec. 15, 1960)

Kansas City Star
- "He Who Owns a Tree Is Wealthy," article (Mar. 19, 1972)
- "Message of Spring," article (Apr. 30, 1972)
- "Field of Finery & Utility," article (Sept. 10, 1972)

Southeast Missourian
- "Maple Grove," article (July 19, 1950)
- "Our Million Dollar Century-old Landmark," article (Aug. 10, 1951)
- "Squirrelia Rodenticum," article (date unknown)
- Weekly newspaper column, "Joy Along the Way," in the *Southeast Missourian*, Cape Girardeau, Missouri (1955–2003)

St. Louis Post-Dispatch
- "Snowy Country Lane," article (Dec. 28, 1953)

St. Louis Globe-Democrat Magazine (Originally *Tempo*)
- "Mother Nature Gets a Sponsor," article (Feb. 4, 1951)
- "Chapel in the Clearing," article (Mar. 25, 1951)
- "Syrup Making Time," article (date unknown)
- "Recipe for Missouri Day," article (Oct. 5, 1952)
- "Autumn Orchards," article (date unknown)

- "Soul Soaking Site," article (Apr. 19, 1953)
- "Birthplace of Missouri Flag," article (date unknown)
- "Bottled Nostalgia," article (Oct. 26, 1952)
- "Love Note from Mr. Drake to Mrs. Mallard," article (Jan. 23, 1950)
- "Jan. Barn," article (Jan. 4, 1953)
- "Feb. Pastime," article (Feb. 15, 1953)
- "Winter Is Here," article (Dec. 13, 1953)

St. Louis Globe-Democrat (daily newspaper)
- "The Best Gift of All," short story (Dec. 24, 1951)

Anthologies

"All the Beautiful Things." *50 Tellable Tales.* Edited by Ruby G. Crumm. Altoona, PA: Dunmire Printing Co., 1952. 151.

"The Bells of Eden Valley." *20 Short Stories You'll Remember.* Edited by Eugene Butler. The Progressive Farmer Company, 1963. 35.

"Christmas Cooking." *Missouri Reader.* Edited by Frank Luther Mott. Columbia, MO: U of Missouri P, 1964. 173.

"A Gift for Molly." *The Lights of Christmas.* Edited by Francis Brentano. NY: Dutton, 1964. 198.

"A Gift for Molly." *50 Tellable Tales.* Edited by Ruby G. Crumm. Altoona, PA: Dunmire Printing Co., 1952. 12.

"Go Fetch the Cows." *The Good Old Days.* Compiled by R.J. McGinnis. NY: Harper & Brothers, 1960. 137.

"Joe-pye." *Days of Grass.* Edited by Rachel Hartman. NY: Channel P, 1965. 41.

"Reflections on Peace." In *This Way of Life.* Edited by Maude Briscoe Longwell. Philadelphia: Farm Journal, 1971. 204.

"River Crossing," *20 Short Stories You'll Remember.* Edited by Eugene Butler. The Progressive Farmer Company, 1963. 42.

"Triple Threat Flashback," *The Writer's Handbook.* Edited by A.S. Burack. The Writer, Inc, 1961. 188.

"The Turkey Caller." *Let's Read!* Edited by George E. Murphy, Helen Rand Miller, Nell Marphy. NY: Henry Holt & Co., 1955. 401.

Other Writings

Christian Home Edition of the Holy Bible. Published by Bible House, Charlotte, North Carolina, 1961. Contains "The Bible For Young and Old," p. 223

Tipoff, monthly publication of Concord Publishing House, Inc. Various reprints including:
- "Christmas in the Kitchen," 1977
- "I Don't Need Silk," 1977
- "The Riches of June," 1977
- "Tadpoles, Meadowlarks, Etc.," 1977

Many might consider it morbid or a gross invasion of privacy to share with the readership the last word Mom said on this Earth. I don't and neither would Mom. Instead, I think she would want people to know what it was so as to provide them with solace and spiritual reassurance.

The word, with eyes closed, was an interrogatory sounding, "Mama?" And, shortly thereafter, God answered.

— *Steve Mosley*